Drew University Studies in Liturgy Series

General Editors: Kenneth E. Rowe and Robin A. Leaver

1. *Pulpit, Table, and Song: Essays in Celebration of Howard Hageman,* by Heather Murray Elkins and Edward C. Zaragoza.
2. *St. James in the Streets: The Religious Processions of Loíza Aldea, Puerto Rico,* by Edward C. Zaragoza.
3. *The Impact of the Liturgical Movement on American Lutheranism,* by Timothy C. J. Quill.
4. *The Language of the Psalms in Worship: American Revisions of Watts's Psalter,* by Rochelle A. Stackhouse.

The Impact of the Liturgical Movement on American Lutheranism

Timothy C. J. Quill

Drew Series in Liturgy, No. 3

The Scarecrow Press, Inc.
Lanham, Md., & London
1997

SCARECROW PRESS, INC.

Published in the United States of America
by Scarecrow Press, Inc.
4720 Boston Way
Lanham, Maryland 20706

British Library Cataloguing in Publication Information Available

Library of Congress Cataloging-in-Publication Data

Quill, Timothy C. J., 1949–
The impact of the liturgical movement on American Lutheranism / Timothy C. J. Quill.
p. cm. — (Drew studies in liturgy ; no. 3)
Includes bibliographical references and indexes.
ISBN 0-8108-3365-4 (alk. paper)
1. Liturgical movement. 2. Lutheran Church—United States—Liturgy. I. Title. II. Series.
BV182.Q55 1997
264'.04173—dc21 97-19273
CIP

ISBN 0-8108-3365-4 (cloth : alk. paper)

The paper used in this publication meets the minimum requirements of American National Standard for Information Sciences—Permanence of Paper for Printed Library Materials, ANSI Z39.48–1984.
Manufactured in the United States of America.

Contents

Editor's Foreword

ONE of the fruits of the liturgical renewal movement in the late twentieth century has been the renewed attention to study of the liturgy in all of the churches. This monograph series aims to publish some of the best of this new scholarship. Fresh studies of Episcopal, Roman Catholic, and Orthodox liturgy are included, along with studies of the full range of Protestant liturgies.

Much liturgical writing to date has concentrated on liturgy as text. This series does not ignore such studies but seeks to reflect more recent thinking that understands liturgy not only against the background of theological principle, liturgical tradition and ritual text, but also in terms of liturgical practice and setting.

Clarity of focus, relative brevity, and freshness of scholarly contribution are the principal criteria for publication in the series. Newly written studies, as well as revised dissertations, form the majority of titles, but edited collections of essays and texts are included when they exhibit a unified topical focus and significantly advance scholarship in the field.

Series Editors:

Robin A. Leaver
Westminster Choir College of Rider University
and Drew University

Kenneth E. Rowe
Drew University

Foreword

RETROSPECTIVELY the twentieth century will be viewed as an extraordinary period of liturgical reform. Although the liturgical movement has its roots in the nineteenth century, it is the twentieth century that embraced and fostered liturgical renewal of an astonishingly broad spectrum. Before the Second Vatican Council of the 1960s the movement was characterized by historical research, theological reflection, and to some extent practical experiments in liturgical reform. In the postconciliar period of the past thirty years or so, most denominations have been involved in a process of liturgical revision, a phenomenon that is unparalleled in the history of Christendom. As the end of the century approaches a number of studies have begun to appear that either attempt to give an overview of the liturgical movement as a whole or provide an assessment of a geographical or denominational aspect within the larger movement. An example of the former is the useful survey *Worship in Transition* by John Fenwick and Bryan Spinks;[1] examples of the later are the sixth volume of the magisterial series *Worship and Theology in England* by Horton Davies,[2] and Robert B. Pleiffer's dissertation on recent liturgical revision in American Methodism.[3] This study of recent American Lutheran liturgical reform by Timothy C. J. Quill shares something of both approaches: it is a detailed investigation

---

[1] John Fenwick and Bryan Spinks, *Worship in Transition: The Liturgical Movement in the Twentieth Century* (New York: Continuum, 1995).

[2] The earlier part of the century was covered in Horton Davies, *Worship and Theology in England*, vol. 5: *The Ecumenical Century, 1900–1965* (Princeton: Princeton University Press, 1965). This has been reissued with an additional sixth part, entitled *Crisis and Creativity, 1965 to the Present*, as *Worship and Theology in England*, vol. 3 (Grand Rapids: Eerdmans, 1996).

[3] Robert B. Pfeiffer, "How Contemporary Liturgies Evolve: The Revision of United Methodist Liturgical Texts (1968–1988)," (Ph.D. dissertation, University of Notre Dame, 1992).

of the liturgical activity of a specific confessional and geographical identity, but it is set within the wider context of the liturgical movement as a whole.

The general survey of Fenwick and Spinks, which betrays the English/Anglican orientation of the authors, is essentially a phenomenology of the liturgical movement, a descriptive rather than an analytical history, that devotes two pages to liturgical developments within American Lutheranism. Timothy Quill presents a more detailed picture, much of it based on unpublished archival sources, which at the same time, especially when discussing the origins of the liturgical movement, is more detailed than the corresponding sections of Fenwick and Spinks.

Particularly valuable is Quill's theological analysis in which he is critical of much of liturgical reform within American Lutheranism, which has tended to follow Catholic practice more closely than Lutheran theology. The Lutheran debate revolves around the concept of a eucharistic prayer, which Luther rejected in his liturgical reforms. Conservative Lutherans appeal to Luther in their objection to a eucharistic prayer, while radical Lutherans, in advocating a eucharistic prayer, state that Luther was liturgically inept. Quill demonstrates that it is possible to create such a prayer without having to denigrate Luther's liturgical competence or to dilute Lutheran eucharistic theology. It is an interesting contribution to the debate, especially since it is likely that American Lutheran liturgies, among the earliest of recent denominational reforms, will soon undergo revision.

Robin A. Leaver
Westminster Choir College of Rider University
and Drew University

Preface

TWELVE years have passed since the Lutheran Church—Missouri Synod published *Lutheran Worship* and seventeen years since the Inter-Lutheran Commission on Worship produced the new *Lutheran Book of Worship*. The two worship books were conceived, developed and finally published amid a time of change and controversy both within American Lutheranism and within the American social milieu.

The task of producing a common book of liturgy and hymnody for all Lutherans in America would prove to be a challenging enterprise. The liturgiologists would have to contend with various national and ethnic traditions (German, Norwegian, Swedish, Slovak, etc.) and divergent theological streams (confessionalism, pietism, and liberalism; high church and low church; American protestantism). One of the major influences on the new hymnals and on the liturgical scholars who produced the new liturgical materials was the modern Liturgical Movement, especially that of the Roman Catholic Church.

Chapters one and two will review the historical and theological elements that formed what has come to be known as the modern Liturgical Movement. Chapter one focuses primarily on the official documents leading up to the Second Vatican Council, the Sacred Constitution itself, and the documents produced for the implementation of the Vatican II reforms. Chapter two will examine the work of two influential theologians. Since Vatican II represented a victory of the Caselian understanding of the liturgy as a celebration of the mysteries of Christ and his Church (ritual "action" [*Handlung*] and "re-presentation" [*Gegenwartigsetzung*]), the second chapter will therefore begin with Odo Casel. Chapter two will then look at Gregory Dix who did much to translate Casel's theology into English.

As an Anglican, his writings had a significant effect on American Lutheranism.

Hymnals/worship books play an important ecumenical role in the church. Chapter three shifts the attention to the historical context in which the new American Lutheran hymnals were produced. It is generally believed that the Lutheran Church—Missouri Synod was primarily responsible for the vision and initiation of a pan-Lutheran book of worship to be completed before the end of the twentieth century. The action of the Missouri Synod at the Detroit Convention (1965) appears to substantiate this view. The convention authorized the president to "pursue a cooperative venture with Lutheran bodies as soon as possible in working toward, under single cover: a common liturgical section in rite . . . and common core of hymns" (*Proceedings*, p. 186). Chapter three will examine the events leading up to this public invitation to the other Lutheran synods and the subsequent withdrawal from the joint venture at the Dallas Convention in 1979. An analysis of available documents demonstrates that it was the American Lutheran Church and the Lutheran Church in America that on a bureaucratic level originally proposed the common Lutheran hymnal. The failure of the *Lutheran Book of Worship* as a truly pan-Lutheran book has had important implications for both the ecumenical agenda as well as for the ultimate directions liturgical attitudes would take in the Missouri Synod. These will be analyzed in chapter three.

In chapter four, the writings of the major Lutheran liturgical leaders will be examined for evidence of being influenced by the liturgical theology of Vatican II, Casel, Dix and others. This chapter will also note the adoption of more visible changes borrowed from the Roman Catholic reforms (freestanding altars, new and modern language texts for the liturgy, alternate eucharistic prayers, simplification of ceremony, the three year cycle of readings, restructuring of the church year, etc.) Chapter five will do the same with the liturgical texts (*Worship Supplement, Contemporary Worship, Lutheran Book of Worship, Lutheran Worship*). These texts will be reviewed under six categories: (1) the tendency to return to the so-called liturgical practices of the early church (thus leap-frogging 1500 years of liturgical practice with its potentially church-divisive theological freight); (2) simplification of the entrance rite; (3) confession and absolution; (4) the unification of the rites of initiation; (5) presiding and assisting ministers and liturgy as the "work of the people"; and (6) the greeting and response. Chapter five will review the introduction of eucharistic prayers into the new hymnals. At various points in chapters five and six, the liturgical theology and practice of the new books will be diagnosed according to the criteria of the *articulus stantis et cadentis ecclesiae,* which is the doctrine of justification by grace through faith.

The reasons for undertaking this book were both pastoral and academic. In the 1970s and 1980s, most pastors in my denomination graduated with but one course in liturgics. The seminary programs were rigorous in exegetical, systematic, and historical theology, yet few seminarians graduated with more than the basic three-hour class in worship. Two years after I graduated, the Lutheran Church—Missouri Synod published a new hymnal titled *Lutheran Worship* (1982). There was widespread ignorance among the clergy and laity as to the liturgical theology, historical precedent, and ritual practice which shaped the new worship book. With the exception of a few, short, introductory pamphlets and booklets, the new hymnal arrived with virtually no manual or textbook which thoroughly explained its historical, theological and practical elements. It would not be until 1993 that the long-awaited *Lutheran Worship: History and Practice* was finally released to an eager church. The first printing was sold out almost immediately.

As a parish pastor I have lived and breathed the liturgical life. The reciprocity of *lex orandi, lex credendi,* the incessant tension between style and substance, and the deepening understanding of liturgy from the standpoint of a radical, sacramental Christology has made it a time of great spiritual and confessional fermentation and development.

My research has been chiefly motivated by pastoral concerns; however, there were academic reasons as well. In 1985 I accepted a call to serve as the pastor of a parish near Concordia Seminary in St. Louis. The proximity of the congregation to the seminary made it possible to enter the graduate program. The Masters in Sacred Theology degree required the writing of a thesis, but the choice of the subject matter grew out of an intense desire to make sense out of the often chaotic and foreign liturgical landscape to be found in the latter part of the twentieth century.

Most of the material I have assembled in this book is not readily available to those interested in the liturgical issues facing the church today. Proximity to archives and a library well stocked with liturgical books and periodicals is beyond reach. Some of the material in this book is new. Some of the issues have already been dealt with in greater detail in assorted books and theological journals. What I have attempted to do is pull together the principal material from a wide variety of sources: journals, books, liturgical texts, tapes, archival documents, unpublished reports and manuscripts. Much of the material is out of print or has never been published.

The purpose of this book is not to repeat what has already been done by other scholars. Rather, it is to bring together, in a "compendium" of sorts, the essential components, in an organized and critical manner, so that the reader gains a clearer understanding of how the contemporary liturgical movement has affected the worship life and piety of Lutherans in America. It will help one understand how it is we got to where we are today. Without a clear and true understanding of the past, one is not able to have a clear and reliable foundation in the present upon which to judge, weigh, and build for the future, that which is true and sure.

I am indebted to many people whose contributions have made this book possible. To all of them I extend my deepest gratitude: my thesis advisor, Ronald Feuerhahn, whose understanding of theology, liturgy, and history along with his encouragement, counsel, and patience were indispensable to the completion of my S.T.M. thesis; my professors at Concordia Seminary in St. Louis—Norman Nagel, whose articulation of the Gospel and the Sacraments laid a solid foundation for all things liturgical—visiting professors Kurt Marquart ("The Evangelical Sacrament"), Roger Pittelko ("Liturgy as Proclamation"), Kenneth Korby ("Holy Absolution"), whose courses deepened my understanding of the profoundly evangelical and sacramental nature of worship—Charles Arand, my thesis reader, and Charles Evanson, who read through this manuscript, offering helpful notations; Susan Hasting and Patricia Ludwig, who possess a deep love for our Lord's Church and his liturgy and also have been gifted with exceptional computer editing talents; Kenneth Rowe and Robin A. Leaver, editors of the Drew Studies in Liturgy series for graciously receiving my manuscript for publication; the beloved members of St. Paul's Evangelical Lutheran Church in New Hartford, Connecticut, and Reformation Lutheran Church in St. Louis, Missouri, for giving me the privilege of serving them as a "steward of the mysteries," dispensing the holy things to the holy ones; mostly I am indebted to Grant and Margaret Quill—since infancy my mother, a woman of deep Christian piety, brought me to the Lord's house where my pastor and father could always be counted on to communicate a sense of deep awe and high delight in the presence of God's holiness and grace, as he chanted the liturgy and proclaimed the crucified and risen Christ Jesus.

I dedicate this book to my wife, Annette, for her encouragement, patience and sacrifice during the endless days of research and writing, and to our precious daughter, Kathryn.

Timothy C. J. Quill
Madison, New Jersey
The Ascension of Our Lord, 1996

Abbreviations

ALC	The American Lutheran Church
CW	Contemporary Worship
CWLH	Commission on Worship, Liturgics and Hymnody
ELCC	The Evangelical Lutheran Church of Canada
ILCW	Inter-Lutheran Commission on Worship
LBW	Lutheran Book of Worship
LCA	Lutheran Church in America
LCMS	The Lutheran Church—Missouri Synod
LW	Lutheran Worship
NLC	National Lutheran Council
SBH	Service Book and Hymnal
SHRC	Special Hymnal Review Committee
TGT	The Great Thanksgiving
TLH	The Lutheran Hymnal
WS	Worship Supplement

1

Historical Origins of the Liturgical Movement in the Nineteenth and Twentieth Centuries

INTENSE research and exhilarating creativity characterized the decade and a half from 1966 to 1982 in American Lutheranism, followed by circumspect moderation and controversy. The modern Liturgical Movement had an overwhelming influence on the liturgical activity of this period. Knowledge of the Liturgical Movement is essential for an understanding of the shaping of *Lutheran Worship* and the *Lutheran Book of Worship.*

> From the viewpoint of Western liturgical development, the four centuries between the Council of Trent and Vatican Council II can be divided into three periods: at the beginning and the end, a half century of intense renewal (1563–1614 and 1903–1962), separated by three centuries of a stability rendered immobile by rubricism.[1]

First Period: The Reformation and Council of Trent

The "sixteenth century is the turning point in the history of liturgical studies."[2] There were numerous contributing factors. The invention of the printing press "made possible the dissemination of critical editions of liturgical texts, translations . . . prayer books as well as commentaries. But interest in the liturgy was stimulated chiefly by the

---

[1] P. Jounel, "From the Council of Trent to Vatican Council II," in *The Church at Prayer: Principles of the Liturgy,* vol. 1, ed. A. G. Martimort, trans. M. J. O'Connell (Collegeville, MN: The Liturgical Press, 1983), 63.

[2] See W. J. O'Shea, "Liturgiology," in *New Catholic Encyclopedia* (New York: McGraw Hill Book Company, 1967), 8: 724.

reform and codification of the liturgical books by the Council of Trent (1545–1563)."[3] The reform of the liturgy by the Lutherans and other "Protestants" forced Rome to take a closer look at the what and how of worship. The reformers opened the door to greater participation by the laity and Rome responded. The Council of Trent commanded that the texts of the liturgy be explained to the people.

Three major issues were raised by the reformers: (1) the sacrifice of the Mass, (2) use of the vernacular in the liturgy, and (3) communion in both kinds. The Lutheran position is articulated most clearly in the Augsburg Confession and Apology (Article XXIV), in the writings of Martin Luther,[4] and in *Examination of the Council of Trent* by Martin Chemnitz.[5]

At the twenty-second session (1562) the "Council solemnly defined the sacrificial value of the Mass as well as the legitimacy of the rites used in its celebration."[6] The decree states,

> And since in this divine sacrifice which is accomplished in the Mass, that same Christ is contained and bloodlessly sacrificed who once, on the altar of the cross, offered Himself a blood sacrifice . . . . For the sacrificial Victim is one and the same, the same now offering through the ministry of the priests who then offered Himself on the cross, the manner of the offering alone being different [section 1, chapter 2]. If anyone says that in the Mass there is not offered to God a true and proper sacrifice . . . let him be anathema. [Canon I] If anyone says that the Mass is merely a sacrifice of praise and thanksgiving . . . let him be anathema. [Canon II].[7]

---

[3] J. M. Carriere, *New Catholic Encyclopedia*, 8: 924.

[4] *Luther's Works*, American Edition (AE) (St. Louis: Concordia Publishing House and Philadelphia: Fortress Press, 1957–86), 36: 11–26, "The Babylonian Captivity of the Church." 133–230, "The Misuse of the Mass." 237–267, "Receiving Both Kinds in the Sacrament." 311–328, "The Abomination of the Secret Mass." 37: 142–144, "That These Words of Christ, 'This is My Body,' etc., Still Stand Firm against the Fanatics." 38: 114–124, "Abomination Concerning the Sacrament." 53: 21–22, 26, 29, "An Order of Mass and Communion for the Church at Wittenberg" (Formula Missae, 1523).

[5] Martin Chemnitz, *Examination of the Council of Trent*, vol. 2, trans. Fred Kramer (St. Louis: Concordia Publishing House, 1978). Fifth Topic: "Concerning Communion Under Both Kinds," 335–435. Sixth Topic: "Concerning the Mass," Section 1, "Concerning the Sacrifice of the Mass," 437–498; Section 7, "Concerning Sacred Things to Be Performed in a Foreign Language," 542–548.

[6] Jounel, 66.

[7] Chemnitz, 440.

In Section VII, "Concerning Sacred Things to be Performed in a Foreign Language," Trent defended the custom of the Roman Church to speak a part of the canon and words of institution in a lowered voice. It also condemned the view "that the Mass ought to be celebrated only in the language of the common people" (Section VII, Canon IV).

Due to lack of time, two important issues were left to the decision of the pope. The first issue concerned communion in both kinds. As early as 1564, Pope Pius IV granted permission to Germany and various countries in Central Europe to commune in both kinds. His successors, however, reversed the process and by 1621 had revoked permission from all countries.[8] In many respects the second issue left to the pope for implementation was of even greater significance to the development of the liturgy. The council charged him with the revision of the Missal and the Breviary.

The words conform, revise, and uniformly describe the enterprise. The books were faithfully to reflect the intentions of the Council. They were not to be new liturgical books but revisions, conforming "to the primitive rule of prayer" *ad pristinam orandi regulam.* They were to establish uniformity in the celebration of rites which meant "that there could be only one way of reciting the psalms in the Church of God and only one rite in the celebration of the Mass."[9] Unification "required a codification of the rules for celebration . . . . As a result, general rubrics were now printed for the first time at the beginning of each of the two books."[10]

Pressure from the theological criticisms of the Lutherans and "Reformed" Protestants, widespread discontentment on the part of the Catholics with the chaotic state of the liturgical practices, coupled with the actions of the Council of Trent led to the middle period (1615–1903), or "three centuries of stability rendered immobile by rubricism."[11] Theodor Klauser is equally blunt in

---

[8] Jounel, 67.
[9] Jounel, 67.
[10] Jounel, 68.
[11] Jounel, 63.

describing this period in a chapter titled "Rigid Unification in Liturgy and Rubricism."[12] Klauser notes that the decree of the Council was carried out swiftly by the Curia. By 1568 Pius V published the *Breviarium Romanum*, and in 1570 the *Missale Romanum*. "The titles given to the new books with the emphasis on the *Romanum* epitomized the situation."[13] All churches had to use the Roman order,

> except in those sees which had their own peculiar liturgy for more than two hundred years . . . (and) further additions and alterations in them were to be exclusively the concern of the Holy See . . . . This act confirmed the process of liturgical centralization, which was further supported by the institution in the reign of Pope Sixtus V of a senior Roman authority for liturgical matters, the so-called Congregation of Rites.[14]

Revision did not stop with the Missal and Breviary but extended to all the liturgical books. This task was virtually completed in 1614 with the publishing of the *Rituale Romanum* in the reign of Paul V.

Middle Period: Three Centuries of Liturgical Stability (1614–1903)

The detrimental effects of these reforms on the worship life of the faithful can hardly be overstated. The spiritual life of the people moved away from the liturgy to the cult of the saints and various individualistic devotions. Klauser's description of the common liturgical practice of this era is revealing.

> Hence while the celebrant "read" the mass at the altar with his back to the people, the faithful were busy with other devotional exercises, mostly of a subjective nature. They sang hymns in the vernacular, whose content had little or even nothing at all to do with the liturgy; they read, wrapped up in themselves, a "mass devotion" or

[12] Theodor Klauser, *A Short History of the Western Liturgy: An Account and Some Reflections*, 2d ed. (Oxford: Oxford University Press, 1979), 117.

[13] Klauser, 118.

[14] Klauser, 118.

> prayed the Rosary silently to themselves. Only at the three main parts of the eucharist: the offertory, the consecration, and the communion did the faithful, raised by the server's bell, turn their attention briefly to the sacred action that was being performed at the altar, in order that they might make certain recommended "affections." Seldom indeed was it the custom for them to take any active part in the sacrifice of the mass by making an inward offering of themselves or by actually making their communion . . . instead of actual communion they were often earnestly exhorted to make an act of spiritual communion.[15]

Lutheran Liturgical Studies in the Nineteenth Century

It was toward the end of this era that Wilhelm Löhe (1808–1872) played a major role in Lutheran liturgical studies. Working out of Neuendettelsau, Germany, he examined about two hundred old agendas in order to find the best *Hauptgottesdienst* for use by the church living in an age of rationalism and spiritual apathy. Löhe also had a significant influence on nineteenth-century American Lutheranism. His involvement with America resulted from a written plea for help (*Notruf*) from Pastor Friedrich Wyneken. "In 1840 there were 400 pastors to care for 120,000 communicant members, grouped in 1200 congregations."[16] Eventually, over 300 missionaries (*Nothelfer*, "emergency helpers") would be trained in Neuendettelsau and sent to North America. In the book *Wilhelm Löhe: Portrait of a Confessional Lutheran Missiologist*, author Rich Stuckwisch notes that Löhe's zeal for missions was motivated by two doctrines. "Insistence on pure doctrine took Löhe ever back to the pure center of all doctrines—Christ and His Universal Atonement of *all men*."[17] Stuckwisch continues, "Löhe found his motivation for missions also in his great love for the Sacrament of the Altar. For Löhe, this Holy Supper is the center of the Church's entire life and activity."[18] To be

---

[15] Klauser, 120–121.

[16] Rich Stuckwisch, *Johannes Konrad Wilhelm Löhe: Portrait of a Confessional Lutheran Missiologist* (Fort Wayne, IN: Repristination Press, 1993), 22.

[17] Stuckwisch, 16.

[18] Stuckwisch, 16.

centered in Christ was to be centered in the Gospel. His profound sacramental Christology found expression in action—in both liturgy and mission. Löhe wrote, "Mission is nothing other than the church of God in action!"[19]

> Pastor Löhe's work as a "missionary" was first of all centered in his pastoral ministry at Neuendettelsau. Here he could practice the Confessional Lutheran orthodoxy he so strongly desired for the whole church. He concentrated in particular on solid, Biblical preaching (a rarity in the age of rationalism) and on faithful pastoral care of his flock. He preached his sermons in the context of dignified, reverent and historically sound liturgical settings. And throughout his ministry, he stressed the Church's Sacramental life, thorough catechesis, visitation and nurture of the sick, and the use of private confession and brotherly discipline.[20]

While in Neuendettelsau, Löhe undertook the study of historical liturgies, including those of the old eastern churches. His goal was to produce an order of service faithful to the old Lutheran agenda. "What prompted him finally to go ahead with this idea was a request from F. C. D. Wyneken and the earliest of Löhe's American missionaries for a German order of service to be used by Lutheran Congregations in America."[21] In 1844 Löhe completed his *Agenda fuer christliche Gemeinden des lutherischen Bekenntnisses.* Löhe had a great impact on the liturgical life of American Lutheranism in the nineteenth century. His influence continues to be felt. Many of his insights are as timely and fresh today as they were over a hundred years ago. A few quotations from his *Three Books About the Church* will demonstrate this. Concerning liturgical form, Löhe wrote:

> These forms are free. Few of them are commanded. Yet despite this freedom, from its very beginning the church has been pleased to select certain forms. A holy variety of singing and praying has

[19] Stuckwisch, 16, quoting from Theodor Schober's *Wilhelm Löhe: Witness of the Living Lutheran Church,* trans. Sister Bertha Mueller from *Wilhelm Löhe: in zeuge lebendiger lutherischer Kirche* (Giessen, Germany: Brunnen-Verlag, 1959), 43.

[20] Stuckwisch, 17.

[21] Stuckwisch, 19.

grown up and a lovely pattern of approach to and withdrawal from the Lord of lords has been established . . . When the liturgy is performed by devout souls it also speaks powerfully to those who are less devout, and the pure confession has no lovelier or more attractive form than when it is seen in the act of prayer and praise.

This was clear at the time of the Reformation. That is why the traditional, ancient, beautiful forms were not abolished but only cleansed from sin and perversions. There are a great number of Lutheran liturgies which unite variety and simplicity. To them are added the glorious number of beautiful, matchless hymns . . . Our church has a great supply of liturgical riches in its storehouses, the only thing it lacks is a proper use of them. . . . A habit must be developed again, and what has become unnatural must become natural through practice. Let us not be afraid to begin!

Let us not be afraid to teach the liturgy! It is taught like the catechism; it can become mere lip service, just as the catechism can, but it does not need to be.

Yet we must beware of misusing our liturgical freedom to produce new liturgies. One should rather use the old forms and learn to understand and have a feeling for them before one feels oneself competent to create something new and better. He who has not tested the old cannot create something new. It is a shame when everybody presumes to form his own opinions about hymns and the liturgy without having thoroughly looked into the matter. Let a man first learn in silence and not act as if it were a matter of course that he understands everything! Once a man has first learned from the old can he profitably use the developments of recent times (in language and methods of speech) for the benefit of the liturgy.

However, we protest against the idea of an *opus operatum* and an overestimation of externals. The church remains what it is even without the liturgy. It remains a queen, even if dressed in beggar's rags.[22]

Despite the fact that he never set foot on American soil, Wilhelm Löhe had a profound effect on the liturgical development and renewal in American Lutheranism. One man who studied at Neuendettelsau before coming to America was Friedrich J. C. Lochner (1822–1902). Lochner would become one of the leading

---

22 Stuckwisch, 18–19.

liturgical scholars among Missouri Synod Lutherans. He was a parish pastor, seminary professor, author, and among the founders of a synodical teacher's college. His major work was *Der Hauptgottesdienst der Evangelisch-Lutherischen Kirche* (1895). Unfortunately it has not been translated into English and remains inaccessible to most Lutherans. When the Lutheran synods in America came together in the 1960s to produce a new, pan-Lutheran hymnal, they would look to the fruits of the modern Liturgical Movement rather than to theology and agendas of the evangelical *Gottesdienst.*

Third Period: Liturgical Reform from Pius X to the Second Vatican Council (1903–1962)

The third period may be termed the modern liturgical movement or simply the Liturgical Movement. Although a twentieth-century movement, its roots go back to the "precursor of the Liturgical Movement," Dom Prosper Gueranger. In 1832, he refounded the Benedictine Abby of Solesmes (France) "as a monastery dedicated especially to the study and recovery of the authentic Gregorian Chant and the church's liturgical heritage."[23] It was the restoration of Gregorian Chant "that attracted the attention . . . of Pope Pius X."[24] His work was primarily concerned with a "romantic return to the 'idealized' worship of the Middle Ages."

First Phase of the Liturgical Movement (1903–1939)

The modern Liturgical Movement may be divided into two parts. Phase one was initiated at the turn of the century when Pope Pius X issued the *Motu Proprio: Tra le Sollecitudini* (1903) on the restoration of church music. Concerns about maintaining and promoting the decorum of the house of God, where the august mysteries of religion are celebrated,[25] amidst widespread abuses led Pius X to produce this decree which explains and promotes proper sacred chant and music.

---

[23] H. Ellesworth Chandlee, "The Liturgical Movement," in *The New Westminster Dictionary of Theology and Worship*, ed. J. G. Davis (Philadelphia: Westminster Press, 1986), 308.

[24] Jounel, 73.

[25] *Tra le Sollecitudini: Motu Proprio* of Pope Pius X on the Restoration of Church Music, November 22, 1903. *Worship and Liturgy: Official Catholic Teachings*, in A Consortium Book series, ed. James J. Megivern (Wilmington, NC: McGrath Publishing Company, 1978), 16.

It was bold and energetic for its day, but by today's standards the encyclical appears very conservative and restrictive. While allowing for "proper" modern musical contributions and some local/national compositions, *Motu Proprio* nevertheless establishes and decrees Gregorian Chant as the "Supreme model." The encyclical also forbids anything to be sung in the vernacular. Although conservative, *Motu Proprio* contained a sentence tucked away in part two that signaled the imminent changes. Pius X urged,

> Efforts must especially be made to restore the use of the Gregorian Chant by the people, so that the faithful may again take a more active part in the ecclesiastical offices, as they were wont to do in ancient times.[26]

The introduction of *Tra le Sollecitudini* contains "what liturgists hail as the 'most famous sentence of our century.'"[27]

> It being our ardent desire to see the true Christian spirit restored in every respect and be preserved by all the faithful, we deem it necessary to provide before everything else for the sanctity and dignity of the temple, in which the faithful assemble for the object of acquiring this spirit from its foremost and indispensable fount, which is the active participation in the holy mysteries and in the public and solemn prayer of the Church.[28]

The concern of the *Motu Proprio* of Pope Pius X on the restoration of church music was not ultimately a concern merely with Gregorian Chant and the proper rules for congregational singing and church music. It was above all else a move to exhort "the faithful to take an active part in the celebration of the mysteries, since this celebration is 'the primary and indispensable source of the true Christian spirit.'"[29] Singing was only the beginning. Frequent and thoughtful communion of the people was the

---

[26] *Tra le Sollecitudini*, 20.

[27] Ernest B. Koenker, *The Liturgical Renaissance in the Roman Catholic Church* (Chicago: University of Chicago Press, 1954), 7.

[28] *Tra le Sollecitudini*, 17–18.

[29] Jounel, 73–74.

ultimate goal. The evangelical critique of this "most famous sentence" would be to ask, "Where is the Gospel?"

Writing at the seventy-fifth anniversary of the encyclical, James J. Megivern concluded, "It is safe to say that there has never been a parallel period in the history of the Christian Liturgy."[30] The *Motu Proprio* may have been a small, tentative step, but within two years Pius X would issue the *Sacra Tridentina: Decree on Frequent and Daily Reception of Holy Communion* (1905), urging all who are present at the Mass to communicate and "not only in spiritual desire, but sacramentally, by the actual reception of the Eucharist" and establishing the necessary conditions for frequent communion.[31] Five years after the *Motu Proprio* the Liturgical Movement was in full stride at the Catholic Conference at Malines, Belgium (1909).

> This conference saw the liturgy as the fundamental means of the instruction of the people in the Christian faith and life . . . (called for the) active participation by the people in the liturgy . . . (and) for a translation of the Roman missal into the vernacular.[32]

Then in 1910 Pius X issued the decree *Quam Singulari*, which opened the reception of Holy Communion to children once they reached the "age of discretion."[33] In 1911 he issued *Divino Afflatu* which revised the Roman *Ordo psallendi* to allow for the weekly recitation of the Psalter and in 1913 the *Motu Proprio, Abhinc Duos Annos* gave Sundays priority over feast days.[34]

Second Phase of the Liturgical Movement (1940–1962)

Between the two world wars the leadership of the movement changed from Belgium to Germany. On the American scene, St. John's College Abbey in Collegeville, Minnesota, was becoming a major center of the Liturgical Movement in the United States. It published a periodical

---

[30] Megivern, xiv.

[31] *Sacra Tridentina*: Decree on Frequent and Daily Reception of Holy Communion, (December 20, 1905). *Worship and Liturgy: Official Catholic Teachings*, James J. Megivern, ed. 27. *Sacra Tridentina* is here in turn quoting from the Council of Trent, session XXII, cap. 6.

[32] Chandlee, 308.

[33] Megivern, *Quam Singulari*, 33.

[34] Megivern, 41.

aimed at the parish clergy named *Orate Fratres*, later renamed *Worship*. The leadership of the Liturgical Movement, however, had moved to Germany and entered a second phase.

> The ideas of worship which the Liturgical Movement actively propagated had come under criticism as being too radical, too much a departure from the tradition of the church . . . too modernist, and lacked a sound basis in the theology of the Roman Catholic Church, indeed was contrary to it.[35]

Whereas phase one was primarily concerned with pastoral needs of the church,[36] phase two would be motivated by the criticism of the movement, some of it justified, to begin "the production of an apologetic for its position."[37] The task of building a credible theology of worship was undertaken by the Rhineland Abbey of Maria Laach. The major figures were Abbot Ildefons Herwegen and Dom Odo Casel. The periodical *Ecclesia Orans* was published in 1918 to promote the movement. Over the next three decades the movement made tremendous gains. Church historians studied the origins and development of liturgies. This led to the study of the liturgy and liturgical theology by such heavyweights as Josef Jungmann, Jean Daniélou, and Louis Bouyer.

> Klosterneuberg also turned to a study of the biblical basis of the liturgy, and inaugurated a biblical movement which has spread widely in the Roman Catholic Church, made important contributions to biblical theology and hermeneutics and has served as a link between Roman Catholics and the Ecumenical Movement.[38]

The transition from phase one to phase two is summarized by P. Jounel:

---

[35] Chandlee, 309.

[36] This was evident from the beginning as Pope Pius X began his *Motu Proprio* of 1903 with the words, "Chief among the anxieties of the pastoral office, not only of this Supreme Chair . . . but of every local church . . . ."

[37] Chandlee, 309.

[38] Chandlee, 309.

> From 1903 to 1914 the reforms of Pius X had preceded and given rise to the liturgical movement; after World War II, however, the developments sponsored by the liturgico-political movement were ratified by Pius XII as he made his own the project of Pius X and adapted it to new conditions. Before 1940 the aim had been to bring the existing liturgy within reach of the people and to promote Gregorian chant. After the war there was a clearer perception of the need for a radical reform of the rites and for a partial introduction of the vernacular into the celebration.[39]

Pius XII charged the Congregation of Rites with preparing a general reform and then in 1947 issued his extensive encyclical *Mediator Dei*.[40] This was followed by a decree from the congregation of Rites authorizing the celebration of the Easter Vigil in the evening instead of on Saturday morning.[41]

> Meanwhile, the growth of the movement for a return to the Bible had been making people more attentive to the Word of God and its use in the liturgy. But if all were to have access to the table of the Word, the Word would have to be proclaimed in the vernaculars. Pius XII did not think the situation sufficiently advanced to justify a sweeping change, and he contented himself with limited authorizations to read the epistle and gospel in the vernacular after they had first been read in Latin. He practiced the same circumspection in opening the door to singing in the vernacular at solemn liturgies (1953).[42]

Reforms of the Second Vatican Council (1963–1970)

The Constitution *Sacrosanctum Concilium* consists of an introduction, seven chapters and brief appendix. The introduction states that the aim of liturgical reform is

> to impart ever increasing vigor to the Christian life of the faithful, to adapt more suitable to the needs of our own times those institutions which are subject to change; to foster . . . union among all

[39] Jounel, 75.
[40] Megivern, 61–127.
[41] Megivern, 128.
[42] Jounel, 76.

> who believe in Christ, to strengthen whatever can help to call the whole of mankind into . . . the Church.[43]

The aim might be epitomized in four words: sanctification, relativity, ecumenism, and evangelism. "Each of the main chapters begins with a short summary statement of biblical theology. For it is in biblical theology that the entire renewal of the liturgy is grounded . . . ."[44]

Chapter 1 lays down "general Principles for the restoration and promotion of the sacred liturgy." Beginning with a discussion of the nature of the liturgy and its importance in the church's life, the opening sentence is that God "wishes all men to be saved and come to the knowledge of the truth" (1 Tim. 2:4). This was accomplished by the Word made flesh who achieved His task of salvation "principally by the paschal mystery of His blessed Passion, Resurrection from the dead, and glorious Ascension . . . ."[45] Just as Christ was sent by the Father, so also were the apostles, who proclaimed the Gospel of Christ's death and resurrection.

> His purpose also was that they might accomplish the work of salvation which they were proclaiming, by means of sacrifice and sacraments, around which the entire liturgical life revolves. Thus by baptism they are plunged into the paschal mystery . . . die . . . are buried . . . raised up with Him.[46]

In the Lord's Supper they proclaim the death of the Lord until He comes. "To accomplish so great a work, Christ is always present in His Church, especially in her liturgical celebrations."[47] The various ways in which Christ is present in the liturgy are enumerated: The Sacrifice of the Mass (both in the person of His minister and under the eucharistic species); in His Word, "since it is He Himself who speaks when the holy Scriptures are read in the church"; and in the people of the Church who gather to pray and sing.

---

[43] Megivern, 197.
[44] Jounel, 77.
[45] Megivern, 199.
[46] Megivern, 199.
[47] Megivern, 200.

> Rightly, then, the liturgy is considered as an exercise of the priestly office of Jesus Christ. In the liturgy the sanctification of man is signified by signs perceptible to the senses, and is effected in a way which corresponds with each of these signs; in the liturgy the whole public worship is performed by the Mystical Body of Jesus Christ, that is, by the Head and His members.[48]

The nature of every liturgical celebration "is an action of Christ the Priest and of His Body," and is a "sacred action surpassing all others; no other action of the Church is equal to it in effectiveness either from the point of view of its basis or in degree."[49] Both the theology and theological terminology used in this document reveal the extensive influence of the liturgical and especially Casel's Mystery Theology on Vatican II. (See chapter 2.)

This does not mean that the Church does not have other important activities. Before one can come to the liturgy, there must be evangelism. The Constitution explains:

> Nevertheless the liturgy is the high point toward which the activity of the Church is directed; at the same time it is the fount from which all her power flows. For the aim and object of apostolic works is that all who are made sons of God by faith and baptism should come together to praise God in the midst of His Church, to take part in the Sacrifice, and to eat the Lord's supper . . . . But in order that the liturgy may be able to produce its full effects, it is necessary that the faithful come to it with proper dispositions, that their minds should be attuned to their voices, and that they should cooperate with divine grace lest they receive it in vain. Pastors of souls must therefore see to it that, when the liturgy is celebrated, something more is achieved than the mere observation of the laws governing valid and licit celebration; it is their duty also to ensure that the faithful take part fully aware of what they are doing, actively engaged in the rite, and enriched by its effects.[50]

The section concludes by encouraging popular personal devotions but advises that they "should be so drawn up that they harmonize

---

[48] Megivern, 200.
[49] Megivern, 200.
[50] Megivern, 201–202.

with the liturgical seasons, are in some fashion derived from it, and lead the people to it, since, in fact, the liturgy by its very nature far surpasses any of them."[51]

Thus we see emerging before us a key understanding of the nature of the liturgical reforms in Vatican II, in that the liturgy calls for a "full, conscious, and active participation of all the faithful in its celebrations." The laity are "a chosen race, a royal priesthood, a holy nation, a purchased people" (1 Peter 2:9) and thus "full, conscious and active participation" is "their right and duty by reason of their baptism."[52]

To accomplish this full participation the Constitution enumerates specific steps to be taken by the Church. The framers of the document fully recognize that the key to success rests with the properly trained leadership. Pastors must become

> thoroughly imbued with the spirit and power of the liturgy . . . professors appointed to teach in seminaries . . . the study of sacred liturgy is to be ranked among the compulsory and major courses in seminaries . . . and taught under its theological, historical, spiritual, pastoral and juridical aspects.[53]

The Constitution states that the liturgy is made up of two elements: "immutable elements divinely instituted, and the elements subject to change."[54] The restoration of texts and rites necessitates changing the latter elements so the Christian people are able "to understand them with ease and to take part in them fully (and) actively."[55]

The Council nevertheless established clear "guiding norms" directing the changes in text and rite. Regulation of the liturgy "depends solely on the authority of the Church, that is, on the Apostolic See . . . (and) no other person, even if he be a priest, may add, remove, or change anything in the liturgy on his own authority."[56]

---

[51] Megivern, 202.
[52] Megivern, 203.
[53] Megivern, 203.
[54] Megivern, 205.
[55] Megivern, 205.
[56] Megivern, 205.

Changes and new forms are to "grow organically from forms already existing,"[57] and "there must be no innovations unless the good of the Church genuinely and certainly requires them."[58]

The Constitution then lists further standards under the headings "Norms Drawn from the Hierarchic and Communal Nature of the Liturgy," and "Norms Based Upon the Didactic and Pastoral Nature of the Liturgy." The former acknowledges that the liturgy pertains to the whole Body of the Church, but she is cautioned that it effects different individual members in different ways. There must be recognition of their "differing rank, office, and actual participation."[59] The latter includes the counsel that new rites

> should be distinguished by noble simplicity; they should be short, clear, and unencumbered by useless repetitions . . . accommodated to the minds of the people . . . and normally should not require much explanation.[60]

It also emphasizes more and varied readings from Holy Scripture. Sermons are to be scripturally and liturgically based, and proclamation in character. Finally, while Latin is to be retained, the use of the vernacular is to be introduced where deemed appropriate and considered advantageous for the people. The territorial ecclesiastical authority (with papal approval) is to determine the extent to which the vernacular is introduced.

Chapter 2 is titled "The Most Sacred Mystery of the Eucharist." The general principles already articulated are now applied to the celebration of the Lord's Supper. Repeatedly the document encourages the "devout and active participation by the faithful." The faithful "should not be there as strangers or silent spectators," but be taught to understand the rite and prayers, and consciously to take part in them. "The rite of the Mass is to be revised in such a way that the intrinsic nature and purpose of its several parts, as

---

[57] Megivern, 205.
[58] Megivern, 205.
[59] Megivern, 206.
[60] Megivern, 208.

well as the connection between them, may be more clearly manifested."[61] To accomplish this the rites are to be simplified, elements that came to be duplicated over time are to be discarded, and "elements which have suffered injury through accidents of history are now to be restored according to the pristine norm of the holy Fathers."[62]

In line with the full active participation of the laity the Council approved the landmark proviso that communion in both kinds may be granted when "the bishops think fit, not only to clerics and religious, but also to the laity."[63]

After pointing out that the two parts of the Mass, the liturgy of the word and Eucharist liturgy, "are so closely connected with each other that they form but one single act of worship," the Council urged pastors to promote more frequent communion, that the faithful "take their part in the entire Mass."[64] Chapter 2 concludes with a list of cases in which concelebration may be allowed.

Chapter 3 concerns "The Other Sacraments and the Sacramentals." The opening paragraph states that these sacraments "not only presuppose faith, but by words and objects they also nourish, strengthen, and express it; that is why they are called 'sacraments of faith.'"[65] Authorization to revise many rites is given. The revision of the rite of Confirmation is to reflect its intimate connection with Baptism.

Chapter 4, which addresses the Divine Office, begins with a brief summary of the theology of the Daily Office. Christ Jesus

> continues His priestly work through the agency of His Church, which is ceaselessly engaged in praising the Lord and interceding for the salvation of the whole world. She does this not only by celebrating the Eucharist, but also in other ways, especially by praying the Divine Office.[66]

---

[61] Megivern, 213.
[62] Megivern, 213.
[63] Megivern, 214.
[64] Megivern, 214.
[65] Megivern, 215.
[66] Megivern, 220.

There is the traditional reference to 1 Thessalonians 5:17, "Pray without ceasing." To enable a better and more perfectly prayed office, various reforms are established. Lauds as morning prayer and Vespers as evening prayer are the two hinges on which the Daily Office turns; hence they are to be considered as the chief hours and are to be celebrated as such. Compline is to be drawn up so that it will be a suitable prayer for the end of the day.[67] Matins is to be retained and adapted for any hour of the day with fewer Psalms and longer readings. Prime is suppressed. The minor hours of Terce, Sect, and None are to be observed in the Choir. Not all clerics are required to pray the entire office but are encouraged to pray at least part of it. Singing the Office is preferred. The laity are encouraged to recite the Office, either with the priests, among themselves, or alone. The vernacular is to be provided. The completion of a revised Psalter is to be hastened. Readings from Scripture are to be arranged to allow for greater quantity and accessibility.

"The Liturgical Year" (chapter 5) is centered on the Lord's Day and the resurrection. Over the course of the liturgical year, the Church unfolds the whole mystery of Christ from incarnation to ascension, Pentecost, and the second coming. "Recalling thus the mysteries of Redemption, the Church opens to the faithful the riches of her Lord's powers and merits, so that these are in some way made present in every age, and the faithful are enabled to lay hold upon them and become filled with saving grace."[68]

The season of Lent has a twofold character which is to be given greater emphasis in both liturgy and liturgical catechesis. Baptismal features in the Lenten liturgy are to be restored as well as the penitential element. The penitential element "should not only be internal and individual, but also eternal and social."[69]

Chapter 6 is titled "Sacred Music" and recognizes the importance of music in the liturgical action. Music "adds delight to prayer, fos-

---

[67] Megivern, 221.
[68] Megivern, 225.
[69] Megivern, 227.

ters unity of mind, or confers greater solemnity upon the sacred rites."[70] The Constitution approves all forms of music as true art if they have the appropriate qualities. "Liturgical worship is given a more noble form when celebrated in song, with the assistance of sacred ministers and the active participation of the people."[71] Gregorian Chant is acknowledged as the proper and preferred form for the Roman liturgy. Polyphony and other kinds of music are permitted if they are in "accord with the spirit of the liturgical action." Congregational singing is to be "carefully fostered." In mission lands appropriate indigenous music is encouraged. "In the Latin Church, the pipe organ is to be held in high esteem."

To implement the reforms of the Constitution *Sacrosanctum Concilium*, Pope Paul VI established a "Consilium" on January 29, 1964. The commission was titled *Consilium ad exsequendam Constitutionem de scra Liturgia* or simply "Consilium." It comprised about fifty cardinals and bishops and more than two hundred experts and thus had a wide international representation. [72]

> The Consilium had a well-defined task: to revise the liturgical books in accordance with the norms set down by the Council, to provide instructions that would educate priests and faithful in the spirit that was to animate the renewal of worship, and also to make the reform gradually become a reality. But while the experts were quite familiar with the liturgical tradition and the sources on which they might draw in order to enrich the Roman body of prayers, they could not have suspected in advance the extent of the change that the use of the vernaculars in the liturgy would bring about.... At the council not a single Father had proposed or even envisaged the introduction of several Eucharistic Prayers into the Roman liturgy. Yet this had been done by 1968.[73]

The first significant document published by the Consilium was *Inter Oecumenici: Instruction of the Sacred Congregation of Rites on Putting into Effect the Constitution of the Sacred Liturgy* (September

[70] Megivern, 228.
[71] Megivern, 228.
[72] Jounel, 79.
[73] Jounel, 80.

26, 1964). In order that the faithful welcome the changes, it noted that renewal proceed "gradually, step by step . . . and explained to them by their pastors by means of planned instructions."[74] Implementation included organizing pastoral activity around the liturgy and the paschal mystery. This necessitates an intimate connection between liturgy and catechesis, education, and preaching.

A significant innovation first introduced by *Inter Oecumenici* in chapter 5 describes "The Proper Construction of Churches and Altars in Order to Facilitate the Active Participation of the Faithful." The freestanding high altar (enabling the priest to celebrate facing the people) is to occupy the central place in the edifice. Celebrant and ministers should not only be seen while serving but while seated as well. The celebrant's chair should not give the appearance of a throne, yet be so situated that when he is seated, it is apparent that he is "truly presiding over the whole gathering." The ambo (pulpit) for the readings should be so positioned that it is clearly seen and heard by all. The construction and furnishing of the baptistery should promote the dignity of the sacrament and lend itself "to the more public administration of the sacrament."[75] The choir and organ should be "so arranged that it is clear to all that the singers and the organist form a part of the congregation, and thus help all to fulfill their liturgical function."[76] Pierre Jounel has since pointed out that "within a short time this instruction would change the arrangement of churches throughout the world."[77]

Concurrent with *Inter Oecumenici* the U.S. Bishops' Commission on the Liturgical Apostolate published a document (October 29, 1964) on understanding liturgical texts in the vernacular. During this same time, many Lutheran and Protestant denominations in America were making the transition from Elizabethan to contemporary English. Although it was disturbing for many, this transition was minor compared to what Roman Catholics were going through. The use of vernacular texts required a rethinking and re-education of

---

74 Megivern, 241.
75 Megivern, 255.
76 Megivern, 254.
77 Jounel, 81.

how the clergy would read and the laity hear the various texts. The result was a very fresh and helpful document that is worthy of study by all denomination—even those who have worshiped in the vernacular for generations. (See Appendix B, "Understanding Liturgical Texts in the Vernacular: A Document from the U.S. Bishops' Commission on the Liturgical Apostolate.")

Inter Oecumenici was quickly followed by *Ecclesiae Semper* (March 7, 1965) for the promulgation of concelebration and communion under both kinds. "Henceforth the presbytery could manifest its unity around the altar, and the faithful could partake of the cup of the Lord."[78]

Liturgical music was addressed in *Musicam Sacram: Instruction of the Sacred Congregation of Rites on Music in the Sacred Liturgy* (March 5, 1967). The Instruction quotes extensively from the Vatican II Constitution on the Liturgy and promotes the use of music appropriate for the local context:

> It should be borne in mind that the true solemnity of liturgical worship depends less on the more ornate form of singing and a more magnificent ceremonial than on its worthy and religious celebration, which takes into account the integrity of the liturgical celebration itself, and the performance of all of its parts according to their own particular nature. To have a more ornate form of singing and a more magnificent ceremonial is at times desirable when resources are available to carry them out properly. On the other hand, it would be contrary to the true solemnity of the liturgy if this were to lead to a part of the action being omitted, changed or improperly performed.[79]

Drawing almost verbatim from the Constitution on the Sacred Liturgy, the Instruction states,

> Liturgical worship is given a more noble form when it is celebrated in song, with the ministers of each degree fulfilling their ministry and the people participating in it. Indeed, through this form, prayer

---

[78] Jounel, 81.
[79] Megivern, 289.

> is expressed in a more attractive way; the mystery of the liturgy, with its hierarchical and community nature, is more openly shown.[80]

Pastors are encouraged to do all they can to involve the laity by assigning to them the appropriate parts of the liturgy; however, this is to be carefully carried out so as not to blur the distinction between priest and laity. The Instruction states:

> The proper arrangement of a liturgical celebration requires the due assignment and performance of certain functions, by which each person, minister or layman, who has an office to perform, should do all of, but only, those parts which pertain to his office by the nature of the rite and the norms of the liturgy. This also demands that the meaning and proper nature of each part and of each song be carefully observed.[81]

For example, in determining the location of the choir, it should be so situated in the church that it is clearly obvious "that it is part of the whole congregation, and that it fulfills a special role . . . whenever the choir also included women, it should be placed outside the sanctuary."[82]

The 1960s ended with a flurry of activity. *Tres Abhinc Annos* dealt with rubrical changes in the Mass. *Eucharisticum Mysterim* (May 25, 1967) discussed theological aspects of eucharistic worship. In commenting on the nature of active participation in the Mass, *Eucharisticum Mysterium* states:

> It should be made clear that all who gather for the Eucharist constitute that holy people which, together with the minister, plays its part in the sacred action. It is indeed the priest alone who, acting in the person of Christ, consecrates the bread and wine, but the role of the faithful in the Eucharist is to recall the passion, resurrection and glorification of the Lord, to give thanks to God, and to offer the immaculate Victim not only through the hands of the priest, but also together with him; and finally, by receiving the Body of the Lord, to perfect that communion with God

[80] Megivern, 287.
[81] Megivern, 288.
[82] Megivern, 292.

among themselves which should be the product of participation in the Sacrifice of the Mass.[83]

The document states that to those who are united to Christ in this sacrifice by faith and charity, "it brings a greater or less benefit in proportion to their devotion."[84]

On November 19, 1969, Pope Paul VI in an address to a general audience concerning the New Mass Rite endeavored to alleviate apprehensions. He addressed the question, "What does this change consist of?" Pope Paul VI answered that it would involve many new ritual prescriptions. He added, "But let us be clear on this point: none of the substance of our traditional Mass has been changed." He continues with what serves as a succinct summary of the Roman Catholic liturgical movement to date.

Some might get the wrong impression .... They might think that the correspondence between the law of praying, *lex orandi*, and the law of believing, *lex credendi*, has been compromised as a result .... But that is definitely not the case—first of all, because the rite and its related rubric are not in themselves a dogmatic definition. They are capable of various theological qualifications, depending on the liturgical context to which they relate. They are gestures and terms relating to a lived and living religious action which involved the ineffable mystery of God's presence; it is an action that is not always carried out in the exact same form, an action that only theological analysis can examine and express in doctrinal formulas, because the Mass of the new rite is and remains the Mass it always was—in some of its aspects even more clearly so than before.

The unity between the Lord's Supper, the sacrifice of the cross, and the re-presentation of both in the Mass, is inviolably affirmed and celebrated in the new rite, as it was in the old. The Mass is and remains the memorial of the Lord's Last Supper, at which He instituted the sacrifice of the New Testament by changing bread and wine into His Body and Blood and willed, by virtue of the priesthood that He conferred on His Apostles, that it be

[83] Megivern, 317.
[84] Megivern, 317.

> repeated identically but in a different manner—that is, in an unbloody and sacramental manner—in perpetual memory of Him until His last coming.
>
> In the new rite you will find clearer light shed on the relationship between the Liturgy of the Word and the properly Eucharistic Liturgy—the latter being the response which realizes and effects the former. You will notice how much emphasis is placed, in the celebration of the Eucharistic service, on the participation of the assembly of the faithful, who are and fully feel themselves a "Church" at the Mass.[85]

Pope Paul also addressed concerns about the consequences the changes would have for those who assist at the Mass. He noted that the desired consequences

> are more intelligent, more satisfying, more real and more sanctifying participation by the faithful in the liturgical mystery—participation, that is, in the hearing of the word of God . . . and in the mystic reality of Christ's sacramental and propitiatory sacrifice.[86]

The theological enterprise of the Liturgical Movement reached its first peak at the Second Vatican Council.[87] It was the first Constitution to be published. H. Ellsworth Chandlee states,

> The Constitution on the Sacred Liturgy contains what is probably one of the best and clearest statements of the theology of the liturgy, its meaning and its function in the life of the church which has as yet been made, a statement which is in its approach thoroughly biblical, patristic, and eirenical . . . the best and most concise statement of the principles and objectives of the Liturgical Movement . . . . Entirely ecumenical in scope . . . must be given thorough study by anyone who wishes to understand the liturgy and the importance of the liturgical renewal of the whole Christian Church.[88]

---

[85] Megivern, 373–374.

[86] Megivern, 374.

[87] On November 14, 1962, the Council passed *De Sacra Liturgia* by the overwhelming majority of 2,162 to 46. Walter M. Abbott, ed., *The Documents of Vatican II* (New York: Herder and Herder Association Press, 1966), 134.

[88] Chandlee, 311.

While Vatican II was a climax of fifty years of work, it proved not to be the culmination of the Liturgical Movement but a tremendous catalyst for future endeavors. It opened the floodgates of liturgical theology studies.

Today, all major traditions of Christianity are affected by and contribute to the development of liturgical theology. Roman Catholic, Lutheran, Orthodox, and even the Reformed churches are involved. If Frank C. Senn is correct in his analysis, then, due to the attention given to the behavioral sciences, North American liturgiology (and worship resources in the American churches) has moved ahead of European pastoral liturgical work.[89] History will determine whether or not Senn's opinion that the focus of leadership of the Movement has shifted to North America is correct. What can be safely said is that the Movement is broadly international and becoming more and more interdenominational. No longer does each tradition work in isolation.

From the perspective of prolegomena, the question of the relationship between liturgy and theology has become a primary if not the primary area of study since Vatican II. Teresa Berger identifies "three particular areas of theological work in which this interest has surfaced: Roman-Catholic liturgical theology, Protestant systematic theology, and ecumenical endeavors."[90] On the question of the relationship of liturgy and theology, Berger summarizes the "bewildering variety" of recent trends and discussions.

> While a Roman-Catholic liturgical theology discusses the relationship of the *lex orandi* to the *lex credendi*, Protestant systematic theology is concerned with doxological and theological language, and the ecumenists wonder about the liturgical context for an emerging doctrinal consensus. It seems obvious, however, that beneath the (terminologically) different discussions there lies a common concern. This concern can be formulated as a new interest in the litur-

---

89 Frank C. Senn, "Teaching Worship in Seminaries: A Response," *Worship* 55 (June 1981): 328.

90 Teresa Berger, "Liturgy: A Forgotten Subject-Matter of Theology," *Studia Liturgica* 17 (1987): 10.

> gical-doxological-hymnic traditions of the churches in relationship to the nature and task of theology.[91]

Writing the above summary in 1987, Berger added, "And lately, there seems to be agreement on the need for further work on the relationship between doxology/liturgy and theology."[92]

The Liturgical Movement is not a passing fad. It is not merely the result of "a new awakening of an aesthetically religious, psychological enthusiasm for cultus, for its ceremonial and ritual, for its external aspects; a sort of new liturgical pietism."[93] The movement has substance and has demonstrated incredible staying power. The above historical overview has shown that the movement did not begin as a "theological" movement (in the sense of being a systematic elucidation and interpretation of worship). Its main efforts were the "practical" revival of the church. Nevertheless, phase one created the necessary conditions for liturgical theology. This was becoming apparent already in the 1960s, when Alexander Schmemann made the observation:

> It became clear that without such theological "reflection" the liturgical revival was threatened either by an excessive submission to the "demands of the day," to the radical nature of certain "missionary" and "Pastoral" movements quite prepared to drop old forms without a second thought or, on the other hand, by a peculiar archeologism which considers the restoration of worship in its "primitive purity" as the panacea for all contemporary ills.[94]

Schmemann's quote effectively articulates how vitally important the theological enterprise is for the practical, pastoral, nitty-gritty of parish worship today.

---

91 Berger, 16.

92 Berger, 17.

93 Alexander Schmemann, *Introduction to Liturgical Theology* (Crestwood, NY: St. Vladimir's Seminary Press, 1986 [original 1966]), 14.

94 Schmemann, 15.

2

The Influence of Odo Casel, Gregory Dix, and Yngve Brilioth in the Development of the Liturgical Movement

Odo Casel and Liturgy as a Celebration of the Mysteries (*Kultmysterium*)

BENEDICTINE monk Odo Casel (1886–1948) of Maria Laach, Germany, was one of the pioneer thinkers of the contemporary Liturgical Movement. His notoriety and influence was attained through his books and editorship of the *Jahrbuch für Liturgiewissenschaft*, which included many of his essays. The most important of his essays and books remains the trenchant *Das Christlich Kultmysterium*.

His special achievement, however, was to bring out the meaning of the liturgy as a celebration of the mysteries of Christ and His Church: the ritual and sacramental deed of the Church makes present Christ's act of salvation.[1] Casel's *fons et origo* was the *religionsgeschichtliche Schule* and especially the Hellenistic mystery cults, which he saw as a preparation for Christ. In search of the "golden age," Casel

> opened the door to phenomenological studies by Christian liturgists; phenomenology underscored the concept of *leitourgia* as "the work of the people;" the emphasis on the corporate nature of worship led to agitation for the vernacular in order to encourage popular participation; and vernacularization required an open-

[1] J. M. Carriere, *New Catholic Encyclopedia*, vol. 10 (New York: McGraw Hill Book Company, 1967); see "Casel, Odo," 176–177.

> ness to contemporary art, music, literature, and architecture. After Casel's death, his rich insights were further developed . . . . Thus his doctrine, with light nuance and corrections, became one of the most valuable elements of contemporary theology on the liturgy, the Sacraments, and the Church.[2]

Casel had both supporters and detractors. Writing in 1954, Ernest B. Koenker discussed the division caused by Casel's theory.

> At present the theory is the subject of widespread debate among dogmaticians and liturgists. It has not been established as dogma; in fact, *Mediator Dei* was promulgated shortly before Casel's death, and some early readers discerned in it a condemnation of the *Mysterientheologie.* But Dom Odo had inquired in Rome and the answer had been: "its merits have to be further discussed and a great deal of scholarly work to be done, before anybody can or will pass judgment on it authoritatively." Meanwhile, a whole French theological school has gone overboard for the new approach: Anscar Vonier, O.S.B., Henri de Lubac, S.J., Jean Daniélou, S.J., Pie Duploye, O.P., P. Doncoeur, S.J., and others . . . . Some accepted it with reservations, for example, Francois Diekamp, J. Butler, Karl Adam, Ch.-V. Heris, and Sohngen. Other outstanding scholars of the movement, including Theodor Klauser and Joseph Jungmann, reject it.[3]

Theodor Klauser expressed great admiration for Casel's learning, richness of ideas, and "eloquence in setting them forth"; however, he did not agree with the direction Casel was taking. Writing in 1965, Klauser acknowledged Casel's impact and shortcoming:

> Casel attracted a great following in his day; his influence was considerable and it still continues to be felt . . . gifted men of this kind and of this stature are much needed both in the world and in the Church. They shake us up and show us new paths and we must be thankful for the effect they have on us, even if we cannot always follow them.[4]

---

[2] Frank C. Senn, *Christian Worship and Its Cultural Setting* (Philadelphia: Fortress Press, 1983), 48.

[3] Ernest B. Koenker, *The Liturgical Renaissance in the Roman Catholic Church* (Chicago: University of Chicago Press, 1954), 104–105.

[4] Theodor Klauser, *A Short History of the Western Liturgy: An Account and Some Reflections*, 2d ed. (Oxford: Oxford University Press, 1979) 27.

Five years after Vatican II, the editor of *Das christliche Opfermysterium* wrote in the introduction of this collection of essays by Casel that *Sacrosanctum Consilium* is "the fairest fruit of everything the pioneers of the liturgical renewal that Odo Casel and the whole school of Maria Laach achieved in their work."[5] On the flyleaf of the volume, Gerhardus van der Leeuw opined that Casel was the most important theologian of the last one hundred and fifty years—with the possible exception of Karl Barth.[6]

As late as 1983, a critical assessment of Casel by Irenée Henri Dalmais, O.P., in *L'Eglise en Prière: Principes de la liturgie* concluded that Casel's "philological" method was seriously defective. Dalmais begins with a lengthy quote from a review of the new French edition of *Le mystere du culte* (1964) by Louis Bouyer which appeared in *La Maison-Dieu: Revue de pastorale liturgique*:[7]

> Dom Casel developed his vision of the soul of early Christianity in a framework that he took over from the comparative history of religions . . . not everything in that framework became outmoded! The basic idea that there is a fundamental structure of the human soul that shines through the most varied rites and myths and, more specifically, that human beings achieve a participation in divine life through mythico-ritual symbols seems to be a permanent gain. No less valuable an acquisition is the vision of life as fundamentally sacred in its fruitfulness as well as in its deaths and rebirths. On the other hand, the assimilation of the Christian "mystery" to a model already formed in the "mysteries" of Hellenistic paganism does not seem acceptable in the terms in which Casel conceived it . . . . It must be said that the assimilation is the result of a mirage: One begins by projecting typically Christian ideas and facts into the data from these religions, then one rejoices to find them there! But the whole process is possible only if one neglects the elementary rules of strict philolog-

---

[5] Oliver K. Olson, "Contemporary Trends in Liturgy Viewed from the Perspective of Classical Lutheran Theology," *Lutheran Quarterly* 26, 2 (May 1974): 112. Olson is quoting from Odo Casel's *Das christliche Opfermysterium* (Graz, Vienna, Cologne: Styria, 1968), 27.

[6] Olson, 112.

[7] Irénée Henri Dalmais, O.P. in *L'Eglise en Prière: Principes de la liturgie* concluded that Casel's "philological" method was seriously defective. Dalmais begins with a lengthy quote from a review of the new French edition of *Le mystere du culte* (1964) by Louis Bouyer which appeared in *La Maison-Dieu: Revue de pastorale liturgique* (no. 80, 1964, 242–243).

> ical and historical criticism. When Dom Casel thinks he is making a semantic analysis of a word like *mysterium*, he never seems to suspect the first rule of any semantic study, namely, that seemingly related texts cannot be interpreted by separating their key expressions from the divergent lexicographical associations they have in different texts. Thus mysterium in the "mystery religions" of Hellenistic paganism, refers directly to an esoteric rite. Mysterium in the New Testament, on the other hand, designates the great secret of divine wisdom, namely, God's plan for human history that can be revealed only by his word, which in fact is his definitive Word: Christ and him crucified. Only as a result of a later transfer did mysterium as used in Christianity come to designate also the rite through which Christ effectively communicates himself. To neglect or minimize the importance of these facts can only lead to serious confusion. As a matter of fact, Casel did clearly see the radical difference between the "mystery religions" and the Christian mystery . . . . What prevented him from drawing all the conclusions from this realization was, in addition to an insufficiently critical method, his radical ignorance of the Judaism of the New Testament period.[8]

Dalmais insists, however, that

> an even more difficult and controverted question is that of the way in which the mystery of salvation is present in the liturgical mysteries. Dom Casel never stopped insisting that what is present is not simply the effect, that is, the grace bestowed, but the redemptive work itself.[9]

Casel's patristic foundations have been demonstrated to be weak; however, Dalmais concedes,

> in its essentials his theology is fully consistent with undoubted patristic teaching. He rejoiced to find this thinking reflected in the teaching of the Encyclical *Mediator Dei*, even though this document expressed reserves with regard to certain views on the way in which the mystery is present (*Mysteriengegenwart*).[10]

---

[8] Quoted from a translation by I. H. Dalmais in *The Church at Prayer: Principles of the Liturgy*, 269–270.

[9] *Church at Prayer*, 270.

[10] *Church at Prayer*, 270.

Within a year after the Vatican II *Sacrosanctum Concilium* was published, Louis Bouyer made this remarkable statement in *La Maison-Dieu*:

> The heart of the teaching on the liturgy in the conciliar Constitution is also the heart of Dom Casel's teaching. The Constitution's constant citation of the patristic, liturgical, and earlier conciliar texts on which Casel based his interpretation, and its interpretation of these texts on the same lines as Casel show a relation of filiation that will strike all future historians.[11]

Casel was a major figure in the development of the theology of the Roman Catholic liturgical movement. To grasp these liturgical developments it is necessary to understand Casel's theory. In the preface to the English edition of *Das Christliche Kultmysterium*, Charles Davis notes that for Casel, "the Christian thing was not a religion but a mystery as the ancients understood the word" and "a 'mystery' was not primarily a mysterious truth beyond our reason but a reality—a divine reality, hidden yet communicated."[12] As a divine reality it was therefore theocentric. God's mystery means three things and one:

1. First of all it is God considered in himself, as the infinitely distant, holy, unapproachable, to whom no man may draw near and live. Yet, by grace he reveals himself to his chosen, yet this is a revelation *in mysterio*. The ancient religions had a "shadowy foreboding of the mystery . . . . Everywhere there is a longing to bring heaven down into the world, to bring man nearer to God, and marry the two hemispheres."[13]
2. Secondly, mystery refers to Christ, the incarnation, and especially the saving deeds (*Handlung*): "The deeds of his lowliness, above all his sacrificial death on the cross . . . [and] above all else, his resurrection and exaltation are mysteries because God's glory is shown through them in the human person of Jesus, although in a manner hidden to the world and open only

[11] *Church at Prayer*, 271.
[12] Odo Casel, *The Mystery of Christian Worship: and Other Writings*, ed. Burkhard Neunheuse [no translator given] (Westminster, MD: Newman Press, 1962), ix.
[13] Casel, 5–6.

to the knowledge of the faithful."[14] For Casel the emphasis is on the role of the saving deeds or saving actions in which the church leads people to salvation. He concludes this second aspect of mystery by saying, "Yet, just as the saving design is not merely teaching, but first and foremost Christ's saving deed, so, too, the church leads mankind to salvation not merely by word only, but by sacred actions; through faith and the mysteries Christ lives in the church."[15]

3. The third usage of mystery applies to the fact that since Christ is no longer visible among us, the post-ascension church meets "his person, his saving deeds, the workings of his grace in the mysteries of his worship."[16]

The Mystery of Christian Worship

Following this brief introduction to a "threefold yet one" understanding of the divine and ineffable (*arreton*) mystery, Casel turns his attention in the second chapter to developing his theory of the mystery of worship in the Christian cosmos. This is followed by an examination of the relationship of the mystery of Christian worship to the mysteries of antiquity, "which lend it their language." As mentioned earlier, Casel's seminal context was the *religionsgeschichtliche Schule.* Given this starting point, his trajectory and destination are fairly predictable. He views the Christian faith as a scheme rather than a religion.

> Christianity is not a "religion" or a confession in the way the last three hundred years would have understood the word: a system of more or less dogmatically certain truths to be accepted and confessed, and of moral commands to be observed or at least accorded recognition. Both elements belong, of course, to Christianity, intellectual structure and moral law; but neither exhausts its essence. Still less is Christianity a matter of religious sentiment, a more or less emotionally toned attitude towards "The divine," which binds itself to no dogmatic or moral system whatever.[17]

---

[14] Casel, 6–7.
[15] Casel, 7.
[16] Casel, 7.
[17] Casel, 9.

Casel claims to find in St. Paul a view of mystery that goes beyond the circumscribed confessions of the church. The mystery is ineffable, yet Casel explains: "We can express the mystery, so conceived, by the one word 'Christ', meaning by it the Savior's person together with his mystical body, the church."[18] Yes, the Christ was "Word made flesh," namely, Jesus, but "The Son of man is raised to be Lord, he is no longer in the flesh of sin, but has become wholly Spirit (*pneuma*); his manhood is utterly transformed by its glorification in the godhead."[19] A Spirit Lord becomes a very important component in a scheme that attempts to disconnect from the Word. Since the saving action of God is an ineffable mystery that cannot be fully expressed, Casel's solution is to keep them as actions which are participated in via the mystery of Christian worship. "The content of the mystery of Christ is, therefore, the person of the God-man and his saving deed for the church; the church, in turn, enters the mystery through this deed."[20] At the center of Christ's saving deeds is the sacred Pasch,

> the sacrifice of the God-man in death on the cross, and his resurrection to glory: it is the Church's sacrifice in communion with and by the power of the crucified God-man . . . . Both of these sacrifices flow together; they are fundamentally one; the Church . . . acts and offers in his strength. Christ living in time made his sacrifice alone on the cross; Christ raised up by the Spirit makes the sacrifice together with his Church which he has purified . . . . It is not as if the Lord, now in *pneuma* were making a new sacrifice with the Church: through the one sacrifice he has reached the term of offering . . . . The church, not yet brought to her completion, is drawn into this sacrifice of his; as he sacrificed for her, she now takes an active part in his sacrifice, makes it her own . . . .[21]

The Roman Catholic understanding of the Church as the "mystical body of Christ" is conveniently drawn upon by Casel at this point. Christ is the head, the Church is the Body. "Bridegroom and bride,

---

[18] Casel, 9–10.
[19] Casel, 11.
[20] Casel, 12.
[21] Casel, 13.

head and members act as one." Christ is the Savior, the one who accomplishes salvation, but "the Church for its part shares in the act of Christ, receiving the influence of every act he does, but receiving actively; healthy members share in the action of a body."[22] Casel understood liturgy as the "fulfillment in ritual of what the Lord did for our salvation . . . . We act out the mysteries as the body of Christ; as his body we do all that the head does." Casel continues,

> In the rite we have an image of Christ's act in which we did not share while it was being fulfilled in time and place. The same thing is true of the last supper. Then Christ said, "this act of sacrifice done once for all time on the cross is here being anticipated in image, and you are to imitate it afterwards in image." The whole church does now what the Lord did at that moment. [23]

The way in which man becomes a member of the mystical body is at baptism where "for the first time, the Christian meets the mystery of worship."[24] Casel does not understand Baptism as a sacred act through which the saving gifts, won by Christ on the cross, are distributed through water and the word and received through faith alone. It is rather the sacred action of a *pneuma*, Christ dispensing the *pneuma* to the body. Casel is clear in his rejection of Paul's doctrine of justification by grace through faith alone. As with all work-righteous and transformational theologies, Casel is very unclear and imprecise in how this active incorporation really works. Since we cannot of our own power become like Jesus, who is the perfect model, Jesus must do it for us. Casel writes:

> But we cannot do this of our own power; only through a saviour; Christ's salvation must be made real in us. This does not come about through a mere application, with our behaviour purely passive, through a "justification" purely from faith, or by an application of the grace of Christ, where we have only to clear things out of the way in a negative fashion, to receive it. Rather, what is necessary is a living, active sharing in the redeeming deed of Christ; passive because

---

[22] Casel, 13–14.
[23] Casel, 104.
[24] Casel, 14.

> the Lord makes it act upon us, active because we share in it by a deed of our own. To the action of God upon us (*opus operatum*) responds our co-operation (*opus operantis*), carried out through grace from him. How is it possible to do this great work where God and man are fellow-actors . . . ? For this purpose the Lord has given us the mysteries of worship: the sacred actions which we perform, but which, at the same time, the Lord performs upon us by his priests' service in the Church. Through these actions it becomes possible for us to share most intensively and concretely in a kind of immediate contact, yet most spiritually, too, in God's saving acts.[25]

Casel demands that "salvation must be made real in us." The articulation of enthusiasm, however, is inevitably unclear. He writes that through the actions we share "most intensively and concretely in a kind of immediate contact, yet most spiritually." What exactly is going on in this admittedly "mystical" sharing is more amorphous than concrete as the qualifiers "in a kind of" and "yet most spiritually" reveal. The editor of *The Mystery of Christian Worship* himself admits, "To determine more precisely the degree of reality which this medial thing has is the thorny task of theology in our day."[26] Casel claims to have clearly located the "substance" of the mystery in chapter 6 of Paul's epistle to the Romans. His eisegesis fails to distinguish between justification and sanctification. He ignores the primary point of the epistle, that the gospel is the power of God for the salvation of everyone who believes, "for in the gospel a righteousness from God is revealed, a righteousness that is by faith from the first to the last, just as it is written; 'The righteous will live by faith.'" Paul highlights this emphasis in chapter 1, verses 16–17 and thoroughly develops it in chapters 3, 4, and 5. Chapter 6 concerns itself with sanctification. Casel's confusion of justification and sanc-

---

[25] Casel, 14–15.

[26] Casel, 207, Editor's Notes on p. 16. Casel attempts to explain more precisely the "degree of reality" in this mystical sharing in a 1941 article in *Jahrbuch für Liturgiewissenschaft*. "In the knowledge born of faith we see in the sacramental image its original, the saving work of Christ. We see it in faith and *gnosis*, that is to say, we touch it, make it our own, are conformed to it through participation and re-formed after the likeness of the crucified and risen Christ . . . . Sacrament and original saving act are not two separated things, but one; the image is so filled with the reality of the original deed that it may rightly be called a presence of it (op. cit. 268)." J. L. W., 15 (1941), 253–269. [ellipsis in original]

tification at this juncture turns baptism into a mixture of law and gospel at the expense of the gospel.

For Casel, baptism marks the initiation into and the beginning of a process of purification of sins and the gift of the *pneuma*. He is very clear at this point: "Let no one, then, think that baptism is only the grace of sins' forgiveness and acceptance as a son, as John's baptism was. Rather, we know that baptism was indeed purification of sins, and the gift of the *pneuma*."[27] Casel admits that baptism forgives sins and gives the initiate acceptance to sonship, but certainty of this gift is tied to the big "if" of *in nos* growth.

> Baptism indeed gave the remission of sins and acceptance to sonship, but communion with the real suffering of Christ by imitation of them. In order that we might all know that Christ did everything he undertook for our sakes, for the sake of our salvation, and suffered in fact not in appearance, and that we become sharers in his pain, St. Paul has called out with such clarity: if we have grown up in the pattern of his death, we shall share also in his resurrection. The word "grown up" (*sumphutoi*) is meaningful; for as the true vine is implanted here, we, too, are engrafted into it through sharing in death by baptism . . . . This special sharing in the life of Christ, both symbolic and real, is what the ancients called mystical; it is something mediate between outward symbol and the purely real . . . the sacrament does not simply give the grace of new life, but preserves "the community of real sufferings by imitation" . . . . So we are right to call mysteries those sacred rites which imitate and pass on the mystery of Christ.[28]

All of this is supposedly possible since by his passion the Lord has become *pneuma* and through the "mystical passion in baptism and the spiritual resurrection which flowed from it,"[29] we have become spiritual men. Just as the risen God-man is now the glorified *Pneuma Christi*, so also in "initiation" (baptism and confirmation), the initiate is "no *mere* man, but man transformed, divinized, new-begotten out of God to be God's child. He carries the life of God

---

[27] Casel, 15.
[28] Casel, 16.
[29] Casel, 17.

within him."[30] He is a member of the High-Priest, Christ, and thus man himself is *christus*, an anointed; a priest who may sacrifice to God the Father. Through Christ this sacrifice "becomes uniquely acceptable and accepted." All of this leads up to the important point:

> There is no religion without sacrifice. Religion is the ordering between God and his creature; God bends down to man, and man climbs up toward God; by taking it and passing it into his possession, God makes the sacrifice holy and consecrates it.[31]

Having attempted to demonstrate an "inmost oneness of being" between Christ and the christs as spirits sharing in the same action of suffering, dying, and rising mystically through baptism,

> it follows that the Church must take a share in Christ's sacrifice, in a feminine, receptive way, yet one which is no less active for that. She . . . sacrifices her bridegroom, and with him, herself. But she does so not merely in faith or in some mental act, but rather in a real and concrete fashion, in mystery . . . .[32]

For a visible community to express this inward oneness and joint sacrificial action necessitates, according to Casel, a common ritual act. The Mass fills the requirements with the priest giving outward expression to the invisible action of God.

To complete this spiritual sharing and total engrafting in the body of Christ, Casel points to the importance of three primary mysteries: baptism, confirmation, and the Eucharist.

> Baptism cleanses from sin by plunging us into the cross; confirmation breathes the new god-life of the *pneuma* into us, and communion strengthens and preserves it, makes the members grow up to their full measure in the body . . . . These three mysteries are, therefore, the most important and most necessary for the life of the church in each Christian.[33]

---

[30] Casel, 18–19.
[31] Casel, 19.
[32] Casel, 21.
[33] Casel, 25.

Liturgy as Cultic Re-Presentation of Saving Event

"Action" (*Handlung*) and "re-presentation" (*Gegenwartigsetzung*) are key words for Casel in his effort to explain how the mysteries work. When Christ and his Church cooperate in the doing of the liturgy, this ritual and sacramental action of the Church makes present (re-presents) Christ's act of salvation. Casel is unequivocal on this point, stating that "liturgical mystery is the most central and most essential action of the Christian religion."[34] Furthermore, Casel claims that Christianity inherited this understanding of mystery from the ancient mystery religions and states emphatically, "Christianity is of its own very essence . . . a mystery religion, and the mystery language its own most rightful possession."[35]

Following the age of Alexander the Great, the synthesis of Greek and Eastern ideas led to the formation of the mystery cults. The form and language of this synthesis, Casel claims, was incorporated by Christianity. Casel, however, distinguishes form and language from content. Form and language give expression to how the mysteries work. For the pagans, the

> fundamental idea was participation in the lives of the gods, who in some way or other had appeared in human form, and taken part in the pain and happiness of mortal men. The believer acted with them by sharing their suffering and deeds portrayed in the rite, and performed in it once more by ritual imitation.[36]

Through this intimate participation the person became a member of the race of gods and was given the assurance that following death he would escape the normal fate of mortals. In the place of Hades' darkness he would attain the blessedness of light.

> Worship in this community was carried out with rich and dramatic symbolism in which the divine actions were performed in a hieratic and formal manner with a rich use of natural symbolism.[37]

---

[34] Casel, 27.
[35] Casel, 34.
[36] Casel, 32.
[37] Casel, 32.

For Casel, the ritual-form of the pagan mysteries is analogous to Christian worship. Like the mystery cults, the Christian mysteries are actions (rituals) which re-present or re-actualize the original saving event. It is important to point out, however, that the Christian content (the original event and its symbols, that is, the mystery of Christ) is not analogous with its pagan counterpart. Casel concludes that the concepts of the ancient mysteries

> remained the prisoners of unredeemed nature, in the slavery of the "world's elements" as St. Paul says of a Jewish-Hellenistic cult [Col. 2:8,20]; they did not lead to the supernatural life of the true God. They were only a shadow, in contrast to the Christian mysteries . . . . An analogy existed for them, as it did for the whole of nature and supernature, and so they were able to lend words and forms to the mysteries of Christ which belonged to that supernature. They did not give existence or content . . . . But they made it possible to give a body to the new and unconceived elements of the New Testament's revelation.[38]

When the Church entered a pagan world in which the "symbolic, strength-giving rites of the mysteries" were an important reality, she did not "end, but rather fulfilled their way of thinking." Nor, in Casel's opinion, would the Church need to transform the world's way of thinking since, as mentioned earlier, he believed Christianity to be "of its own essence . . . a mystery religion." Going even further, Casel added, "The ancient church lived in mystery, and needed to construct no theory about it."[39] The editor of Casel's *Das Christliche Kultmysterium* accentuates this view:

> It is most important to keep this in mind. The all-important fact is that Christianity is a mystery religion in virtue of its own very nature and the liturgy of mysteries is the central and essential activity of this religion.[40]

---

[38] Casel, 33.
[39] Casel, 36.
[40] Casel, 208 (editor's note from page 34).

Casel goes to great lengths to explain the workings of his pagan-Christian ritual form. He gives this primary definition of mystery:

> The mystery is a sacred ritual action [*heilige kultische Handlung*] in which a saving deed is made present through the rite [*Heilstatsache unter dem Ritus gegenwart wird*]; the congregation, by performing the rite, take part in the saving act, and thereby win [*erwirbt*] salvation.[41]

In Casel's opinion, the best of the ancient world made a positive contribution to Christianity, which in turn gave a wholly new meaning to the mystery-type. The new meaning is the redemptive life and passion of Jesus Christ. A most important point at which the new content was connected to the mystery-type occurred with the Lord's directive to the disciples to "do this in remembrance of me."

> This sacred rite with its full divine content is what the disciples are to "act in memory"; they are to make real again the passion of their divine master . . . . Christ has given his mystery to the church's care; she acts it out, and thereby fulfills his action, which has become hers. So Christ and the church become one in act and passion: the mystery is made a new and eternal covenant.[42]

Worship consists of prayer, sacrifice, and mystery. Whereas prayer lifts the thoughts and wishes before God, and sacrifice is essentially a gift to God, mystery "seeks to place itself in a still deeper relationship"[43] to God or the gods in order that the worshiper may obtain life and salvation through his or her participation in the saving action made present again. Since every age is in need of salvation and life, "the epiphany goes on and on in worship; the saving, healing act of God is performed over and over."[44] This is

---

[41] Casel, 54. See also Odo Casel, *Das Christliche Kultmysterium*, 3d ed. (Regensburg-Verlag vorm Friedrich Putstet: Gregorius-Verlage, 1948), 102. "*Das Mysterium ist eine heilige kultische Handlung, in der eine Heilstatsache unter dem Ritus gegenwart wird; indem die Kultgemeinde diesen Ritus vollzieht, nimmt sie an der Heilstat teil und erwirbt sich dadurch das Heil.*"

[42] Casel, 59.

[43] Casel, 53.

[44] Casel, 53.

accomplished through ritual action and ritual remembrance (*anamnesis*) that re-presents the initial saving act.

> Worship is a means of making it real once more, and thus breaking through to the spring of salvation. The members of the cult present again in a ritual, symbolic fashion, that primeval act; in holy words and rites of priest and faithful the reality is there once more. The celebrant community is united in the deepest fashion with the Lord they worship; there is no deeper oneness than suffering and action shared. Thereby they win a share in the new life of God; they enter his chorus, they become gods. The mysteries' way is, therefore, the way of ritual action as a sharing in the gods' acts; its aim is union with godhead, share in his life.[45]

The way of the mysteries is the way of ritual action. The aim is union with God. The method is action/sharing in the god's acts. "Man enters into a cultic act which is the symbolic re-presentation and actualization of spiritual realities and events."[46] Casel states:

> The Christian mystery is the memorial of Christ's saving act through worship in rite and word. The mystery is no mere recalling of Christ and his saving deed; it is a memorial in worship. The church does what the Lord did, and thereby makes his act present. Christ himself is present and acts through the church, his *ecclesia*, while she acts with him. Both carry out the action.[47]

This sharing in God's saving action requires anamnesis (going back by remembering). The doing is, therefore, a re-presentation (a mystical *repraesentatio*; *Gegenwartigsetzung*; a making-present-again of the whole saving work of Christ)[48] that makes the liturgy

---

[45] Casel, 53.

[46] Koenker, 110. In a footnote, Koenker refers to the article "Glaube, Gnosis und Mysterium," *Jahrbuch für Liturgiewissenschaft*, XV (1941), 195 ff.

[47] Casel, 141.

[48] In *The Liturgical Renaissance in the Roman Catholic Church*, Ernest Koenker's thorough research points out variations on Casel's theory among leading contemporaries. "Francois Diekamp, Abbot Anscar Vonier, and Eugene Masure all admit the re-presentation of Christ's passion and death but hesitate to follow Dom Casel when he affirms this for the whole life of Christ, from the Incarnation to the Ascension. According to another group, including Karl Adam and J. Butler, 'It is not the death of Christ himself which is rendered present in the cult but his will to offer himself and be a propitiation.' 111. There

not only the place of effect, but the place of cause and effect. "Not just faith in the once dead prince is to save the faithful; his saving act is to be a continual, lasting, mystical, and yet concrete presence in the church."[49] In *Mysterientheologie* the "do this in remembrance," is not something psychological or ethical, but as Ernest Koenker points out,

> It is rather ontological action, a *signum efficax*, a reality which efficaciously heightens man's natural existence through an activity in a higher sphere; as such, of course, it works *ex opere operato*. The symbol really and actually is in the supernatural-divine order what in its outward, natural appearance it signifies.[50]

> Liturgy is both cause and effect.

> Christ has given his mystery to the church's care; she acts it out, and thereby fulfills his action, which has become hers. So, Christ and the church become one in act and passion.[51]

This understanding of the way mystery works is especially apparent in the sacrifice of the mass, where

> The act of Christ in the Christian sacrifice consists in his presenting once more his act of sacrifice and redemption beneath the veil of symbols; the share of the faithful expresses itself in the co-sacrifice, especially in the prayer which surrounds the sacrifice; therefore, the *eucharistia* plays so important a role in the

---

was also strong opposition from G. Sohngen of the Braunsberg Academy. "A controversy arose between Casel and Sohngen . . . . Dom Odo conceives of the work of redemption as not only present in its effects (*realitas efficientiae*), but the work itself is made present as an act or event. Sohngen conceives of the sacramental presence as a *perfectum praesens*; the event is made present, not objectively, but in its effects; the sacrament is a symbolic action which applies grace stemming from the work of Christ to the faithful. 'The sacramental representation is not a reality in itself; fundamentally, it is nothing other than a current of grace, *kein stehendes, sondern ein geschehendes Symbol*.' For Sohngen the historic work itself is not rendered present, since as historical occurrences the redemptive acts participate in the fate of everything historical—they are singular and cannot be repeated. Rather, it is the fruit of the redemptive acts that is made present, the applied grace and other effects of the sacraments." 112.

[49] Casel, 58.

[50] Koenker, 107.

[51] Casel, 59.

> mass . . . . The objective act of Christ and the concomitant act of the congregation sharing in his experience, his thanks, his praise and his sacrifice form together the Christian Eucharist, the prayer of sacrifice, the high-point of Christian worship.[52]

Cognizant that Christ sacrificed for sins once for all (Heb. 7:27), Casel nevertheless attempts to formulate a scheme in which the real saving acts of Christ are brought to those in the present. In the words of James F. White, "Odo Casel had opened new possibilities in portraying the mass as a time mystery rather than a spatial one."[53] Casel theorizes:

> Through participation in the mysteries, we enter into the image and so reach the archetype. Thus, the Mass not only represents the death of Christ and communicates to us the effects of his sacrifice; it is an active image of the Pasch of Christ, makes us immediate members of what once took place in and upon him. It is therefore within the power of the Mass to bring us into the same temporal dimension with the saving deeds of Christ, and to place us in their immediate presence.[54]

Later he added:

> We act out the mysteries as the body of Christ; as his body we do all that the head does. In the rite we have an image of Christ's act in which we did not share while it was being fulfilled in time and place. The same thing is true of the last supper. Then Christ said, "this act of sacrifice done once for all time on the cross is here being anticipated in image, and you are to imitate it afterwards in image." The whole church now does what the Lord did at that moment.[55]

Finally, Casel posits that since God is present, and since "he has no past and no future" but "is the everlasting point in which all hold together . . . . Hence with him there is only one Today."[56] In

---

[52] Casel, 72–73.
[53] James F. White, *Introduction to Christian Worship* (Nashville: Abingdon Press, 1980), 231.
[54] Casel, 101.
[55] Casel, 104.
[56] Casel, 142.

the mystery of worship we pass through a door in the presence of God and into that ineffable realm where "there is neither past nor future, only present."[57]

Early Lutheran Reactions: Sasse, Brunner, and Otto

In a discussion of our Lord's words "in remembrance of me," Hermann Sasse (writing in *This Is My Body*, 1959) agrees that "in remembrance" here is unlike any other remembering since in the Sacrament our Lord gives us his true body and blood.

> This makes us not only contemporaneous with him, but unites us with him in a way that transcends everything we otherwise call remembrance. The centuries that separate us from his earthly days, and from the time of his death and resurrection, disappear.[58]

Sasse, however, immediately points out that our Lord's death occurred "once for all" (*ephapax*, Rom. 6:10; Heb. 7:27; 9:12; 10:10). The Lutheran Cassandra from Australia rejects the description of the Lord's Supper as an "unbloody repetition," an "'instauration' of the sacrifice of the cross." Sasse warns,

> Even the ambiguous word "representation," which has become very popular with modern theologians under the influence of the Liturgical Movement, is dangerous and quite unsatisfactory, because it endangers the uniqueness, finality and sufficiency of Christ's sacrifice on Calvary. . . .[59]
>
> This must be said here because even Lutherans are beginning to speak of the Sacrament of the Altar as a "re-presentation" of the sacrifice of Christ in the sense that an event of the past is made present. The "presence" in this Sacrament, however, is not the presence of an event or an action which occurred in the past ([*passio Christi*]), the suffering of Christ), but it is rather the Presence of Christ's body and blood, of his true humanity and true divinity ([*Christus passus*], Christ who has suffered for us). It is this Real Presence of the crucified and risen Lord, who gives us his true body

---

[57] Casel, 142.

[58] Hermann Sasse, *This Is My Body: Luther's Contention for the Real Presence in the Sacrament of the Altar* (Adelaide: Lutheran Publishing House, rev. ed. 1977), 308.

[59] Sasse, 309–310.

> and blood to eat and to drink that lends to the remembrance of his death a reality and actuality such as we do not find otherwise in the recollection of a historical event.[60]

Who are these Lutherans of whom Sasse speaks? Rudolf Otto, German scholar and contemporary of Casel, is credited by Peter Brunner as being the first to call attention to the "cultic anamnesis" in Holy Communion. Commenting on Otto's essay—"*Vom Abendmahl Christi*"—(1917), Brunner concludes,

> [H]is insights regarding the anamnesis-event . . . may really be termed a prophetic anticipation of the results of an investigation which, in detail, is still in progress today, the basic thought of which (rendering the salvation-event present through cultic anamnesis) may be assumed, however, as firmly established.[61]

Brunner also repeatedly speaks of the salvation-event becoming present; however, he carefully attempts to do so in a manner appropriate to Lutheran theology. He concludes,

> Thus, in the act of Holy Communion, bracketed with its proclamation, the historical salvation-event concentrated in Jesus' cross is indeed present for us with its redemptive gift "through effective representation."[62] By virtue of the anamnesis-character of Holy Communion, Rudolf Otto's statement applies: "With, in, and under the celebration of the Lord's Supper, Golgotha becomes event here and now—not through our imagining, but through Jesus' institution."[63]

In a dilative footnote on the usage of re-presentation, Sasse points out that word *repraesentare*

> was introduced into the terminology of the church by Tertullian, the father of ecclesiastical Latin. He understood "representation" as

---

[60] Sasse, 309.

[61] Peter Brunner, *Worship in the Name of Jesus*, trans. Martin H. Bertram (St. Louis: Concordia Publishing House, 1968), 329, n. 172. *Zur Lehre vom Gottesdienst der im Namen Jesu versammelten Gemeinde*, in Leiturgia, 1954.

[62] Brunner, 329. Brunner is quoting Rudolf Otto's *Reich Gottes und Menschensohn* (Munich, 1934), 255.

[63] Brunner. Brunner here quotes R. Otto's *Sunde und Urschuld* (Munich, 1932), 121.

> "manifestation" or "public declaration." (See G. Dix, *The Shape of the Liturgy*, 255 f.)

In the footnote Sasse makes this pertinent summary and judgment:

> Aquinas calls the celebration of the Sacrament an "image representing the passion of Christ (*imago . . . repraesentativa passionis Christi*)" *Suma Theol.*, III, Q. 83, Art. I. Neither in this nor in other passages does Thomas have in mind what certain modern theologians, especially of the Benedictine school of Maria Laach (like the late Odo Casel, *Das christliche Kultmysterium* . . . and numerous other publications), understood by *re-praesentatio*, namely, that an event of sacred history, like the passion of Christ, is present again in the Sacrament, Casel, op. cit., 102). This much debated theory rests upon the assumption that the Hellenistic mystery-cults in which certain mythical occurrences, like the death and resuscitation of a deity, are made present, "re-presented," must be regarded as "a shadow of things to come" (Col. 2:17), namely, of the true mysteries (Sacraments) of Christ. This assumption and the whole theory must be rejected. How can the mythical experiences of non-existing deities be compared with the historical events of Christ's death and resurrection?[64]

Sasse points to Gottlieb Sohngen's *Symbol und Wirklichkeit im Kultmysterium* (1940) as the best criticism of the *Mysterien-Theologie* theory. He also refers the reader to Gregory Dix, who "has convincingly refuted the view of an essential influence of the mystery-religion upon the Christian Eucharist" in his book *The Shape of the Liturgy*.[65]

Casel places the words "mystery" and "liturgy" side by side and for him they mean the same thing from different points of view.

> *Mystery* means the heart of the action, that is to say, the redeeming work of the risen Lord, through the sacred actions he has appointed: liturgy, corresponding to its original sense of "people's work," "service," [Casel here follows a narrow etymological

---

[64] Sasse, 309, n. 35.

[65] Sasse, 309. Sasse points the reader especially to page 64 in Dix's book (page 65 in second printing).

approach] means rather the action of the church in conjunction with this saving action of Christ's.[66]

Writing in the first half of the twentieth century, Casel was reacting to both rationalism and a wave of mysticism. His answer to the individualistic mysticism of his day was to counter with a call for communal mysticism. His definition of this liturgical mysticism contains key elements in his understanding of worship. Liturgical mysticism is

> the mysticism of the ordinary worship of the church, carried out and regulated by its priests; a mysticism therefore, of sacred action, Spirit-informed, the property of the congregation led by proper authority, where the Lord himself shares its work with his bride and leads her to the eternal Father.[67]

In view of this rationalism and individualistic pietism, Casel considered his approach to be theocentric since "in the first place the mystery is defined by a revelation (epiphany) from God." Another important characteristic of mystery is that it is

> not concerned with race or nation, but with the individual, yet in such a fashion that this individual comes immediately into a community, under a religious authority.[68]

A theme repeated throughout *Kultmysterium* is the importance of the proper hierarchy of priest holding the immediate and authoritative place of Christ and the rest of the faithful participating according to his rank. Casel cautions:

> From thence it comes that the whole church, not merely the clergy is to take an active part in the liturgy, each according to sacred order, in his proper rank, place, and measure. All members are truly, sacramentally conjoined to Christ their head; every believer because of the sacramental character he received in baptism and confirmation, has a part in the priesthood of Christ the head. This

[66] Casel, 40.
[67] Casel, 50.
[68] Casel, 54.

> means that the layman does not merely assist with private devotion and prayer at the priest's liturgy, but is, by his objective membership in Christ's body, a necessary and real sharer in the liturgical fellowship . . . . Laymen can never assume the service of the consecrated priesthood; every rank must keep its place . . . the outward expression of this is the reservation of sanctuary for priests, the choir for monks and virgins, and the people. Many of the difficulties of the liturgical renewal would disappear with a careful observance of the ancient notion of hierarchy.[69]

Gregory Dix and Liturgy as Action

With the publication of *The Shape of the Liturgy* in 1945, Dom Gregory Dix (Benedictine monk of the Church of England) would become one of the most influential leaders of the Liturgical Movement. His insights have affected the liturgical revisions undertaken by almost every denomination over the course of the past fifty years.[70] His sweeping impact on the English-speaking Lutherans in the United States has been profound. Dix's major contribution

> has become a fundamental working principle in the liturgical studies: one understands the origin, growth, and theology of the ancient rites by inquiring primarily into their "shape," or basic patterns, before making other inquiries which are sometimes fruitless, as was the search for the text of "the" primitive anaphora. Even though Dix's views on some matters may be difficult to sustain today, in *The Shape of the Liturgy* he did much to create the state of liturgical study as it is still pursued.[71]

Even Herman Sasse acknowledged Dix's accomplishments:

> One of the most convincing and impressive results of Dom Gregory Dix's *magnum opus* is the proof that what he calls "the shape of the liturgy," including the most important formulas, is preserved throughout the centuries and makes the liturgy one.[72]

---

[69] Casel, 48.

[70] Dom Gregory Dix, *The Shape of the Liturgy* (London: A & C Black, 1945; reprint New York: The Seabury Press, second printing 1982), 11. Dix begins, "The origin of this essay was a paper read before the Cowley Fathers during their General Chapter in August of 1941."

[71] Dix, 765. These observations are part of the "Additional Notes" that appear in the back of the 1982 American edition and were written by Paul V. Marshall.

[72] Sasse, 49.

Both Dom Odo Casel and Dom Gregory Dix worked within the shadow of the *religionsgeschichtliche Schule*. On the first page of his introduction, Dix writes,

> It is only within recent years that the science of Comparative Religion has fully awakened to the value of the study of "ritual patterns" for the appreciation of any given system of religious ideas and its necessary consequence in human living—a "culture." The analysis of such a pattern and the tracing of its evolution opens for the historian and the sociologist the most direct way to the sympathetic understanding "from within" of the mind of those who practice that religion, and so to a right appreciation of the genius of their belief and the value of their ideas and ideals of human life.[73]

Since the Eucharist is the central and primary Christian "ritual pattern," Dix undertook the enormous task of examining the majority of the available liturgies. There is a great variety in the "doing" of the liturgy from place to place and time to time; nevertheless, Dix claims that "by careful analysis there is to be found underlying most of these varying rites and all of the older ones a single normal or standard structure of the rite as a whole."[74] Dix calls this standard structure the *shape* of the liturgy. The purpose of Dix's research was

> to give some sort of answer to the main question: Can we hope to penetrate through this (fourth–fifth century) period of growing uniformity, and behind that through the period of the unordered growth of local traditions (in the third–fourth century) back to some sort of original uniformity? Can we hope to find in the primitive church, say in the second century, coherent universal principles which can guide our own ideas about liturgy? Was there

---

[73] Dix, xi. Since Dix is studying the "'ritual pattern' of the eucharist action," he is not so much concerned with what is said as what is done. He is not primarily a theologian or even a pure historian, but a liturgist, a student of Comparative Religion, and a believing Christian. He adds the footnote, "The technique of the liturgist must be fully as 'scientific' in its methods as that of the *religionsgeschichtliche Schule* in Germany. But I think it will be obvious to anyone carefully studying their works that they lost much in insight into their material by not sharing the belief of those who produced it." xiv–xv, n. 1.

[74] Dix, xiii.

> anything, for instance, in what is vaguely called "the early church" which might serve as a standard or model by which the perplexities of Prayer Book revision in the twentieth century England might be lessened?[75]

Dix believes that there is, and states: "This book has been written partly in order to show that there is."[76] Dix's method was to work backward from later to earlier texts. He rejected the popular approach that searched for an *Uranaphora*, the original "apostolic" fixed text of the Eucharistic Prayer. He was convinced, however, that there was good reason to believe that the common outline he discovered in the eucharistic prayers of the great rites (Syrian, Egyptian, Roman, etc.) "is of genuinely apostolic tradition."[77] This common outline identified by Dix consisted of four actions: taking, blessing, breaking and sharing.

The outline or "shape" of the liturgy must be understood in "action" terms. Dix points out that the typical view of both priest and layman is that the Eucharist is primarily "something said, to which is attached an action, the act of communion." The reverse was true of those living before the fourth century. They regarded "the rite as primarily something done, of which what is said is only one incidental constituent part, though of course an essential one."[78] Dix reiterates in very clear terms:

> The first main distinction, then, which we have to bear in mind, is that the apostolic and primitive church regarded the Eucharist as primarily an action, something "done," not something "said"; and that it had a clear and unhesitating grasp of the fact that this action was corporate, the united joint action of the whole church and not of one celebrant only.[79]

---

[75] Dix, 208.

[76] Dix, 214.

[77] Dix, 5. Dix points to others who opposed the traditional school (who kept up the search for the "original," "primitive," "lost" text): "Some of the greatest names of liturgical scholarship—Tommasi in the seventeenth century, Forbes . . . and Ceriani in the nineteenth century, Brightman, Armitage Robinson and Lietzmann in the twentieth, and above all, Edmund Bishop . . . ." 211.

[78] Dix, 12.

[79] Dix, 15.

Dix begins his description of the classical shape of the liturgy with a brief chapter on the *synaxis*. The primitive core of the liturgy falls into two parts, the *synaxis*, which is Greek for "meeting," and the Eucharist proper (or "thanksgiving"). These two parts correspond to the Service of the Word and the Service of Holy Communion. According to Dix they were separate things with separate origins. The *synaxis* was in its shape a continuation of the synagogue service, while the Eucharist was "of directly Christian development," though according to Dix and others, it had a Jewish meal background (Passover sacrifice meal, *kiddush*, or *chaburoth*).[80]

As seen above, Dix initiates his study of the Christian Eucharist service by a comparative study of the available liturgies. Working phenomenalistically, he identified a four-action shape as the common, unifying characteristic. With this theory in hand he works his way back to the source of Holy Scripture. His opening sentence concerning what the "received" text has to offer is quite revealing: "The last supper of our Lord with His disciples is the source of the liturgical Eucharist, but not the model for its performance."[81] Granted, Matthew, Mark, and Luke are historical narratives describing the events of that night when Jesus was betrayed. Paul's account in 1 Corinthians 11, on the other hand, was written in answer to liturgical abuses in the early Church and begins, "For what I received from the Lord (Ἐγὼ γὰρ παρέλαβον ἀπὸ τοῦ κυρίου), I also passed on (παρέδωκα) to you: The Lord

---

[80] Dix, 36. In chapter 4, in the section titled "The Lord's Supper," Dix begins, "Our Lord instituted the Eucharist at a supper with his disciples which was probably not the Passover of that year, but an evening meal twenty-four hours before the actual passover." Great attention is then given to the fact that the last supper was a Jewish "religious meal" of some sort. The type best conforming to the situation was the "formal supper of the *chaburah* (plural, *chaburoth*, from *chaber* = a friend). These *chaburoth* were little private groups or informal societies of friends banded together for purposes of special devotion and charity, existing within the ordinary Jewish congregation . . . ." Dix does mention in a footnote that "the almost universal conclusion of modern investigators (that it was not a Passover), has, however, recently been challenged in Germany, and it is only fair to say that the question is not yet finally settled." 50, n. 1. Paul Marshall's 1982 "Additional Notes" at the end of the book add, "The weight of modern scholarship takes the view adopted by Dix, that the Lord's Supper was not a Passover meal." But he hedges, "Whether the meal was Passover or *chaburah*, the bread and cup were common to both." 767, n. 6.

[81] Dix, 48.

Jesus, on the night he was betrayed, took bread . . . ." First Corinthians is an apostolic epistle, not a liturgical agenda complete with rubrics. It is, however, more than mere historical narrative. The Apostle Paul appeals to the Words of the Lord as passed on in the liturgy to locate the one, common, essential thing necessary to restore unity to the chaotic liturgical practices in Corinth. It is not found in common action but in the body and blood of the Lord. Paul's approach to liturgical renewal is theological and Christological.

Dix's Four-Action Shape

The heart of Dix's entire thesis is given in the opening paragraph of chapter 4:

> The new testament accounts of that supper as they stand in the received text present us with what may be called a "seven-action scheme" of the rite then inaugurated. Our Lord (1) took bread; (2) "gave thanks" over it; (3 broke it; (4) distributed it, saying certain words. Later he (5) took a cup; (6) "gave thanks" over that; (7) handed it to His disciples, saying certain words.[82]

Dix then postulates that the seven actions were merged into a four-action shape once the *chaburah* meal dropped off.

> With absolute unanimity the liturgical tradition reproduces these seven actions as four: (1) The offertory; bread and wine are "taken" and placed on the table together. (2) The prayer; the president gives thanks to God over bread and wine together. (3) The fraction; the bread is broken. (4) The communion; the bread and wine are distributed together.
>
> In that form and in that order these four actions constituted the absolutely invariable nucleus of every eucharistic rite known to us throughout antiquity from the Euphrates to Gaul.[83]

---

[82] Dix, 48.

[83] Dix, 48. Paul Marshall notes: "Virtually all scholars have adopted Dix's technique, of seeking a primitive shape rather than a primitive text, but there have been instances where their research has compelled some writers to define the primitive shape in terms somewhat different from (than) those adopted by Dix.

The chief issue for many people has been Dix's understanding of the "taking" of the elements as the germ of the offertory, which he saw as an act of self-sacrifice upon the part of each

Four actions: (1) taking (offering), (2) blessing (praying), (3) breaking, and (4) sharing (communion). Dix theorizes that the sequence of acts "emerged from its association with a meal in the 'Lord's supper,'" and "consisted always of four essential acts, all of which were derived from the Jewish customs of the *chaburah* supper." Dix explains:

> 1. The offertory, the "taking" of bread and wine, which in its original form in the four-action shape was probably derived from the bringing of contributions in kind for the *chaburah* meal.
> 2. The prayer, with its preliminary dialogue of invitation, derived directly from the *berakah* or thanksgiving which closed the *chaburah* meal.
> 3. The fraction, or breaking of the bread, derived from the Jewish grace before all meals.
> 4. The communion, derived from the distribution of the broken bread at the beginning and the cup of blessing at the end of the supper of every Jewish *chaburah*.[84]

Dix concludes:

> The liturgical Eucharist consisted simply of those particular things in the ordinary *chaburah* customs to which our Lord at the last supper had attached a new meaning for the future. These had been detached from the rest of the *chaburah* ritual and perpetuated independently.[85]

---

worshiper. Some of the offertory sentences of the 1979 *Book of Common Prayer* of the Episcopal Church reflect this view, as does the first offertory prayer of the *Lutheran Book of Worship*. This is not the case in the new Roman Liturgy. Joseph Jungmann adopted Dix's theory in the main, but wrote of the first action as "preparing bread and wine." (*The Mass*, [Collegeville, 1976] 20.) The new Roman rite does include an offertory procession of the faithful, but the accompanying texts refer to the elements brought for the eucharistic sacrifice, not to the people's self-oblation.

Dix's views of the offertory have been least successful in his own church. The *Alternative Services Book* (1980) labels this action "the preparation of the gifts," and the one suggested offertory verse (used only when there is a collection of the people's offerings) keeps the emphasis on God's gifts rather than the assembly's. The entire liturgy is offering-shy: In none of the four eucharistic prayers of the new English rite ("A") is there any offering of bread and cup or of the lives of the worshipers. Even the A.S.B. version of the eucharistic prayer of Hippolytus has had the oblation completely removed (and the epiclesis shifted to a position prior to the Institution narrative!)" Marshall concluded: "It can be said that Dix's own thinking on the self-oblation was not perfectly clear . . . ." 769–770, n. 21.

[84] Dix, 103.

[85] Dix, 103.

Of the four actions, Dix identifies two (praying and sharing) as the most important to the nature of the Eucharist liturgy. Ironically, with the selection of these two "actions," Dix is back full circle to words (there is no praying without words) and the body and the blood (sharing is not the primary thing in communion; the primary and determining thing is what is shared, namely, the body and blood, οὐχὶ κοινωνία ἐστὶν τοῦ αἵματος τοῦ Χριστοῦ . . . τοῦ σώματος τοῦ Χριστοῦ? 1 Cor. 10:16).

Dix has returned to the necessity of words in determining the meaning of a liturgy which is primarily action. Frank Senn credits Gregory Dix with the "now-widely held view that the eucharist prayer originally said all that needed to be said about the meaning of the rite."[86] In chapter 7, "The Eucharistic Prayer," Dix explains this important observation:

> We have seen that the Eucharist is primarily an action, our obedience to our Lord's command to "Do this"; and that this action is performed by the Shape of the Liturgy, the outline of the service viewed as a single continuous whole. We have also seen that the meaning of this action is stated chiefly in the great eucharistic prayer, which formed the second item of that "four-action shape" of the Eucharist which has come down almost from apostolic times. Since this prayer was originally "the" prayer, the only prayer in the whole rite, it was there that the whole meaning of the rite had to be stated, if it was to be put into words at all in the course of the service. We have also noted that, while the tradition as to the outline of the rite was always and everywhere the same, there was no original fixity about the content and sequence of this prayer. Its text was subject to constant development and revision, so that it varied considerably from church to church and from period to period, and even (probably within narrower limits) from celebrant to celebrant.[87]

This important quote is representative of the approach taken by the majority of contemporary liturgical scholarship. "Do this," is

[86] Frank C. Senn, *New Eucharistic Prayers: An Ecumenical Study of Their Development and Structure* (New York: Paulist Press, 1987), 3. In *The Shape of the Liturgy*, 119, Dix writes: "The eucharist prayer was originally intended to embrace in its single statement the meaning of the whole rite, from the offertory to the effects of receiving communion."

[87] Dix, 156.

interpreted as a referent to the entire four-shape action of the liturgy. Grammatically, however, "Do this" agrees with eating and drinking, not taking, praying, or remembering. Certainly it is unthinkable that one would not give thanks for the gift of the body and the blood. Certainly the eating and drinking will be done in remembrance of all our Lord did (from incarnation to ascension) for our salvation. Certainly the liturgy will include these elements. Giving thanks and recalling the Gospel are not unique to the Sacrament. What is unique is the promise that when we eat and drink the bread and wine, we partake of the very body and blood of Jesus Christ. It is a concrete, sacramental "for you." It is the very giving out of the forgiveness of sins (or the denial of forgiveness and thus damnation).

This is not to say that it is only the eating and drinking that makes the sacrament. It is a misunderstanding of the term *usus* to equate it solely with *sumptio*.[88] It also includes the verba. The Formula of Concord, Solid Declaration clarifies this.

> But this blessing or recitation of Christ's words of institution by itself, if the entire action of the Lord's Supper as Christ ordained it is not observed (if, for instance, the blessed bread is not distributed, received, and eaten but is locked up, offered up, or (carried about), does not make a sacrament. But the command of Christ, "Do this," which comprehends the whole action or administration of this sacrament (namely, that in a Christian assembly we take bread and wine, consecrate it, distribute it, receive it, eat and drink it, and therewith proclaim the Lord's death), must be kept integrally and inviolately, just as St. Paul sets the whole action of the breaking of bread, or of the distribution and reception, before our eyes in 1 Cor. 10:16.[89]

The emphasis of the Lutheran Confessions is on the Words of Institution and the eating and drinking of the body and blood. The meaning of the whole action is that which St. Paul identifies as the "whole action of the breaking of bread . . . the distribution and

---

[88] Hermann Sasse, *We Confess the Sacraments*, We Confess Series, vol 2, trans. Norman Nagel (St. Louis: Concordia Publishing House, 1985), 135.

[89] *The Book of Concord: The Confessional Writings of the Evangelical Lutheran Church*, trans. & ed. Theodore G. Tappert (Philadelphia: Fortress Press, 1959), 584.

reception. I Cor. 10:16" The meaning of the action is that which Christ himself has given. The Solid Declaration continues,

> In this context "use" or "action" does not primarily mean faith, or the oral eating alone, but the entire external and visible action of the Supper as ordained by Christ: the consecration or words of institution, the distribution and reception, or the oral eating of the blessed bread and wine, the body and blood of Christ.[90]

Nowhere is our giving of thanks mentioned as primary or essential. After all, "It is not our faith which makes the sacrament, but solely the Word and institution of our almighty God and Savior, Jesus Christ . . . . "[91] Concerning the mandate "This do," Norman Nagel observes that in the biblical text

> We are not bidden to pray, sit, kneel, stand, have a meal, have a Passover or a memorial. We are bidden to eat and to drink the body and blood of Christ.[92]

Nagel also writes:

> If Jesus bade his apostles to go on doing, what did he mandate? We look for the verbs in the imperative. If we gather these, we find they are "Take and eat" and "Drink." The only other imperative is the one at the end, "This do, as often as you drink it, in remembrance of me." They are bidden to drink, and this is to be done remembering him (adverbial relationship to the main verb, the imperative) . . . . But how could we not pray, or ponder the Passover to end all Passovers, or rejoice when our Lord has us together with him at his table now, and so at the feast of the Lamb who was slain with all his saints? There are biblical promptings for these. There are also devotional promptings that ponder how many grains are made into one bread, and how many grapes into one cup. (*Didache*, 9,4) This can make some fine preaching, but, as Luther observed, such pious reflections on similitudes and signs

---

[90] Tappert, 584.

[91] Tappert, 585.

[92] Normal E. Nagel, "Holy Communion," in *Lutheran Worship: History and Practice*, ed. Fred L. Precht (St. Louis: Concordia Publishing House, 1993), 309.

> do not hold against temptation, devil or death; the words and the body and the blood of Christ do.[93]

The theory of the Eucharist as primarily action relies heavily upon the connection of "do this" with "in remembrance of me." As we have already seen, this was a major premise explored by the proponents of the *Mysterientheologie*, primarily by Dom Odo Casel. It was in the area of anamnesis that a very fascinating link between Dom Odo Casel and Dom Gregory Dix was pointed out by Massey H. Shepherd Jr. as early as 1958. In an essay titled "The History of the Liturgical Renewal," Shepherd gives an account of the wide impact of Maria Laach, especially through the two publications *Liturgiegeschichtliche Quellen und Forschungen* ("Sources and Studies in the History of Liturgy") and *Jahrbuch für Liturgiewissenschaft* ("Yearbook for Liturgical Research"). According to Shepherd,

> They have stimulated once more creative discussion of sacramental theology in the Roman Church, such as has not been known since medieval scholasticism. Outside the bounds of the Roman Church, it may be sufficient to note Casel's influence upon such diverse scholars as Rudolf Otto, Gregory Dix, and Charles Harold Dodd.[94]

Shepherd concludes his brief description of Casel's *Mysterientheologie* by quoting Ernest B. Koenker's "admirable summary."

> In the liturgical rites of sacrifice and sacrament we meet the mystical making-present-again of the *totum opus redemtionis*; not only the Passion of Christ but his whole life, from the Incarnation to his Second Coming, is rendered sacramentally present in the cultic mysteries. It is not an empty commemoration or pious meditation; neither is this action something psychological or ethical. It is rather ontological action, a *signum efficax*, a reality which efficaciously

---

[93] Nagel, "Holy Communion," 309.

[94] Massey Hamilton Shepherd Jr., "The History of the Liturgical Renewal," in *The Liturgical Renewal of the Church*, ed. Massey Hamilton Shepherd, Jr. (New York: Oxford University Press, 1960), 32–33. The book consists of six addresses delivered at a Liturgical Conference held in Madison, Wisconsin, May 19–21, 1958. Among the contributors are Theodore Otto Wedel and Arthur Carl Piepkorn.

> heightens man's natural existence through an activity in a higher sphere; as such, of course, it works *ex opere operato*.[95]

What is extremely interesting is Shepherd's observation that Dix borrowed from Casel. He places this summary of anamnesis in Dix next to Koenker's summary of Casel.

> Possibly the best translation of Casel's theology into English is Dom Gregory Dix's exposition of the *anamnesis* or "memorial" in the Eucharist "as meaning a 're-calling' or 're-presenting' of a thing in such a way that it is not so much regarded as being 'absent,' as itself presently operative by its effects.[96]

Dix insists that the "meaning of this action is stated chiefly" in the Eucharistic Prayer "which has come down almost from apostolic times." There is no need to question the practice of the ancient churches' using the Eucharistic Prayer (with great freedom and variety) to extol the gifts given in the Lord's Supper. It is a different issue to begin the examination with the biblical account of the instruction. If this is the starting point, one would not look to the "action" of prayer in which to find the meaning for the Lord's Supper because neither Matthew, Mark, Luke, or Paul include the content of the prayer. What they do include are the important things. The Lord's words of institution tell us what the supper does. It is his body and blood, given and shed for the communicant to eat and drink for the forgiveness of sins. This we are told. These words come from the Lord's time. These words come from the Lord's mouth.

In place of this, the four-shape action approach would have us look elsewhere for the meaning of the sacrament. Responding to the absence of any record for what our Lord said when he gave thanks, Dix maintains

> the words of His "Thanksgiving" are not recorded for us. Why should they be? They were as familiar to every Jew as the Lord's

---

[95] Shepherd, 33. Shepherd quotes from Ernest B. Koenker's book *The Liturgical Renaissance in the Roman Catholic Church*, 107.

[96] Shepherd, 34.

> prayer is to us. "Let us give thanks," He began. And when they had intoned their responses, "Blessed art Thou, O Lord our God," He chanted, "Eternal King, Who feedest the whole world with thy goodness . . . " and so the sonorous phrases they all knew by heart.[97]

All of this rests on the speculation that it was a *chaburah.*

Yngve Brilioth's Five Meanings of the Liturgy

If the meaning of the "action" is to be stated chiefly in the Eucharistic Prayer, the question still remains, what is the meaning of the meal? The answer to this was articulated by Yngve Brilioth (1891–1959), who was a contemporary of Dix. In the book *Eucharist Faith and Practice, Evangelical and Catholic,* Brilioth explores two questions:

1. Can the Eucharist of the church still be derived from the action of Jesus in the night he was betrayed?
2. Can any particular view of the Eucharist be claimed, on the basis of the New Testament, as the norm and standard by which all subsequent developments are to be judged?[98]

Brilioth claims to answer in the affirmative. He offers four main meanings or "antitheses" of the Eucharist: (1) Thanksgiving, or Eucharist; (2) Communion-fellowship; (3) Commemoration, or the historical side; (4) Sacrifice, including the act of Memorial, and the Church's self-oblation. A fifth element is then added, (5) Mystery, which according to Brilioth "embraces and unites all the others, and bridges the gap between the one act of the Savior and the innumerable Eucharists in which that act is apprehended in the experience of faith, and its benefits appropriated."[99] Charles J. Evanson offers a critique of Brilioth in which he concludes:

---

[97] Shepherd, 57.

[98] Yngve Brilioth, *Eucharist Faith and Practice, Evangelical and Catholic* (London: Society for Promoting Christian Knowledge, 1930), 2.

[99] Brilioth, 17. Charles J. Evanson, "Worship and Sacrifice," *Concordia Theological Quarterly* 42 (October 1978): 347, writes: "It was the appearance of Archbishop Brilioth's *Eucharistic Faith and Practice: Evangelical and Catholic* . . . which first brought the Lutheran Eucharist to the direct attention to non-Lutherans, and at the same time whetted the appetite of many

> Since the Gospels are themselves witnesses to a variety of theological emphases, one can posit only that there can be no real norm whatever outside the consensus of the extant liturgies themselves. Far from seeing the Scriptures as norm and standard, it appears that these writings themselves will admit to no norm.[100]

We have already noted a similar attitude toward Scripture in Casel. Oliver Olson points out that Dix also wrote his *magnum opus* from a low view of Holy Scripture.

> Only if we understand the distaste within the Oxford Movement for "the authority of the Word of God," which they understood in a Zwinglian sense, and only if we understand that part of the enthusiasm for reviving medieval ceremonies was a means for defying a government which presumed in the 1874 Public Worship Act to regulate the spiritual life of Christians, can we understand why Dix's book has become so popular despite its shaky argument. By giving a kind of doctrinal finality to which the ritualists had been doing, the *Shape of the Liturgy* became a kind of Declaration of Independence, around which the Anglo-Catholics could rally.[101]

Thus in similar ways, Casel and Dix, "by adopting the method of understanding the liturgy by observing its external forms, came to put great emphasis on the notion of 'action.'"[102] Olson posits that "we can safely assume that the constant emphasis within the Liturgical Movement on 'action' has been inspired by these two men or by reasoning similar to theirs."[103] The truth of Olson's claim will be

Lutherans for what they now came to regard as a more complete, balanced, adequate, and even catholic form of Eucharistic worship. Brilioth's work has been pivotal, of more significance even than the major labors of Dom Gregory Dix. Unfortunately, the work of neither of these "giants" is without faults. In the case of Brilioth, it must be noted that he fell heir to the destructive critical work of Spitta, Schweitzer, et al. As heir to a methodology which made it impossible for him to make any authoritative statement about what the congregation *ought* to believe and how it *ought* to worship . . . he was forced to face two important critical questions (see text above). . . . Unfortunately, on the basis of his methodology, Brilioth is not equipped to answer either of these important questions satisfactorily. For him, the New Testament has dissolved into independent and perhaps even conflicting 'theologies.'"

100 Evanson, 349–50.

101 Oliver K. Olson, "Contemporary Trends in Liturgy Viewed from the Perspective of Classical Lutheran Theology," *Lutheran Quarterly* 26 (May 1974): 120.

102 Olson, 121.

103 Olson, 121.

fully substantiated in chapters 4 and 5, which examine the literature and liturgical texts in American Lutheranism.

Brilioth also made use of the phenomenological method. Bryan Spinks has demonstrated that Brilioth was responsible for the perpetuation of the myth that Martin Luther's liturgical reforms of the Mass showed "little creative power." Concerning the *Formula Missae* Brilioth concludes, "Here, therefore, the pruning-knife must be more rigorously applied; and of the latter half of the service only a torso is left."[104]

Spinks shows how numerous influential English and American liturgical textbooks produced during the past fifty years have uncritically accepted the notion of Luther as a careless liturgical scholar. Spinks begins:

> The English-speaking student who inquires into the liturgical work of Luther will soon discover that in the general textbooks on liturgical history there is a consensus of opinion that in this particular field, the Wittenberg Reformer was conservative, hasty, and singularly inept, and that when it came to reform the canon, his method was one of drastic curtailment, amputation and displacement.[105]

Spinks documents how such scholars as W. D. Maxwell (1936), Bard Thomson (1962), Louis Bouyer (1968), G. J. Cuming (1969), C. Jones, G. Wainwright and E. Yarnold (1978), James F. White (1980), G. Wainwright again (1980), Donald Bridge and David Phypers (1981), and even Luther D. Reed (1959) promote this view of Luther. But what is surprising is that they all simply repeat, without question, the findings of Brilioth.[106] It would prove an easy though superficial task for the members of the Inter-Lutheran Commission on Worship to argue for a restoration of the full Eucharistic Prayer in the new hymnal by uncritically pointing to the full weight of scholarship.

---

[104] Brilioth, 116.

[105] Bryan Spinks, *Luther's Liturgical Criteria and His Reform of the Canon of the Mass*—Grove Liturgical Study 30 (Bramcote Notts., England: Grove Books, 1982), 7.

[106] Spinks writes: "In the face of such formidable consensus, it might seem that any dissent from this estimate of Luther's work must be highly questionable. However, a careful

In *Luther's Liturgical Criteria and His Reform of the Canon of the Mass*, Bryan Spinks points to the work of Vilmos Vajta as a valuable attempt "to escape the 'comparative liturgy' type of study"[107] of Luther and instead start from a point that takes Luther's theology seriously. Vajta pointed out that

> Luther regarded worship as primarily a work of God and only secondarily as a work of man. . . . Vajta also emphasized the hitherto neglected contrast that Luther made between *Beneficium* and *Sacrificium*.[108]

Spinks goes on to examine Luther's *Formula Missae* of 1523 and *Deutsche Messe* of 1526. He concludes:

> In Luther the words are a proclamation of the gospel. The reformed canon, then, is a deliberate new composition. The reason for the new canon is to be found in Luther's doctrine of justification by faith and its relations to the command "Do this in remembrance of me." The old canon was in obedience to the command, for throughout it spoke in terms of "We do." It was a response to God's action in Christ, seeking by faithful obedience and repetition and intercession, to enter into the sacrifice of Christ. This seems to have been precisely Luther's objection. For Luther, the sacrifice of the cross and forgiveness of sins were God's gifts to man which could only be received with thanksgiving. It could not be actively entered into by man, whether by imitation or by intercession. "Do this in remembrance of me" was to proclaim again what God had done for man, and Luther seems to have concluded that the most effective way of doing this was by letting God himself speak in the word of institution. Thus Luther's reformed canon replaced "We do" with "He has done." His

---

examination of the footnotes and bibliographies of these works reveals an interesting fact. All make use of, or cite as authoritative, a single work by the Swedish Lutheran scholar, Bishop Yngve Brilioth." ([n. 5 adds] "All these sources quote Brilioth, but then the newer works quote predecessors as an added authenticity. E.g. Abba cites Maxwell and Brilioth; Cuming quotes Brilioth and Maxwell; Senn quotes Bouyer and Brilioth, Eugene Brand seems to have depended on L. D. Reed.") An investigation of Brilioth reveals that we are not dealing with the opinions and results of independent investigations by numerous scholars, but simply the constant repetition of successive scholars of the views promulgated by Brilioth. Repetition of these views do not make them assured results of liturgical scholarship!" 11.

107 Spinks, 15.

108 Spinks, 15.

starting point was "*Dominus Dixit.*" As he explained: "He sent forth his word, and thus (*sic*) healed them," not: "he accepted our work and thus healed us." . . . If this explanation of Luther is correct, then words such as "conservative," and "pruning-knife" or "hatchet job," are completely inadequate and even misleading. Far from being a conservative and unimaginative liturgiologist, Luther was in fact giving radical liturgical expression to justification by faith, and deserves to be regarded as a serious Reformation liturgist.[109]

Pointing to the wider context, Spinks concludes that

What Luther in his reform of the canon teaches contemporary liturgists is that past forms and patterns, however venerable, are not inviolate and may, in the interest of a sound theology, be done away with, "no matter who takes offense."[110]

[109] Spinks, 37. Spinks quotes AE 36: 39.
[110] Spinks, 41. Spinks quotes AE 36: 254.

3

The Failed Attempt to Produce a Pan-Lutheran Book of Worship

VIRTUALLY all the literature on the history of the *Lutheran Book of Worship* and *Lutheran Worship* perpetuates the view that the vision of a pan-Lutheran book of worship, before the end of the twentieth century, was the idea of The Lutheran Church—Missouri Synod. The view appears to be substantiated by the action of the 1965 Detroit Convention of the LCMS, which authorized the president to "pursue a cooperative venture with Lutheran bodies as soon as possible in working toward, under single cover: a common liturgical section in rite . . . and common core of hymns."[1]

This chapter will examine the events leading up to the public invitation of 1965 and the subsequent withdrawal from the joint venture at the Dallas Convention in 1979.[2] An analysis of pertinent documents offers evidence that it was not the Missouri Synod but the Lutheran Church in America and the American Lutheran Church who on a bureaucratic level originally proposed the common Lutheran hymnal. The evidence suggests that the LCMS worship commission opted to use very irregular means in order to move the Missouri Synod into what the commission perceived was a very controversial position.

In its day *The Lutheran Hymnal* was a remarkable success. It provided The Lutheran Church—Missouri Synod (including the

---

[1] *Proceedings of the 46th Regular Convention of the Lutheran Church—Missouri Synod,* Detroit, Michigan, June 16–26, 1965, 186.

[2] For historical background and influences of the Liturgical Movement prior to 1960 see Jeffrey J. Zetto, "Aspect of Theology in the Liturgical Movement in the Lutheran Church—Missouri Synod, 1930–1960" (Th.D Thesis, Christ Seminary Seminex, St. Louis, 1982).

synods of the Synodical Conference) a quality English liturgy and hymnody during the last phase of its transition from a German- to an English-speaking church.[3] As is the case with all hymnals, *TLH* was not perfect. The book was marred with problems ranging from poor hymn translations to "anglican thumps"[4] in the liturgy. On the other hand *TLH* preserved two important qualities that had been major motifs in the publication of earlier LCMS hymnals. "These were: (1) a concern for a confessionally, yet evangelically orthodox hymnody; (2) vigorous encouragement of the use of the rhythmic form of the chorale as the best means for recapturing the vital musical expression of Reformation times."[5]

The Lutheran Hymnal may be judged a success on the basis of three important criteria: (1) it was a joint Lutheran endeavor; (2) it was almost universally accepted by the LCMS within a mere four years after publication;[6] (3) after a decade and a half of use it was still effectively serving the synods of the Synodical Conference. A survey conducted by the Committee on Hymnology and Liturgics between 1956 and 1959 determined:

> [T]he investigations have shown that an overwhelming percentage of our congregations desires that a thoroughly revised edition of *The Lutheran Hymnal* be not published at the present time. While many fault our hymnal, in some cases very severely, the majority of our people treasure it highly.[7]

---

[3] Paul T. Dietz, "The Transition from German to English in the Missouri Synod from 1910 to 1947," *Concordia Historical Institute Quarterly* 22, no. 3, 119. From 1930 to 1956 there was a noticeable increase in the transition from German to English in the LCMS. In 1930, 58 percent of the services were held in English. In 1946, 85 percent were in English for a gain of 27 percent.

[4] *The Lutheran Hymnal* incorporated the poorly pointed Anglican chants for the liturgical portions of the hymnal. An "anglican thump" results when there are two syllables on the final note of the seventh measure. For example, the Gloria in Excelsis (*TLH*, page 17) ends with two points on the fourteenth measure, "glory."

[5] Carl Schalk, *The Roots of Hymnody in the Lutheran Church—Missouri Synod* (St. Louis: Concordia Publishing House, 1965), 7.

[6] In the convention report of the Committee on Hymnology and Liturgics, chairman W. G. Polack wrote: "*The Lutheran Hymnal* has become the official hymnal of the synods of the Synodical Conference. The fact that this volume has been distributed in more than 850,000 copies, at this writing, means that it has become almost universally introduced in the churches of this body." *Reports and Memorials of the 39th Regular Convention of the Lutheran Church—Missouri Synod*, Saginaw, Michigan, June 21–30, 1944, 275–76.

[7] "Report of the Committee on Hymnody and Liturgics," *Reports and Memorials of the 44th Regular Convention of the Lutheran Church—Missouri Synod*, San Francisco, California, June 17–27, 1959, 559.

In view of this survey, the committee, along with representatives of the Synodical Conference, expressed the opinion that a thoroughly revised edition should appear in about another ten years.[8] The Committee on Hymnody and Liturgics left the 1959 convention with a new name, The Commission on Worship, Liturgics, and Hymnody (CWLH) and with a new challenge to produce a successor to *TLH*. But would their efforts succeed to the extent reached by the 1940 committee? With a generous amount of time, talent, and synodical support at their disposal, the commission proceeded with optimism and great expectations. Two years later, however, profound changes would begin taking place within the synod's worship commission. The first hint of this change can be detected from two significant documents dating from 1961 and 1962. The first is a three-page progress report written by W. E. Buszin. This report, apparently directed to the Institute of Liturgical Studies of Valparaiso, tells of a secretive meeting between the LCMS and representatives of the LCA and ALC.

> Together with members of Synod's Committee on Doctrinal Unity, representative members of the Commission of Worship, Liturgics and Hymnology have met with the chairman and one other member of "the churches cooperating in the Commission on the Liturgy and the Commission on the Hymnal of the Lutheran bodies which have published the *Service Book and Hymnal*." Both sides agreed that the meeting be unofficial in every way and that due caution be taken when telling others of this meeting.[9]

Prior to this point in time, the CWLH minutes describe the activities of the commission absorbed in producing a revised edition of *TLH* for the synods of the Synodical Conference. Now, for the first time, the 1961 progress report hints at a radical change in the agenda. From here on out, the commission would strive more and more toward the publication of a new hymnal which would

---

[8] "Report of the Committee," 559.

[9] "Progress Report of the Commission on Worship, Liturgics, and Hymnology," by Walter E. Buszin, CWLH chairman, June 3, 1961 (Concordia Historical Institute, St. Louis, Missouri, 111.1k.13, Box 1), 2.

hopefully encompass all Lutheran bodies in America. Also accompanying this shift would be a new method of operation in which the CWLH used highly irregular tactics, hidden agendas, and a furtiveness that stretches the proprieties of churchmanship. The Buzsin progress report continues:

> The number of those is growing rapidly who believe it to be highly desirable that but one set of official service books and one official hymnal be used by all Lutherans of America. Bearing in mind that advances would be made only with due caution, all present agreed that it would be inadvisable to hurry matters and that for the time being, no official steps be taken. Our guests, who met with us in St. Louis, proceeded to Chicago and there met with their commissions in plenary session. The commissions decided unanimously to invite us to attend their next annual meeting in spring of 1962 as guests and observers.[10]

In light of the previous concern for caution, plus the total absence of information concerning what was discussed in Chicago, the sudden events at the next meeting of the CWLH at Concordia Seminary, St. Louis, in October of 1962 are both unexpected and astonishing. The guest list at this meeting was impressive. The agenda began with general remarks by synodical president, Dr. Oliver Harms, concerning the attempt of the synod to "establish unified forms of thinking and working."[11] Executive Director Walter F. Wolbrecht then suggested:

> That in planning for future activities, the commission might keep in mind answers to the following questions: What is the purpose and plan of the commission? With regard to the relationship of the commission to the Synodical Board of Directors, Dr. Wolbrecht pointed out that long-range plans should be developed first. Short-range plans should grow from the long-range plans . . . He sug-

---

[10] "Progress Report of the Commission," 2. There are no references to the Chicago meeting in subsequent CWLH minutes.

[11] "The Minutes of the Commission on Worship, Liturgics and Hymnody," October 18–20, 1962, Concordia Seminary, St. Louis, Missouri (Concordia Historical Institute, 111.1k.13, Box 1), 1.

> gested that an attempt be made to influence the worship and liturgical activities of other Synodical Boards and Departments . . . and other extra-synodical boards and groups.[12]

In retrospect, the counsel of Dr. Wolbrecht to the worship commission appears to be challenging the men to focus beyond the mere revision of *TLH.* Such long-range thinking would affect how the hymnologists approached the short-range liturgical labors demanding their immediate attention. The remarks of commission chairman Walter Buszin, who spoke after Walter Wolbrecht, certainly support this conjecture. The minutes record, "With regard to our relationship to the other two Lutheran groups, it was stated that we hope to see the day when all Lutheran groups will have common materials."[13] Later in the day, just prior to adjournment, the minutes report an incident which suggests that the invitation to pursue quickly a cooperative hymnal venture, originally came from the Lutheran Church in America and the American Lutheran Church.

> A note delivered by Pastor Sebold reported that in a telephone conversation with a third party, Henry E. Horn, Chairman of the Commission on Liturgy of the LCA and ALC, had asked to have conveyed to the commission his ernest desire and hope for a common liturgy and hymnal for all Lutherans in North America in the near future. He feels that, although there will be on both sides men who feel rather hesitant about it, this is not an impossibility. He would like to see some informal discussions on the subject soon, and he expressed the hope that the project for a common book will not have to be postponed until after another separate Lutheran (Missouri) service hymn book is published.[14]

Confirmation of these activities would have to wait until the publication of the *Commentary on the Lutheran Book of Worship* in 1990. In chapter 1, under the section on The Inter-Lutheran Commission

---

[12] "The Minutes of the Commission," 1.

[13] "The Minutes of the Commission," 1. Buszin continued by saying, "This seems to be the feeling which is general in all Lutheran groups." This raises the question as to whether his rationale for such an assertion was based in any way on the sentiments expressed at the June 3, 1961 meeting in Chicago.

[14] "The Minutes of the Commission," AA-14.

on Worship, author Philip Pfatteicher offers this observation on how the new hymnal came to be.

> Meanwhile, following the publication of the *Service Book and Hymnal* (1958), the Commission on Liturgy and Hymnal of the American Lutheran Church and the Lutheran Church in America turned to future developments in liturgy and hymns. Henry E. Horn, who chaired the commission, explained that, faced with a deadlock between only two churches—one of which, the American Lutheran Church, voted in bloc—the commission sought ways whereby the three Lutheran bodies could work together. Conversations between Henry Horn and Walter Buszin, who chaired the Lutheran Church—Missouri Synod commission, explored ways and means for establishing a common commission. The only way this could be accomplished was to have the Missouri Synod commission propose it *de novo* on the floor of the church convention. Then the invitation could be extended to the other two church bodies. The new commission may therefore be understood as an extension of the work of the Commission on Liturgy and Hymnal.[15]

In less than three years the delegates of the LCMS would convene in Detroit and adopt Resolution 13-01, which resolved:

> That we authorize the President . . . to appoint representatives to pursue a cooperative venture with other Lutheran bodies as soon as possible in working toward, under single cover: (a) a common liturgical section in rite, rubric, and music; (b) a common core of hymn texts and musical settings . . .[16]

What was begun by bureaucratic invitation to the Missouri Synod amid cautious whispers grew with remarkable speed to become a bold public invitation from the Missouri Synod. It is pertinent to examine the manner in which the two sides reached unofficial consensus and in which the LCMS worship commission succeeded in getting the synod to not only join the venture but "publicly" initiate it

---

[15] Philip H. Pfatteicher, *Commentary on the Lutheran Book of Worship* (Minneapolis: Augsburg Fortress, 1990), 4–5. Pfatteicher footnotes the source of this information as a letter to the editor by Henry Horn in *Lutheran Partners* 3:1 (January/February 1987):7.

[16] *Convention Workbook*, Detroit, 1965, 186.

at Detroit. Six months after the Henry Horn invitation, a consultative meeting between the synods took place in Chicago between the CWLH and the Commission on Liturgy and Hymnal of the National Lutheran Council. The CWLH report states:

> Pastor Henry E. Horn, NLC Commission Chairman, had extended an invitation to Dr. Buszin for members of the Synodical Conference Commission to take part in a Special Order of Business at 10:00 A.M. on Thursday "for the purpose of discussion on matters of mutual concern."[17]

During the discussion, Dr. Edgar S. Brown of the LCA introduced a resolution calling for the establishment of a "semi-official 'ad hoc' committee of nine members, three from each of the church bodies represented (ALC, LCA, LCMS) to be approved by the respective church bodies or officials, to deal with matters of mutual interest." Although Dr. Brown's resolution was not adopted, nonetheless it does represent a third effort on the part of a non-Missouri Synod official to initiate a joint-hymnal committee with the anticipated approval from the respective church bodies or officials. Due to "'misgivings' over the 'semi-official' nature of the committee and possible implications; a less formal and more flexible type of consultative arrangement was suggested."[18] The nature of the cooperative venture would be established at the afternoon session with the adoption of the following resolution:

> BE IT RESOLVED that we favor a consultative relationship between the Commission on the Liturgy and Hymnal, and the Commission on Worship, Liturgics and Hymnody . . . for the purpose of study of matters of mutual concern and interest . . .[19]

The most enlightening information resulting from the consultative meeting is found in the "unofficial observations" of the LCMS

---

[17] "Report on the Consultative Meeting" on Thursday, April 25, 1963, Chicago, between the Commission on Liturgy and Hymnal (NLC) and the CWLH (Concordia Historical Institute, file 111.1K.13, Box 1), 1.

[18] "Report on the Consultative Meeting," 2.

[19] "Report on the Consultative Meeting," 3.

which were attached to a document titled "Report on the Consultative Meeting." In addition to other reactions, Secretary Martin L. Seltz included the following six goals under the sub-title "Possible Long Range Goals."

1. To envision the two streams, NLC and SC (Synodical Conference), as approaching each other more and more closely in worship materials—without appreciable sacrifice in quality—until if God so wills, they might blend into one.
2. To keep these streams, while distinctively American, from wandering too far from world Lutheranism, especially the German stream.
3. To initiate such a possible blending of the two streams with less controversial matters, such as Introits, Graduals, Psalms, and the like (as suggested by Dr. Bergendoff)—then work from there toward the center.
4. To move very slowly and carefully, however, toward the main body of hymnal and liturgy, striving for mutual high standards of quality and true harmony in doctrinal approach. (This is where tensions might be anticipated; they will need to be patiently lubricated and evangelically resolved—which could be a long and trying process.)
5. To recognize and utilize our consultative relationship in working with the "holy Books of the Church" as another vital instrument of the Holy Spirit—together with other Commissions conferring in doctrinal matters—in leading us to strive for true unity on the basis of Scripture and Confessions.
6. In the mean time, to proceed with our contemplated revisions of the Lutheran Hymnal and service books (to be published by 1967–70?)—with the prayerful hope that they may be a very strong and positive factor in determining the course of any future common stream.[20]

[20] "Report on the Consultative Meeting,," 5. Concerning goal 2, history shows that the commission succeeded quite well, to the chagrin of the ALC. In a February 2, 1987, personal interview with then Executive Secretary of the LCMS Commission on Worship, Dr. Fred L. Precht pointed out that before pulling out of the joint project, the LCMS succeeded in effecting the hymnody of the *Lutheran Book of Worship* with a preponderance of German chorales. Point of information concerning goal 3, Conrad Bergendoff was an LCA clergyman from Augustana College, IL.

These six statements clearly reveal the goal, malady, and means of the CWLH. The goal was a quality pan-Lutheran hymnal which retained strong German Lutheran traits. The malady was the tensions caused by the lack of doctrinal consensus. The means was to begin working together on "less controversial matters," but with the premeditated goal of working slowly and carefully toward the main body of liturgy and hymnody.

Given these goals, the CWLH would have to decide what to do with the revision of the *TLH* that Synod was expecting. A cryptic parenthesis in the sixth goal foreshadows the eventual scuttling of the project. Until then, the work of revising *TLH* would proceed, but the expected date of completion was stretched from 1967 to 1970 with a conspicuous question mark added. Goal six makes it clear that the energies being put into *TLH* revision were actually (or contingently) intended for a new book. One questions how long the hymnologists would be able to carry out effectively their duties given the parameters of conflicting goals. Sooner or later their production schedule would have to come to grips with the obvious. That point would be reached and addressed in a meeting of the CWLH subcommittee on September 26–27, 1963. The minutes of that meeting show the members wrestling with the problem and determining a course of action.

> Dr. Buszin indicated that the committees' authorization is to revise *The Lutheran Hymnal*, not to prepare a new book. It was noted, however, that the changes now under way in subcommittees would amount to a new book, not merely a revision. Basic to the salvation of the dilemma would be Synodical resolutions instructing the commission to publish a new book. If a discussion could be held with representatives of all Lutheran groups on the possibility of producing a Pan-Lutheran hymnal, for instance in 1980 . . . as suggested by Mr. Lindemann (CWLH board member), and if this goal were adopted by all synods, *The Lutheran Hymnal* could be reprinted by our Synod with minor revisions at this time for Missouri Synod's use, and the committee could direct its attention and share its work with committee working for a common hymnal.[21]

[21] "Minutes of the Sub-Committee on Liturgics of the Commission on Worship, Liturgics and Hymnody," September 26–27, 1963, Secretary George Hoyer (Concordia Historical Institute, file 111.1K.13, Box 1), 1.

How would this be done? The subcommittee determined that it would be necessary for the next meeting of the CWLH to discuss thoroughly the possibility of a common hymnbook and then

> formulate a memorial to the next synodical convention directing the administration of Synod to appoint and authorize a committee to work for a common hymnal and to approach other synods to appoint similar committees for the development of such a hymnal for publication in 1980 on the anniversary of the Book of Concord.[22]

Meetings then took place between representatives of the LCMS worship commission and the *Service Book and Hymnal* Committee and agreement was reached to develop plans for the production of a pan-Lutheran book. Nevertheless, work on *TLH* revision would continue.

At this time a representative from the worship commission also consulted with the synodical administration. CWLH minutes dated May 14–16, 1964, describe the meeting:

> Professor Hoyer reported on his meeting with Dr. Wolbrecht in which he (Hoyer) suggested consideration of the publication of a pan-Lutheran hymnal. He stated that the suggestion was received somewhat favorably and also that the idea was not at all frowned upon by Synodical Officials.[23]

With the next synodical convention only a year away, the CWLH determined it was of "extreme importance [to give a] clear and impressive statement regarding the activities and plans of the commission in the 1965 synodical report."[24] In the Detroit *Convention Workbook* the CWLH reported its intention to complete the revised edition of *TLH*, adding, "The target date of 1970 appears to be an attainable goal for the completion of the task."[25] Oddly enough, in spite of the extensive space and detail given to the plans for *TLH*

---

22 "Minutes of the Sub-Committee," 1.

23 "Minutes of the Commission on Worship, Liturgics and Hymnody," May 14–16, 1964, Concordia Seminary, St. Louis (Concordia Historical Institute, file 111.IK.13, Box 1), 3.

24 "Minutes of the Commission," 3.

25 "Report of the Commission on Worship, Liturgics, and Hymnody," *Convention Workbook (Reports and Overtures) 46th Regular Convention of the Lutheran Church—Missouri Synod*, Detroit, Michigan, June 16–26, 1965, 389.

revision, tune-text melody line edition, plus organist, keyboard, and choir editions, none of this ever materialized. Once Resolution 13-01 was passed and approved the joint-hymnal project, the committee immediately dropped *TLH*. The intermediate need for revised worship materials for which *TLH* revision was intended was instead met by the publication of a supplement to *TLH*.[26] The worship committee also diplomatically endorsed the production of a pan-Lutheran hymnal. The report stated:

> The commission is cognizant of the concerns of certain groups and many individuals in the church who have expressed themselves as favoring the production of a common hymnal for the Lutheran Church in this country, possibly to appear . . . in 1980.[27]

It should be pointed out that a large number of memorials urging the synod to produce a common hymnal were submitted to the convention by congregations, pastoral conferences, and synodical districts.[28] In view of this "grass root" support, the CWLH report stated:

> The commission furthermore wishes to go on record as favoring the ultimate publication of common liturgical materials which would be in possession and use of all Lutheran bodies in America.[29]

Considering all the meetings and communications it had with representatives of the worship commissions of the LCA and ALC, it appears highly irregular that the CWLH should include the following statement in its *Convention Workbook* report:

---

[26] Resolution 2-08, "To Publish Supplement to 'The Lutheran Hymnal' for Field Testing," *Convention Proceedings: 47th Regular Convention of the Lutheran Church—Missouri Synod, New York,* New York, July 7–14, 1967, 90.

[27] Resolution 2-08, 389–90.

[28] Resolution 2-08, 392–94. Of the ten memorials submitted favoring a common hymnal, five were from congregations, two were from pastoral conferences (New Jersey State Pastoral Conference and the Pastoral Conference of the Southeastern District), and three were from districts (Atlantic, Ontario, and English). Four unpublished overtures proposing a joint hymnal were also submitted (306). One memorial was printed which encouraged Synod to publish its own hymnal as "originally planned."

[29] Resolution 2-08, 390.

> There has been no indication from groups outside the Synod that they are willing and anxious to work toward the publication of a common hymnal at this time. In fact, there is reason to believe that such a proposal would be resisted since it would be interpreted by many as an inadequacy on their part or the recently published *Service Book and Hymnal*.[30]

The convention voted to go ahead with the joint hymnal, and by November, President Harms had received a favorable response from the LCA, ALC, and SELC.

> At the time of this resolution [LCMS Detroit Convention, Res. 13-01] the *Service Book and Hymnal* was a mere seven years old. The ALC and the LCA might well have rejected the offer of a new service book, especially when the spectacular acceptance of the *SBH* is recalled. The fact that both churches responded positively is probably due to several factors including: (1) The time was a high point in inter-Lutheran relations, the Lutheran Council in the U.S.A. was soon to be founded, fellowship between the ALC and the LCMS was soon to be declared. (2) Although the *SBH* was generally received, there were questions. Many of Scandinavian background felt their traditions were slighted. Many regarded the language archaic and the music not of contemporary taste. (3) Lutherans by the 1960s were feeling the full effects of the liturgical scholarship. The liturgical changes arising out of Vatican II helped create questionings among Lutherans about just what was sacrosanct in the liturgy and produced a dissatisfaction with many forms and hymns. The final result of all these factors was that the ALC and the LCA accepted the proposal from the LCMS.[31]

Dr. Harms also announced that at the November [1965] meeting of the CWLH, "he was appointing the entire worship commission as representatives of the LCMS for inter-Lutheran meetings in accordance with Detroit Resolution 13-01."[32] At the invitation of

30 *Convention Workbook*, Detroit, 1965, 390.

31 William G. Rusch, *A Background Paper for a Theological Review of Materials Produced by the Inter-Lutheran Commission on Worship* (January 1977), 15–16.

32 "Minutes of the CWLH," November 4–5, 1965, meeting at 210 N. Broadway, St. Louis (Concordia Historical Institute, file 111.1K, Box 1), 2.

Dr. Harms, representatives and observers from six American Lutheran bodies met in Chicago on February 10–11, 1966.[33]

Thus the original invitation to produce a joint Lutheran hymnal came from the LCA and the ALC, whose liturgical leaders worked in consort through the National Lutheran Conference. Three district invitations were extended through bureaucratic channels: (1) Henry Horn's telephone invitation to the CWLH in October of 1962; (2) Henry Horn's invitation to Dr. Buszin and the members of the Synodical Conference Commission to meet in Chicago in April of 1963 to discuss "matters of mutual concern"; and (3) Edgar Brown's invitation/resolution to form a semi-official "ad hoc" committee of nine members who in turn were to be approved by their respective church bodies. The six-part "Possible Long Range Goals" formulated in response to the April 1963 invitations were a virtual blueprint for moving the synod stealthily into an admittedly controversial situation.[34]

Given the available evidence, it is reasonable to conclude that (1) the LCMS did not extend the original invitation that led to the common hymnbook; (2) a study of the events leading up to Missouri's public invitation at Detroit in 1965 indicates that the CWLH followed questionable procedures; and (3) their efforts did not bring about greater unity.

Over the next decade the ILCW worked toward the production of a new hymnal which would eventually be titled *Lutheran Book of Worship*. As late as 1973 and 1975, the LCMS convention committee received no negative overtures requesting the Missouri Synod to pull out of the joint project. In 1973 one overture expressed a desire for the traditional wording to be used in the

---

[33] The papers presented at the meeting were published under the title *Liturgical Reconnaissance: Papers Presented at the Inter-Lutheran Consultation on Worship*, ed. Edgar S. Brown, (Philadelphia: Fortress Press, 1968). See also Pfatteicher's *Commentary on the Lutheran Book of Worship*, 6–7.

[34] While the minutes and reports cited do provide authentic and highly credible evidence; nevertheless, the conclusions lack corroborative external documentation (with the exception of Henry Horn's *Lutheran Partners* letter). The minutes of various LCA, ALC or National Lutheran Council commissions and committees could possibly offer such verification. When the archival time restrictions have expired on the personal manuscripts of the key administrative personalities such as Dr. Harms and Dr. Wolbrecht, then another excellent external source of information may be available.

Nicene Creed and Lord's Prayer.[35] Even as late as 1975 the few overtures submitted involved constructive yet supportive criticism. Only one memorial suggested that the new hymns may contain theological content that should be questioned.

In February and March of 1977 an extensive study of the attitudes of the membership of Synod toward the new hymnal was undertaken by the independent firm Charron Research and Information, Inc. Of those who were familiar with the new hymnal, the study concluded that "a majority of both groups (clergy and laity) express positive feelings toward the new hymnal."[36] A significant and growing minority, however, was beginning to make its feelings known. Six months prior to the 1977 Dallas convention, the *Concordia Theological Quarterly* (published by the faculty of Concordia Theological Seminary, Ft. Wayne) contained an article titled "The Deepening Liturgical Crisis," in which it called the products of the Inter-Lutheran Commission on Worship "doctrinally impure in every case."[37] The article also called for the synod to follow the lead of the South Wisconsin District resolution (adopted at its June 1976 district convention) and for "withdrawal from plans for an inter-Lutheran hymnal and to concentrate on developing a new hymnal for our Synod."[38]

Dallas Resolution 3-04A: To Deal with the Proposed *Lutheran Book of Worship*

When the Missouri Synod gathered for a convention in Dallas during the summer of 1977, one of the primary items of business con-

---

[35] *Convention Workbook (Reports and Overtures), 50th Regular Convention of the Lutheran Church—Missouri Synod*, New Orleans, July 6–13, 1973, 79.

[36] Charron Research and Information, Inc., *Lutheran Church—Missouri Synod: A Program of Assessment and Recommendation* (St. Louis: July 1977), 59. This special report was prepared for the Department of Worship under the authorization of Mr. John P. Schuelke, administrative officer, board of directors, LCMS. The data were collected in a study conducted for the Synod in February and March of 1977. To the question: "At this time, would you say you are generally positive or negative toward the new hymnal?" Response of "Man in Pew:" 52% positive, 30% negative, and 17.8% don't know. Response of "Man in Pulpit:" 58% positive, 39.5% negative, and 2% don't know.

[37] Judicius, "Theological Observer: The Deepening Liturgical Crisis," *Concordia Theological Quarterly* 41:1 (January 1977), 50.

[38] Judicius, 50.

cerned the production of the new hymnal. It had been thirty-seven years since the appearance of *The Lutheran Hymnal* (1940). The *Lutheran Book of Worship* was scheduled for publication in December of 1978.[39]

The content of the resolution can be divided into two main points (see Appendix C for complete text of resolution 3-04A). Point one consists of the second "Resolved," which called for the establishment of a "blue ribbon" committee (later referred to as the Special Hymnal Review Committee or SHRC), and of the third "Resolved," which directed the committee to review the final draft of *LBW*. The third "Resolved" also stated that the purpose of the review was to formulate a recommendation to the 1979 convention. The committee was to recommend one of three options: (1) adopt the final draft of *LBW*, (2) adopt the final draft of *LBW* with specified modifications, or (3) reject *LBW* and propose that an alternative new hymnal for the LCMS be developed.[40]

The second main point of the text is mentioned in the fifth and sixth resolves. The convention requested the ALC, LCA, and ALCC to postpone publication of *LBW* until the review of the final draft was completed. At this point, if the "blue ribbon" committee determined *LBW* to be "unsuited for use in the LCMS, the Commission on Worship [was] directed to gather materials for a new hymnal for the LCMS."[41]

A look at the history of American Lutheranism reveals that the development and use of hymnals (for both liturgy and hymnody) have implications that go beyond synodical and denominational borders. Richard D. Wolf points to the Liturgy of 1748 and the Hymnal of 1786 and concludes,

---

[39] *Proceedings of the 52nd Regular Convention of the Lutheran Church—Missouri Synod*, Dallas, Texas, 1977, 58. See also Robert Sauer, "The Special Hymnal Review Committee," *Lutheran Worship: History and Practice*, ed. Fred L. Precht (pre-publication manuscript) in chapter 4, page 1. Sauer was chairman of the Special Hymnal Review Committee. He writes: "No subject was debated at greater length than the proposed *Lutheran Book of Worship* during the . . . Dallas [convention]. Almost one hundred overtures from congregations and other entities of the Synod questioned further involvement in the pan-Lutheran effort. Very few indicated support for the project that had been initiated by the Synod in convention at Detroit in 1965."

[40] *Proceedings*, Dallas, 1977, 127.

[41] *Proceedings*, Dallas, 1977, 127.

> Worship according to an agreed-upon, common liturgy has always been an important factor in the creation and maintenance of unity among Lutherans, and has at times played no small role in producing an atmosphere conducive to actual union.[42]

Again in the first half of the nineteenth century the common liturgy was recognized as a step toward greater unity. In the official actions regarding the liturgy (1839–49) the Ministerium of Pennsylvania resolved

> That we rejoice in the translation of our German Liturgy into the English language by the Evangelical Lutheran General Synod . . . and we trust that this may contribute to greater harmony and to more fraternal relations between us and them and the whole church.[43]

The fear of many in the LCMS that a joint hymnal would lead to greater unionistic practices and perhaps merger with synods of marked theological diversity was not without historical justification. As late as 1966, William Seaman's report on "The *Service Book and Hymnal* Since 1958" boasted to the representatives of the new Inter-Lutheran Commission on Worship that "It has often been said that the *Common Service Book* did more to create the United Lutheran Church in America than any committee, commission, constitution, or convention."[44] Seaman adds: The *SBH* had been a powerful instrument in creating spiritual unity within the church which exceed all our hopes and expectations.[45] Philip Pfatteicher also states: "The use of one book encouraged and facilitated the merging of church bodies."

Such concerns are contained within the document itself. The fourth "Whereas" refers to both "theological questions" and "fellowship implications."

> WHEREAS, Theological questions have been raised by agencies and members of the LCMS (e.g., CTCR, faculty members of the two

---

[42] Richard C. Wolf, *Documents of Lutheran Unity* (Philadelphia: Fortress Press, 1966), 32.
[43] Wolf, 95–96.
[44] Edgar S. Brown, *Liturgical Reconnaissance*, 110.
[45] Brown, 110.

seminaries, worship material reviewers) concerning the proposed *Lutheran Book of Worship* (e.g., commemorations, eucharistic prayer forms, adequacy of expressions, optional use of "he descended to the dead" in the Apostles' Creed, theological implications of hymn text alterations, confirmation promise, fellowship implications).[46]

The progress toward external unity with the ALC peaked with the declaration of altar and pulpit fellowship at the 1969 Denver convention. The actual moment that a tide begins to change is usually difficult to determine with precision. After it has changed, given time, it becomes more and more obvious. So it was for the delegates in Dallas. On July 19, 1977, they adopted Resolution 3-02A in which the LCMS declared itself to be in a state of "fellowship in protest" with the ALC on account of doctrinal disagreements.[47] On the other hand, an amendment to change resolution 3-02A to read, "That the LCMS declare with regret that fellowship with the ALC at the synodical level does not exist on account of the doctrinal differences listed above," was declined.[48] Two days later the weary delegates gathered for their last evening session. They were now in a state of "fellowship in protest" with the ALC, and they were faced with the prospect of sharing a joint hymnal (that their own synod had "officially instigated") which was due to be published before the end of the next year.

The fifth "Resolved" appealed to the ALC, LCA and ELCC to postpone production of *LBW* without assurances that the LCMS would ever see its way clear to approve it, with or without modifications. It would not be long and the Missouri Synod would have its answer. By September of 1977 the seven-person "blue ribbon" committee had already elected Dr. Robert C. Sauer chairman of the committee and had requested information from the ILCW as to what modifications could yet be made in *LBW*. A letter to Robert Sauer dated September 26, 1977, said:

> [I]t will already be too late by the time of the next meeting of the Special Hymnal Review Committee to make any changes that

[46] *Proceedings*, Dallas, 1977, 127.
[47] *Proceedings*, Dallas, 1977, 126–127.
[48] *Proceedings*, Dallas, 1977, 126.

> would require the shifting of space requirements. Such changes would be the deletion of a hymn or of entire stanzas of hymns, the addition of a paragraph to a service, etc. Changes of words or phrases in the liturgy could be made into the final proofing process which are scheduled for completion by the end of January. Such changes would be the restoration of the original form of the footnote on the Apostles' Creed, the change of a term etc.[49]

With only a token effort on the part of the ILCW, the Special Hymnal Review Committee moved ahead and by the close of its December meeting "unanimously resolved to recommend to the congregations of the Synod that *LBW* be accepted with modifications,"[50] and if approved by the July 1979 convention in St. Louis, the new hymnal should be published as quickly as possible under the tentative title *Lutheran Worship*.[51]

The effects of Resolution 3-04A would be both immediate and long range. That the action would involve internal strife was already apparent when a standing vote was necessary to defeat a substitute motion to receive the new publication "as one of the resources for worship available to the congregations, subject to successful completion of the doctrinal review process."[52]

Within four months the resolution would effect the resignation of six of the seven members of the Commission on Worship. The commission had stated its position already in the 1977 *Convention Workbook* report by saying, "The commission further believes that *LBW* is wholly faithful to Scripture and the Lutheran Confessions."[53] The report included an extensive appendix responding to the accusations against the new hymnal and concluded, "The commission recommends *LBW* to the use of congregations of the Synod with enthusiasm and conviction."[54] In a Religious News Service

---

[49] *Report and Recommendation of the Special Hymnal Committee* (St. Louis: Concordia Publishing House, n.d.), 3.

[50] *Report and Recommendation*, 4.

[51] *Report and Recommendation*, 6.

[52] *Proceedings*, Dallas, 1977, 128. The narrow vote was 548 to 501.

[53] *Convention Workbook of the 52nd Regular Convention of the Lutheran Church—Missouri Synod*, Dallas, 1977, 58.

[54] *Convention Workbook*, Dallas, 1977, 59.

release in the *Washington* (D.C.) *Post,* the six resigning members of the commission were quoted as saying, "the question of fellowship, rather than alleged doctrinal error, is the real reason for delaying approval of the worship book."[55]

Within a month, the charges of delaying leveled against the SHRC would be muted. The "blue ribbon" committee would urge the synod to publish its own hymnal. While Vice President Sauer was reported by the Associated Press to have "denied that strained relations with the ALC were the key issue behind the dispute,"[56] nevertheless, Sauer did make it clear that fellowship concerns were involved as well as theological problems. The United Press International reported that Dr. Sauer "condemned an ecumenical effort . . . to make the book acceptable to even a non-Lutheran audience."[57] The response of the Rev. E. Theo. DeLaney (Auxiliary member of the Commission on Worship) to the January article in the *Concordia Theological Quarterly* would support Sauer's contention. DeLaney wrote:

> The selections (of the commemoration of saints in Contemporary Worship 6) includes those of the ecumenical tradition who have shaped the churches of the Reformation, but representatives of other movements of the church are also included as testimony to the variety of God's gifts to his people . . . . A narrowly defined orthodoxy has been consciously avoided, for one of the principal purposes of the calendar is to suggest the size and diversity of the cloud of witnesses.[58]

DeLaney's explanation is in defense of such men as Toyohiko Kagawa, John Calvin, Pope John XXIII, Albert Schweitzer, and

---

[55] *Washington* (D.C.) *Post* (November 25, 1977) article from newspaper available at Concordia Historical Institute, St. Louis, file 111.1B "Commission on Worship."

[56] *Des Moines* (Iowa) *Register,* Associated Press (November 17, 1977) article from the newspaper available at Concordia Historical Institute, St. Louis, file 111.1B, "Commission on Worship."

[57] *Milwaukee* (Wisconsin) *Sentinel* (St. Louis, MO, December 13, 1977) Article from newspaper available at Concordia Historical Institute, St. Louis, file 111.1B "Commission on Worship."

[58] E. Theo. DeLaney, "Response to Judicius," *Concordia Theological Quarterly* 1:77 (no copyright). Unpublished article of 13 pages, single spaced. Copy available at Concordia Historical Institute, St. Louis, file 111.1B "Commission on Worship."

Soren Kierkegaard.[59] That the majority of the members of the LCMS would not approve of a new hymnal that encouraged them to adorn their altars with white paraments in memory of these "saints" became apparent by the action of the delegates in adopting Resolution 3-02A.

In 1979 the LCMS in convention chose to produce its own hymnal. By the second half of the 1980s the ALC and LCA would be walking down new roads which involved Eucharist and/or pulpit sharing with the Reformed, Episcopal, and Roman Catholic churches. In 1987 the ALC, LCA, and AELC would merge to form the Evangelical Lutheran Church in America. The last-minute decision for the LCMS to pull out of the project left many people in the ALC, LCA, and ELCC bewildered. It was also the cause of hurt and anger for some in the LCMS, including many who had worked on the ILCW and Worship Commission. The unfortunate timing was due to the internal struggle within the LCMS in the 1960s and 1970s. Given the extensive press coverage it received in both the religious and secular media, the reversal did not take anyone by surprise. On the fifteenth anniversary of the *Lutheran Book of Worship* Philip H. Pfatteicher wrote:

> So, even though their book was but twenty years old, the ALC and the LCA eagerly agreed to the LCMS proposal. (At the end of the ten-year production the Lutheran Church—Missouri Synod of course withdrew from the joint project, but that is another story.)
>
> More was at stake than genuinely pan-Lutheran co-operation. For Lutherans in North America, co-operation on a common book of worship led inevitably to merger. The point of having one book is to have one church. The Common Service Book of 1918 was a prelude to the formation of the United Lutheran Church in America (ULCA), merging the bodies that prepared the Common Service of 1888: The General Council, the General Synod, and the General Synod South. The *Service Book and Hymnal* of 1958 was a preparation for the formation of the ALC and the LCA and later of the Evangelical Lutheran Church in Canada. *The Lutheran Book of Wor-*

[59] Inter-Lutheran Commission on Worship, *Contemporary Worship 6: The Church Year Calendar and Lectionary* (St. Louis : Concordia Publishing House, 1973), 35–46.

> *ship*, from which the Missouri Synod withdrew its support at the late stage of the process, led to the formation of the Evangelical Lutheran Church in America (ELCA), merging the Association of Evangelical Lutheran Churches (AELC), the ALC and the LCA and the formation of the (new) Evangelical Lutheran Church in Canada (ELCiC). Some say that the Missouri Synod's dawning awareness of that process of unification was the reason for their withdrawal from the project: to share one book with other Lutherans in North America would seem to leave little reason for continued separation and that was unacceptable to key figures in the LCMS.[60]

With the adoption of the 1979 Resolution 3-01, "To Adopt *Lutheran Worship* as an Official Hymnal of the LCMS," the synod was being consistent with its historical understanding and practice of church fellowship. A report on a series of open conferences held between the leaders of the LCMS, ALC, and LCA between 1972 and 1977 revealed a wide theological divergence in such key areas as the Gospel, fellowship, and biblical interpretation.[61] For example, in the ALC the expression "doctrinal consensus" means "agreement in the proclamation and teaching of the gospel . . . . A relatively small group in the ALC would understand it to mean agreement in every article of the Christian faith . . . ."[62] The LCA expressed even greater latitude by saying, "'Consensus' describes agreement on doctrine, on what must be preached in and by the church in proclaiming the gospel. It does not presuppose that all parties have the same theology."[63] The LCMS defined its position on "consensus" by quoting from the Formula of Concord,

> as to the schisms in matters of faith, however, which have occurred in our time, we regard as the unanimous consensus and declaration of our Christian faith and confession (especially against the Papacy . . . and other sects) the Unaltered Augsburg Confession, Apology, and Smalcald Articles.[64]

---

[60] Philip H. Pfatteicher, "Still To Be Tried," *Lutheran Forum* 27 (November 1993): 22.

[61] Lutheran Council in the USA, *The Function of Doctrine and Theology in Light of the Unity of the Church* (New York: Lutheran Council in the USA, 1978).

[62] *Function of Doctrine*, 18.

[63] *Function of Doctrine*, 20.

[64] *Function of Doctrine*, 24.

Compared to *The Lutheran Hymnal*, the *Lutheran Book of Worship* fared poorly. The final product was not a joint hymnal reaching a greater audience than previously accomplished in the Missouri Synod or in the history of American Lutheranism. It was actually a step backward, as it caused a division between the LCMS and the churches of the Synodical Conference. Although the Synodical Conference had been disbanded, the various synods still shared a common hymnbook in *TLH*. Not only did *LBW* fail to be universally accepted by the congregations of the LCMS, but it contributed to making the Missouri Synod a three-hymnal Synod.

The use of three hymnals within the Missouri Synod since 1978, *TLH* (32% usage), *LBW* (7.9%), and *LW* (49%), split the Synod three ways and opened the door for yet further division in prayer books and practice.[65]

> The same survey revealed that the use of supplemental hymnals makes up the remaining 11% within our Synod. This figure is up an alarming 8.6% from the 1989 survey. This translates into approximately 250 parishes per year leaving Lutheran hymnals.[66]

At the same time *Lutheran Worship* was being introduced into the local congregations of the Missouri Synod, the Church Growth Movement was also spreading. This product of American Protestant "Evangelicalism" brought with it a foreign theology of worship (Arminian) that took advantage of the sentiments of many who were frustrated by the adjustments required in learning to use the new hymnal. For those interested in "growing a church" the new hymnal was best kept in the pew rack while new liturgies were produced weekly and printed in full ("liturgy" and "contemporary" hymn texts) in throw-away handouts. Much of this foreign material is theologically inappropriate or at best simply inane. Anti-hymnal

---

[65] Richard C. Resch, "Hymnody as Teacher of the Faith" (unpublished paper, ca. 1992). Resch notes the source of these figures: *A Use Survey Among Congregations of the Lutheran Church—Missouri Synod*, Summer 1991. Conducted by Donald L. Brown, Research Specialist, Concordia Publishing House.

[66] Resch.

and anti-liturgical attitudes caused many congregations simply not to buy *Lutheran Worship*.

While uniformity is to be sought and has certain benefits, nevertheless, diversity among liturgical traditions has always been the norm through the centuries. It would therefore be inaccurate to charge the LCMS decision to produce its own hymnal as separatistic or sectarian. Resolution 3-04A was an attempt to retain the best of its evangelical and confessional tradition in matters liturgical.

4

Influence of the Liturgical Movement on the Liturgical Literature of American Lutheranism

ONE year before the publication of the *Lutheran Book of Worship* a timely paper was prepared by William G. Rusch in order to explain "[t]he present LCA process of a theological review of the materials produced by the Inter-Lutheran Commission on Worship." As stated in the preface, "To understand the work of the commission, the history of the Lutheran liturgy in North America and the liturgical scholarship during the last hundred years should be described."[1] Rusch described how the liturgical work which led up to the Common Service of 1888 was primarily an attempt to build on the "pure Lutheran liturgies of the sixteenth century." *The Lutheran Hymnal* (1941) continued in this approach. A shift took place in 1945 when work began on the *Service Book and Hymnal* (1958).

> The character of the liturgy is less traditionally Lutheran than the Common Service. The commission for the *Service Book and Hymnal* did not feel obligated to repristinate the Common Service. While working from this Lutheran basis and with other

[1] William G. Rusch, "A Background Paper for A Theological Review of Materials Produced by the Inter-Lutheran Commission On Worship," January 1977 (Bound copy available in Concordia Seminary Library). William Rusch was Associate Executive Director, Division of Theological Studies, Lutheran Council in the U.S.A. Following an overview of the new theological influences guiding the work of the ILCW, the majority of the paper consists of a theological review of the booklet titled *Liturgical Texts*. Rusch explains, "The methodology to be followed here is to take each item of the new service book, examine any theological debate that has occurred at that point, and determine what can be noted of the theology underlying the text."

> Lutheran materials, the commission also recovered some liturgical forms from the early church, thus combining traditions from the Eastern and Western churches . . . . "The Preface to the Liturgy" discloses that Lutherans had been influenced by the renewal of liturgical scholarship in this century that crossed denominational lines and sought recovery of features of the worship of the early and Eastern church. By the year 1960 the vast majority of American Lutherans were using the *SBH*, a book rooted in the Common Service but at important points moving beyond it. Another large segment of Lutherans, the Lutheran Church—Missouri Synod, was employing a different book, *The Lutheran Hymnal*, which shared much with the *SBH* in their common parentage in the Common Service and yet did not include the more ecumenical features of the *SBH*.[2]

In a chapter titled "A Description of Liturgical Scholarship During the Last Hundred Years," Rusch draws attention to the fact that non-Lutheran scholarship had a "direct bearing" on the liturgical developments of American Lutheranism. He writes, "Patently this is an enormous subject that can be no more than noted here, and yet it is one of great import for understanding theologically new liturgical materials." [3] Rusch then devotes a page and a half to some of the most influential scholars and works, for example, F. Probst, Louis Duchesne, Edmund Bishop, Henry Bradshaw Society and the Alcuin Club, F. E. Brightman, O. Cullmann, J. Jeremias, H. Lietzmann, Y. Brilioth, G. Aulen, V. Vajta. He notes *Leiturgia* and *Handbuch des evangelischen Gottesdienst* and states, "Important periodicals such as *Liturgiegeschichte Quellen, Liturgiegeschichtliche Forschungen, Jahrbuch für Liturgiewissenschaft Ephemerides*, circulated the ever increasing volume of liturgical research."

Rusch lists the primary effects of the scholarly studies on the liturgical life of the Roman Catholic Church:

1. Recommendations of frequent communion;
2. Communion of children at an early age;
3. Encouragement of congregational singing of Gregorian chant;

[2] Rusch, 9–10.
[3] Rusch, 10.

4. Introduction of Easter Vigil in 1951;
5. General reform of the Holy Week Services in 1955;
6. Partial reform of the rubrics in 1956. The reforms of the liturgy by Vatican II were an outcome of this liturgical scholarship.

Among other items called for by the 1963 Constitution were

7. Active participation in the liturgy by all the faithful;
8. A general restoration of the liturgy itself from theological, historical, and pastoral points of views;
9. Inclusion of more Scripture;
10. Vernacular.

The implementation of the Constitution included

11. Freestanding high altar;
12. Sermons at all Sunday and feast day masses.[4]

In addition to the extensive influence from the continental studies in the fields of "Christian archaeology and patristic studies," Rusch made special note of the developments in the Anglican Church. (1) In 1927 the Church Assembly considered a new Prayer Book whose prayer of consecration included an epiclesis on the elements. (2) In India and Africa other rites in the Anglican Church

> sought to clarify the structure of the liturgy and to restore as much as possible the primitive elements which were either omitted or obscured in the existing Prayer Books. These rites almost exclusively looked to pre-Reformation materials, often to the Eastern church.[5]

(3) Gregory Dix's *The Shape of the Liturgy* appeared in 1945. Rusch opines,

> This volume did much to prepare the ground for a basic reconsideration of the liturgy. This was a key factor in the production of the Liturgy of the Church of South India in 1950. This liturgy included as full a participation as possible by the faithful in the liturgy,

---

[4] Rusch, 11–13.
[5] Rusch, 13.

> including congregational response in the Prayer of Consecration, an intercession in the form of a litany and provision for an Old Testament lesson before the Epistle.[6]

(4) In 1958 the Lambeth Conference urged a revision of the Prayer Book to recover further the worship of the primitive church.[7] Rusch continues:

> It is precisely this overwhelming amount of new research on the liturgy and practical developments within other churches that were factors which influenced the commissioners of the *Service Book and Hymnal* to move cautiously beyond the Common Service and obtain liturgical forms from the early church. This liturgical scholarship continued after the appearance of the *SBH* in 1958. It was soon contributing to a number of bilateral ecumenical dialogues and making possible agreements on baptism, the eucharist and ministry that only a few decades earlier would have been judged unlikely by most knowledgeable individuals. These bilateral agreements in turn affected new work done on liturgical materials.[8]

Luther Reed also pointed to the new research of liturgical scholars in Europe and America necessitating a "thoroughgoing revision" of his book *The Lutheran Liturgy*.[9] Reed stresses the desirability of the Eucharistic Prayer, noting his pleasure that it was included in the *Service Book and Hymnal*. He disparagingly likens Luther's liturgical reforms to "drastic action . . . cutting into the Canon like a surgeon and removing everything except the Verba . . . ."[10] He also quotes Bishop Brilioth's deprecating opinion of Martin Luther:

> "The pruning knife of the Reformation" had to clear away "the disfiguring outgrowths of the Roman Mass," but "the richer treasures of the older liturgies were not recovered. Thus the operation left a

---

[6] Rusch.
[7] Rusch, 13–14.
[8] Rusch 14.
[9] *The Lutheran Liturgy* was first published in 1947. The revised edition appeared in 1959.
[10] Luther D. Reed, *The Lutheran Liturgy: A Study of the Common Liturgy of the Lutheran Church in America* (Philadelphia: Fortress Press, rev. ed. 1959), 346.

gaping void . . . a central problem of the Lutheran Rite still awaits its solution [*sic*]."[11]

As for the present situation, Reed observes the shift in Roman Catholic thought from "spatial considerations to conceptions of action" in the Mass. "The Eucharist is regarded primarily as a 're-presentation' of our Lord and of his actions in the Upper Room."[12] Accordingly, the Lutheran elimination of "all surrounding prayer forms left the Verba standing alone in stark, if strong, simplicity," and thus "intensified the medieval conception of consecration by a fixed formula, and in a single moment in time."[13] Having pointed out the "liabilities" of both the Roman Catholic and Lutheran practices, Reed recommends going back to the early church and proffers Gregory Dix's "Four-Action Shape" scheme.

> In the restoration of a form of Eucharistic Prayer in the Common Liturgy, we return to the earlier pre-Roman conception, according to which the church sets apart the elements in a blessing or thanksgiving which includes four actions in imitation of our Lord's actions at the Last Supper. These actions are: taking, blessing (or giving thanks), breaking, and distributing. This is indeed all one action. Its comprehensive character helps free us from the erroneous conception of consecration limited to a moment and effected by a formula.[14]

William Rusch attempted to show the state of liturgics in American Lutheranism in the early 1960s and how it arrived at this point. He concluded:

---

[11] Reed, 349. Yngve Brilioth was a bishop of the Swedish Lutheran Church. Reed is quoting Brilioth's *Eucharist, Faith and Practice*, 125. For a critical analysis of the Brilioth-Reed opinion of Luther's liturgical reforms see Bryan Spinks, *Luther's Liturgical Criteria and His Reform of the Canon of the Mass*, Grove Liturgical Study 30 (Bramcote, Notts., England: Grove Books, 1982).

[12] Reed, 353.

[13] Reed, 354–355.

[14] Reed, 355. Reed makes no mention of Gregory Dix in reference to the "Four-Action Shape" popularized by Dix in his book *The Shape of the Liturgy* (1945). The book does appear two pages earlier in a bibliography appended to the section "A Eucharist Prayer Desirable." It also appears in the lengthy bibliography at the end of the book on page 787. Five references under Dix are included in the index. Three refer the reader to his book *The Treatise on the Apostolic Tradition of St. Hyppolytus of Rome*; two refer the reader to *The Shape of the Liturgy*.

> It has been observed that by 1960 an immense amount of scholarly activity was being carried on within the Christian community that both directly and indirectly had an influence on the liturgy.[15]

He notes that *The Lutheran Hymnal* and the *Service Book and Hymnal* had gone far in achieving liturgical unity among American Lutheranism. It was all of the above that contributed to the context in which the Lutheran Church—Missouri Synod, in convention, invited the other Lutheran bodies to cooperate in a joint hymnal in 1965.

Twelve years after the completion of the *Lutheran Book of Worship* (1978), the impressive 558-page *Commentary on the Lutheran Book of Worship* (1990) was published. Written by Philip H. Pfatteicher,[16] the volume carries the revealing subtitle *Lutheran Liturgy in Its Ecumenical Context.* Chapter 1 is titled "Convergence and Cooperation" and begins,

> A study of the liturgy used by Lutherans in North America during the transition from the twentieth to the twenty-first century may properly begin not with a Lutheran person or event but with the principal work of a Roman Catholic bishop of Rome....
>
> The conciliar documents summarized in a concise and provocative way the fruits of decades of scholarship and thus laid the foundation for specific reforms of the church's practice....
>
> The scholarly research which this document reflected, buttressed by the liturgical movement of the twentieth century, was not peculiar to the Roman Church nor limited to it. Scholars of various traditions and diverse lands and many denominations had been moving in similar directions.[17]

Pfatteicher points out that the Episcopal Church in the United States is also part of the convergence of traditions as are, more recently, the Presbyterians and United Methodists. Finally he acknowledges,

---

[15] Rusch, 15.

[16] The Inter-Lutheran Commission on Worship existed from 1966 to 1978. Philip H. Pfatteicher served on the Liturgical Text Committee from 1968–78 as a representative of the Lutheran Church in America.

[17] Philip H. Pfatteicher, *Commentary on the Lutheran Book of Worship* (Minneapolis: Augsburg Fortress, 1990), 1–2.

> The Lutheran church in North America could not help being influenced by these developments as well as by the work of its own scholars in Scripture, history, systematic theology, and liturgy; it, too, shared in the emerging ecumenical consensus of the latter half of the twentieth century.[18]

The *Commentary on the Lutheran Book of Worship* presents a very positive view of the Roman Catholic Church. According to Pfatteicher, Vatican II

> showed the Church of Rome to be not the monolithic monarchy many thought it to be but rather a living body capable of remarkable change, renewal, and renovation—a model for the rest of Christianity. Moreover, the churches of the Reformation, and Lutherans especially, saw in the working and the documents of the council an acceptance of basic principles of the sixteenth-century Reformation: the primacy of grace, the centrality of Scripture, the understanding of the church as the people of God, the use of the vernacular language. It was as if the Lutheran Reformation had made its point at long last. Indeed, some Lutherans observed that the place in the modern world where the principles of the Reformers were most clearly at work was the Roman Church. This thrilling discovery challenged deep-seated prejudices and stereotypes and evoked an atmosphere of heady optimism.[19]

Almost a decade prior to the Vatican II (*Sacrosanctum Concilium*, December 1963), Ernest Koenker expressed similar enthusiasm and "heady optimism" over the effects of the Liturgical Movement on the Roman Catholic Church and ecumenical "rapprochement." The closing sentences in his book *The Liturgical Renaissance in the Roman Catholic Church* anticipate the sentiments of Pfatteicher.

> Under favorable conditions the Liturgical Renaissance will extend its objectives and its sphere of influence . . . . The movement may go on to personalize, to individualize, and to Christianize the sacraments and sacramentals in such a way that the old magic sacramentalism of the Roman Catholic Church will be completely overcome.

---

[18] Pfatteicher, 3.
[19] Pfatteicher, 1–2.

> A new, evangelical spirit may be infused into the relationship between priest and people and their bishop; even the concept of the papacy may be spiritualized and Christianized. If the renaissance can continue unhindered, there may be a new "Liturgical Springtime" of the Roman Catholic Church—an awakening, the importance of which many would not now dream.[20]

Eleven years before the formation of the ILCW, Koenker's book brought to American Lutherans a very thorough and accurate overview of the theology behind the Roman Catholic liturgical movement. He articulated the primary theological thinking behind the Roman Catholic liturgical movement: the mystical Body; the active participation of the faithful; the church year: the divine office and freestanding altar with priest facing the people; emphasis on the general priesthood; return to earlier centuries for a liturgical model; the person and work of Christ; the *Mysterientheologie* of Odo Casel and others, and the innovation of re-presentation as an action to address the time-space dilemma of the sacrifice of the Mass; agitation for the vernacular; Gregorian Chant and emphasis on congregational singing; and "rapprochement in divided Christendom." Three years after Vatican II and the same year the Inter-Lutheran Commission on Worship was established (1966), Koenker's book would be reprinted by Concordia Publishing House with a new introduction by the author. In the preface to this edition, Koenker writes:

> When the volume was published in 1954, no one could have foreseen the remarkable changes in legislation, mentality, and atmosphere which have taken place in Rome during the last decade .... Theologically one age has passed and another is well under way .... Twenty years ago ... I might have projected fifty or a hundred years for the realization of the revisions and reform. Yet suddenly and dramatically, quiet Pope John convened a Council and cut off scores of years from the anticipated slow pace.

Koenker quotes an unnamed Austrian Jesuit working in Rome in connection with Vatican II in November of 1964: "We have seen

---

[20] Ernest B. Koenker, *The Liturgical Renaissance in the Roman Catholic Church* (Chicago: The University of Chicago Press, 1954), 201.

more changes in the past three weeks than in the previous 1600 years." Koenker then adds,

> Because of the Council's official backing, the Liturgical Movement has received a forward thrust which now makes the mentality of the 1940s in the Church closer to the Catholicism of the Middle Ages than to the Catholicism-come-of-age today.... The power of the Gospel is present in the Roman Catholic Church, reshaping and renovating static forms and structures in a way quite unimaginable a decade ago. We face . . . a spiritual renaissance. The Liturgical Movement has not only been vindicated by Vatican II. It has taken further revolutionary strides through the Council. The movement has become of immense significance for the entire Roman Catholic Church, and for Christendom and society as a whole. This is due first of all to its openness to the world as God's world and to the other Christian communities as truly churches; but even more fundamentally its impact stems from its Christocentric and biblical orientation, and its consequent recovery of the corporate nature of the Church and her worship and of the calling and priesthood of the laity.[21]

Koenker's overall evaluation of the movement is very optimistic. He offers the sympathetic view that "Among the various trends and movements . . . within the Body of Christ, today, the Liturgical Movement must be given an honorable place."[22] He is referring here to the liturgical movements not only in the Roman Catholic Church but also in the Anglican, Lutheran, and Reformed churches, and among America's various Protestant denominations. He quotes from the proceedings of the Evangelical Academy conference at Bad Boll, *Ökumenisch oder katolisch*, in which author Wilfried Lempp "points to the Liturgical Movement in the Roman Catholic Church as a spiritual development which the Evangelical Church must greet with distinct gladness."[23] Koenker admits that his "study will reveal a decided sympathy for the aims and objectives of the movement."[24]

---

[21] Ernest B. Koenker, *The Liturgical Renaissance in the Roman Catholic Church* (St. Louis: Concordia Publishing House, paperback edition, 1966), v–vii.

[22] Koenker (CPH), v.

[23] Koenker (CPH), vi.

[24] Koenker (CPH), vi.

Koenker also laments the passing of the initial founders of the modern Liturgical Movement whose names he notes along with the date of their death: Virgil Michel, 1938; Ildefons Herwegen, 1946; Anton Baumstark, 1948; Odo Casel, 1948; Alcuin Deutch, 1951; Heinrich von Meuers, 1953; and the great Pius Parsch, 1954.[25] Koenker was concerned that the next generation lacked equivalent training in "sound liturgical-historical scholarship." He noted that "with the exception of the Benedictine foundations, only the Liturgy Program at the University of Notre Dame introduces sound liturgical study on the North American continent."[26]

In 1959, Concordia Publishing House published Ernest Koenker's *Worship in Word and Sacrament*. This was the same year that the Lutheran Church—Missouri Synod began the revision of *The Lutheran Hymnal*, and one year after the publication of the *Service Book and Hymnal* (1958). The book was directed toward the "average intelligent and concerned layman," and was a call for "a great deal of study and re-thinking" of worship. This re-thinking was to emphasize "the praise and thanksgiving aspect of the Eucharist, to tie Bible and liturgy, preaching and Sacrament together." Although the task would not be easy, such study and re-thinking would be necessary, wrote Koenker, before "the Liturgical Movement within the Lutheran Church will gain its desired influence and the ancient, objective liturgical forms will convey their traditional message."[27] In many respects, *Worship in Word and Sacrament* is an outstanding little book. It points out the negative influences on the liturgy in America: secularism, protestantism, individualism, man-centered and experience-based worship. Koenker develops the rich emphasis of the presence of Christ in worship that is both word and sacrament. He makes it clear that "Something actually occurs in worship because the promises of God and his gifts are not empty, commemorative signs. They actually bestow what they promise."[28] He properly

---

[25] Koenker (CPH), 200.

[26] Koenker (CPH), 200–201. Koenker was a professor at Valparaiso University, which had contacts with its fellow Indiana university Notre Dame.

[27] Ernest B. Koenker, *Worship in Word and Sacrament* (St. Louis: Concordia Publishing House, 1959), 6.

[28] Koenker, *Worship*, 100.

stresses the rhythm of worship being from God to man and then from man back to God. Koenker writes: "we must remember that in its primary sense worship is God's action in Christ; only secondarily is it man's action."[29] The order of the two "actions" is correct. Koenker identifies the primary "action" to be God's action "in the events described in the prophetic and apostolic Scriptures," and inextricably bound up in Christ. The usage of the verb "action," however, portends the influences of Casel, Dix, and others. In chapter 6, "What May We Expect From Liturgical Renewal?" Koenker identifies a question all major denominations will have to address when they experiment with imported forms and customs: "How does the *Mysterientheologie* in Roman Catholic and Anglican circles call for re-examination of the meaning of *mysterium* and *sacrifice*?"[30] Koenker hints at the answer by asking another question: "Why does there seem to be such a ubiquitous interest in liturgical restoration?"[31] The answer is that sociologically, "in Nietzsche's terms, 'God is dead' for many of our contemporaries . . . . He is cut off from the everyday events of life or is 'far away and long ago' . . . apparently absent and unnecessary in our world . . . ." Koenker then frames this cultural problem as it applies to worship in the form of a theological question: "Has the all-powerful God, who judges as well as sustains us, become a reality in the lives of our people?"[32] Here Koenker turns the attention to the theology of action and mystery.

> The Liturgical Movement sees the ancient worship forms of the church as a testimony—in act, rather than by the proliferation of words—to the reality of God in the universe . . . . The movement should be seen as one aspect of the effort in recent years to meet the inroads of secularism in the church.[33]

Koenker stresses that the Liturgical Movement is not primarily interested in forms but in the reality of God. By forms he means the "classic" liturgies of the ancient church and of the sixteenth century

[29] Koenker, *Worship*, 11.
[30] Koenker, *Worship*, 64.
[31] Koenker, *Worship*, 65.
[32] Koenker, *Worship*, 66.
[33] Koenker, *Worship*, 66–67.

whose restoration is of such interest to scholars. Responding to those who are clamoring for original, contemporary liturgies, he encourages them to write them if they are able. But Koenker adds,

> New liturgical creations lack the structure and depth of the ancient Eucharist . . . . A healthy conservatism demands a progress in keeping with the ancient and traditional religious patterns. There are elements and emphases in these patterns that are imperishable. These should be revived and stressed.[34]

Just what these "patterns" are, Koenker does not say. One suspects he is alluding to the shape and actions of Gregory Dix. Furthermore, the section on "Outward Appearance and Spiritual Reality" echoes the "Caselian-mystery" model:

> In this sense the symbols of the liturgy point beyond themselves to the historical events in the Bible. God *was active in history* . . . . The Eucharist celebration represents the saving acts of God in history. God is active in the Christ-mystery of this celebration, communicating His gifts to men, but this communication has an historical basis.[35]

Further light is shed on the freight of the word "represent" in the later hyphenated usage of the word.

> Sunday after Sunday and in festival after festival the saving acts of Christ's life were re-presented in the liturgy. It was not one's own, individual religious feelings that were celebrated, as in the case of the naturalistic religions, but through the great hymns of the church, through the lections, canticles, and preaching, the historical events of our redemption were recounted.[36]

What does the "Liturgical Renewal" mean for the Lutheran Church? Koenker presses the point that "For the Lutheran Church the first impetus must be directed toward a study of historical

---

[34] Koenker, *Worship*, 68–69.
[35] Koenker, *Worship*, 88.
[36] Koenker, *Worship*, 96.

resources of the ancient church and the Reformation period, and these sources must be related to the present situation."[37] He points to the fact that liturgical scholarship among Lutherans in America and Germany have "deepened our understanding of liturgical practice, particularly of the early church, the Reformation period, and the period of deterioration under Pietism and Rationalism."[38]

On the other hand, Koenker stresses that "The Liturgical Movement does not lead to Rome," but will lead to the Lutheran Church being more "'catholic' in the best sense of the Word." He also notes that "Roman Catholic observers have seen the movement in Lutheran circles as an endeavor, within the limits of the Lutheran Confessions, to re-emphasize certain common Christian elements rather than as a steppingstone to the Holy See."[39]

Hermann Sasse was not as optimistic. In 1959, Augsburg Publishing House published *This Is My Body: Luther's Contention for the Real Presence in the Sacrament of the Altar.* Sasse observed the remarkable spread of the Liturgical Movement "throughout Christendom irrespective of the borderlines of churches and denominations."[40] He approved of the fact that it promoted the early church practice of regular communion by all. This was especially desirable in Europe where contemporary developments had devastated church attendance in general, not to mention communion attendance. Sasse was hopeful the Liturgical Movement would lead to a revival of the Sacrament in the Church. He remained doubtful, however, that its effect on Lutheranism would be in any way beneficial.

> The question remains, however, whether this movement would also lead to a revival of the sacrament in the Lutheran sense. The

---

[37] Koenker, *Worship,* 64.

[38] Koenker, *Worship,* 72.

[39] Koenker, *Worship,* 70.

[40] Hermann Sasse, *This Is My Body: Luther's Contention for the Real Presence in the Sacrament of the Altar* (Adelaide: Lutheran Publishing House, rev. ed. 1977), 281. The first draft of the book was finished in 1954, but logistic and editorial difficulties delayed publication until 1959 by Augsburg Publishing House in Minneapolis.

Sasse also expressed criticisms of the influence of the Liturgical Movement on Lutheranism in two articles: "Liturgy and Lutheranism," *Una Sancta* 8.3 (1948): 6–18, and "The Liturgical Movement: Reformation or Revolution?" *Una Sancta* 17.4 (1960): 18–24.

> influence exerted on the Lutheran church by the modern Liturgical Movement seems to point more to a strengthening of romanizing tendencies than to a new understanding of Luther's profound perception of the inseparable connection between the Sacrament and the Gospel. Thus, the question whether or not the Lutheran doctrine on the Sacraments is still tenable remains a serious problem, even if Christendom as a whole should experience a revival of its sacramental life. An entirely different understanding of Baptism and the Lord's Supper might be the result of such a movement even within our own church. The question appears to be twofold: the problem of the doctrine of the Lutheran Confession, and the problem of the exegetical basis of this doctrine.[41]

As the 1950s drew to a close, the state of affairs in American Lutheranism was captured in the presentations made at an ecumenical liturgical conference held in Madison, Wisconsin, in 1958.[42] The opening address by Theodore Otto Wedel, titled "The Theology of the Liturgical Renewal," credits the Benedictine monastery at Collegeville, Minnesota, with introducing him to the Liturgical Movement and to the *Jahrbuch für Liturgiewissenschaft.* Major attention is given to the importance of Dom Odo Casel and the *Mysterientheologie.* Wedel concludes:

> Whatever the critical evaluation of Dom Casel's theology may eventually turn out to be, I feel certain that his insights will not be ignored. His use of the word "mystery" in place of the word "sacrament" is in itself significant. The older Greek term *mysterion* had a much wider meaning. It meant first of all, an action, a representation of an event, a recalling of the past so as to make it real in the present . . . *anamnesis.* According to Dom Casel, it is precisely this action-memorial of the sacrifice of Christ which is the offering or sacrifice of the Mass. The offering *is* the *anamnesis* itself. A past event becomes really present now. The very nature of a sacrament is this real presence of a past event in ongoing time.[43]

---

[41] Sasse, 281–2.

[42] The six addresses given at the conference were published in the book *The Liturgical Renewal of the Church,* ed. Massey Hamilton Shepherd Jr. (New York: Oxford University Press, 1960).

[43] Shepherd, 5.

The Mystery Theology school argues that the older, pre-medieval understanding of the sacrament was primarily a real presence in action rather than a thing. "Dom Casel and his followers argue, the Eucharistic real presence miracle . . . is first of all a time-miracle, not a space-miracle." Next Wedel adds:

> It is therefore quite understandable that representatives of the *Mysterientheologie* find this view of the Eucharist as a time-sacrament lingering long in the Church in the age of the Fathers. Proof of reticence with regard to admission of space symbols into the worship life of the Church is written large in the iconoclastic controversies of the seventh and eighth centuries.[44]

He points out that to date, no statues of Christ or the saints are found in any Greek Orthodox Church. [45]

The *Mysterientheologie* is enticing to Catholicism. The ecumenical possibilities are intoxicating. The Mystery Theology appears to offer new hope in explaining the sacrificial nature of the Mass in a way that Rome was unable to do in the sixteenth century. It also offers auspicious promise for untangling the Roman Church from the web of transubstantiation. Wedel writes:

> If we turn to the "mystery theologians" for light on this issue of the real presence conveyed to us by way of a spacial symbol, as well as by symbols in the category of time, we discover that they, too, do not ignore the problem. As already noted, Dom Casel refers repeatedly to the official Roman dogma of transubstantiation and takes it, as it were, in his stride. He is aware of the fact that the Eucharist is not only a re-presentation of the sacrifice of Christ, but also a Holy Communion. Just how Roman Catholic liturgiologists would deal with the problem of according full weight to the verb *is* in "This is my Body," if they were freed from the tyranny of Aristotelian metaphysics, we do not know.[46]

One place to start would be to give the Body its full weight. That is what our Lord tells us that we have. Of his words we can be most

---

[44] Shepherd, 6.
[45] Shepherd, 6.
[46] Shepherd, 11–12.

sure. Exchanging the man-made theory of transubstantiation for a theory of "trans-action" does not lead to certainty but to ambiguity. The predilection for using the more vague terminology of "presence" and "mystery" instead of the dominical and concrete "Body and Blood," suggests an inexact theology. The dilemma caused by the problems and priority of time symbols versus a spatial symbol are unsolvable. It is best to drop the symbol talk and go with what is certain. What is certain is what our Lord says. He said, "receive, eat, this (τοῦτο) is my body (σῶμα)" and "drink of it, all of you, for this (τοῦτο) is my blood" (Matt. 26:26, 28). Everything points to and gives weight to the body and blood. Even the word "this" points to the body and the blood as it is in grammatical agreement with the neuter words *body* and *blood* rather than with the masculine bread (ἄρτον) and cup (ποτήριον).

Ecumenical aims have been and continue to be a driving force in the contemporary Liturgical Movement. Hence there is an extra advantage in leap-frogging 1500 years of church history (shades of fundamentalism) to the "golden age" of the early church. There one is to search for the "pure" liturgies, liturgies of "action" unstained by the controversies of the great schism of East and West and by the division of the West during the Reformation. The ecumenical allure also served as a catalyst for the sudden opening of the doors for liturgical renewal in American Lutheranism in the mid-1960s. Much of the suspicion and outright antagonism to things liturgical (not to mention widespread ignorance and apathy) among American Lutheran clergy and laity was overcome amidst the euphoria of the ecumenical winds carried in by the public invitation of the Missouri Synod to the ALC and LCA to join in producing a new common book of worship.

The problems in searching for a model among the archeological fragments of the early church are manifold. This is not the early church. Fifteen hundred years of history cannot be bleached from the fabric of the *Una Sancta* as if one were exchanging one preferred color for another. Historically, the doctrine of justification has been the criterion for all liturgical reform, renewal, and restoration undertaken in the Lutheran evangelical tradition. It was not the search for the classical anaphora prototype. It was not a vague theory about seven actions compressed into four that gives shape to the liturgy. It was not sacrificial action and anamnesis that served as the unifying core of worship. It was and is the body and blood which are received for the forgiveness of sins. It was and is our Lord's Word of law and gospel. It was and is a radical, incarnation Christology, at the center of which is God's grace in Christ. "We have seen his glory . . . full of grace and truth" (John 1:14). The criterion for liturgical change is not based on a method which begins with the fragments of ancient liturgies and works backward to the apostolic and dominical Word. When a theologian's interpretation of the practices of the early church determine the nature and shape of the liturgy, the end product will only be as good as the skill, integrity, and bias of the particular scholar. In the case of the Roman Catholic mystery paradigm, Lutherans ought to be leery of where it may lead. Wedel gives his opinion:

> Yet this is precisely the clue which the pre-medieval understanding of the Eucharist as real presence of the dramatic action of Cross and Resurrection as an integral whole may contain. Accord priority to real presence in this Eucharist *action*, and real presence in the symbols of the sacrificial victim naturally follows. But to cite Dom Casel himself: "Only the presence of the sacrifice as action gives meaning to the presence of the One sacrificed." Or, to cite further: "The secondary significance of the Eucharist, namely, its claim to be supernatural food, derives from its primary significance as an offering; for the Holy Communion is a partaking precisely of *sacrificial* food (*Opferspeise*), Body and Blood of a crucified Lord."[47]

There were European Lutheran theologians who saw the danger of shifting from the justification criterion to anthropocentric criteria. The temptation to adopt any form of sacrifice in the Lord's Supper is rejected by the Norwegian Carl F. Wisloff. His timely book *The Gift of Communion* was translated into English in 1964 and was a virtual road map through many of the complexities of medieval as well as modern Roman Catholic eucharistic theology. His presentation of Luther's rejection of the sacrifice of the mass would be help-

---

[47] Shepherd, 12.

ful to those confronted with the action-mystery-sacrifice influences of the Roman Catholic liturgical movement.

It is significant that the third address at Madison in 1958 was given by Arthur Carl Piepkorn of The Lutheran Church—Missouri Synod, whose presentation was titled "The Protestant Worship Revival and the Lutheran Liturgical Movement." He clarifies the situation as it stood in 1958 with the observation: "The Lutheran Liturgical Movement is frequently equated with and condemned as preoccupation with aestheticism, ritualism, or ceremonialism."[48] Piepkorn does not deny that there is an interest in these areas, but he insists that the "chief concern of the Lutheran Liturgical Movement has been and is a theological and practical one."[49] He also denies a significant influence from the European Liturgical Movement.

> I repeat that the liturgical movement in the Lutheran Church on this continent is an indigenous one, evoked by American rather than by European conditions. Compared to the Church in Europe, the Lutheran Church in America has for the past century been on the whole consistently more Biblical, more Catholic, more Lutheran, and more Orthodox, in the sixteenth- and seventeenth-century sense.[50]

As for the impact of Roman Catholicism on Lutheranism, Piepkorn observes: "A common characteristic of the Lutheran liturgical movement is a cordial lack of enthusiasm for Roman Catholicism."[51] Piepkorn admits, however, that "usable results of Roman Catholic scholarly research are received with gratitude; and friendly interpersonal relations with individual liturgically minded Roman Catholics are carefully cultivated."[52] Piepkorn points out that opponents of the Lutheran liturgical movement "have so often and so violently accused the movement's propo-

---

[48] Shepherd, 86.
[49] Shepherd, 86.
[50] Shepherd, 87.
[51] Shepherd, 88.
[52] Shepherd, 88.

nents of popery and Romanizing," that "representatives of the Lutheran liturgical movement have developed a kind of anti-Roman sensitization."[53]

The observation that there was a lack of enthusiasm for things Roman in the late fifties and early sixties is contiguous to the intense and enthusiastic preoccupation with the unparalleled rapprochement among the American Lutheran Churches and the production of new Lutheran worship books.

1958 ~ *Service Book and Hymnal* published.
1959 ~ Lutheran Church—Missouri Synod synodical convention approves revision of *The Lutheran Hymnal*.
1960 ~ Formation of the American Lutheran Church.
1962 ~ Formation of the Lutheran Church in America.

There is no doubt that the attention and energies of American Lutherans during this period were focused primarily on Lutheran unity and Lutheran liturgical revision. It is quite clear, however, that one eye remained ever attentive to the remarkable developments taking place in the Roman Catholic liturgical movement. This is noted in the preface to *Liturgical Reconnaissance: Papers Presented at the Inter-Lutheran Consultation on Worship*. That Lutherans from the three major synods (ALC, LCA, and LCMS) should be coming together in 1965 (at the request of a LCMS convention resolution) to produce a pan-Lutheran hymnal is quite amazing. In retrospect the acknowledgement of the influence of the Roman Catholic liturgical movement is also quite astonishing. Even though the ALC and LCA had the new *Service Book and Hymnal* (a mere six years old) this did not deter the ALC and LCA from enthusiastically joining in the new pan-Lutheran hymnal endeavor. Edgar S. Brown Jr. justifies yet another worship book in the preface to *Liturgical Reconnaissance* with the comment that "events throughout Christendom, notably the liturgical reforms arising out of Vatican II, conspired to create an uneasiness, if not a dissatisfaction, with much of the liturgical forms and hymnody then in use." He continues, "Language was

[53] Shepherd, 88–89.

considered to be archaic, music often ill-suited to contemporary society of the 1960s."[54]

The contribution to the book *Liturgical Reconnaissance* by Walter E. Buszin (representing the Synodical Conference) concedes both a Roman Catholic and Reformed influence.

> The Missouri Synod has always concerned itself with purity of doctrine. Its insistence on such purity has contributed in large part to its fame, as well as to the ridicule to which it has been exposed in the past. To this day this remains a characteristic of the Lutheran church and applies more to its hymnody than to its liturgical work. However, in more recent years it has coursed its way also in liturgical practice, finding its sources chiefly in the practices of the Roman Catholic church and of the Reformed denominations. In the field of hymnody doctrinal indifference has expressed itself chiefly in the sentimental and fundamentalistic hymnals which have been adopted chiefly in certain mission fields of the church.[55]

Overall, *Liturgical Reconnaissance* only hinted at the impact that the Roman Catholic and Anglican liturgical movements were having on the liturgical developments in American Lutheranism. Edgar S. Brown of the LCA concluded his article with the admission:

> That there is a growing influence of developments founded upon modern scholarship in scripture, liturgy, theology, and sociology, which yearns to break out of the more traditional molds usually identified with the so-called Oxford Movement and all of its companionate developments. Language is undergoing scrutiny, as is the *very shape of the rite itself* [emphasis mine]. There is a conscious recognition that the liturgy is truly *"the peoples' action"* [emphasis mine] and therefore the people should do more.[56]

Liturgical Reconnaissance includes a statement adopted by the 1960 Convention of the United Lutheran Church in America as a guide

---

[54] Edgar S. Brown Jr., ed., *Liturgical Reconnaissance: Papers Presented at the Inter-Lutheran Consultation on Worship* (Philadelphia: Fortress Press, 1968), vii–viii. The consultation took place in Chicago, Illinois, February 10–11, 1966.

[55] Brown, 85–86.

[56] Brown, 32.

to its congregations in the theology and practice of the Sacrament of the Altar. The statement shows Caselian influences. Concerning the sacrament as memorial, the statement reads:

> The memorial aspect of the sacrament is, however, to be understood not in sheer chronological concepts as mere recollection of a past event which becomes dimmer as time goes on. Only the believer (or he who is offended) may become contemporary with the saving events of Calvary in any age . . . so faith alone can perceive this memorial as more than a memory of a past event devoutly recalled and symbolically re-enacted.[57]

Concerning the real presence the document states:

> The term "real presence" was historically intended to protect the sacrament against spiritualizing interpretations and to insist that the *entire deed* [emphasis mine] of God in Christ for man's redemption is present there.[58]

Liturgical Reconnaissance also included a statement authorized by the Commission on Worship of the LCA to give guidance to the ministers and congregations in the conduct of the liturgy entitled "Action in Worship." Section 2 is titled "The Conduct of Worship by Two or More Ministers." It begins by acknowledging that most members of the LCA have never seen a service conducted by more than one man, except in the case of a synod meeting or large rally. The document warns of dividing up the service like a pie in which each clergyman is to receive an equal size slice so to avoid "bruised sensitivities." It attempts to give the rationale for the assignment of the variable parts (sermons, lessons, psalms, bids to prayers) to other participating clergy, reserving the invariable part (the Ordinary) in its entirety to the Officiant (also called the Principal Minister, the Celebrant, or less desirably, the Liturgist). The document uses the terms "Assisting Clergy" or "Assisting Ministers" and recognizes the fact that in some places a deacon and also a sub-deacon

---

[57] Brown, 36.
[58] Brown, 37.

assist and notes that it is customary in some places for a layman to assist with the Cup. At this point the demand for the inclusive use of lay persons as "Assisting Minister" is absent. The groundwork does however anticipate *LBW* stress on the inclusive participation of the laity in the leadership of the liturgy. The progress report of the Synodical Conference's "Commission on Worship, Liturgics and Hymnology," written by Herbert F. Lindemann for the "Committee on Liturgical Texts" makes a statement about the inclusion of the Eucharist Prayer which in retrospect is quite surprising, given the fact that it would become the wail most often caterwauled against the ILCW:

> One of the significant decisions arrived at during the past triennium has been the *approval* on the part of the Commission of the *principle of the Eucharistic Prayer* [emphasis mine]. In agreement with this, it is our hope that in any subsequent Order of the Holy Communion a Eucharist Prayer will be included.

The report indicates that four Eucharistic Prayers have already been "approved by the committee," and others are in the "process of preparation."[59]

With the publication of the *Worship Supplement* in 1969, *Contemporary Worship* in 1970, and various books and articles published by the liturgical leaders of the Inter-Lutheran Commission on Worship in the 1970s, the radical extent of the Roman Catholic liturgical movement would become very evident. The titles alone of two books speak volumes: *The New Mood in Lutheran Worship* (1971) and *Worship: Good News in Action* (1973).[60]

The New Mood provides insight into the new theology of worship that found expression in the *Worship Supplement* and *Con-*

---

[59] Brown, 125.

[60] Herbert F. Lindemann, *The New Mood in Lutheran Worship* (Minneapolis: Augsburg Publishing House, 1971). Lindemann (LCMS) was a member of the "Liturgical Texts Committee" for the revision of *TLH* and served on the "Liturgical Texts Committee" of the ILCW from 1967–78. He was chairman of the ecumenical Consultation on Common Texts and was a member of the international *Societas Liturgica*. Mandus A. Egge, ed., *Worship: Good News in Action* (Minneapolis: Augsburg Publishing House, 1973). The book contains the addresses of "eight leaders in worship renewal" at an Inter-Lutheran Conference on Worship in Minneapolis (June 11–15, 1973).

temporary Worship provisional booklets. The author, Herbert F. Lindemann (LCMS), was prominent in the drafting of the *Worship Supplement* and "among the catalyst group which brought the Inter-Lutheran Commission on Worship into being."[61] Lindemann's book provides a progress report on the ecumenical developments that colored the "new mood." The most visible changes introduced into the Roman Catholic Church by Vatican II are mentioned in brief:

> Free standing altars, The Mass in the vernacular, new texts for the liturgy, including alternate eucharist prayers, simplification of ceremonial, a three-year cycle of readings, restructuring of the church year, and others.[62]

The ILCW would be playing variations on all of these themes. It was to be a time of unprecedented liturgical cooperation between the separated brethren since "[t]hey were working on the same tasks and were operating with very similar approaches. Their proposals for liturgical reform were often so much alike that liturgies seemed to be almost interchangeable."[63] In fact, Lindemann acknowledges:

> This has in fact happened, and happened repeatedly; in Lutheran services eucharist prayers of Roman Catholic origin have been used, as well as liturgies produced by the Taize brethren, the Presbyterian church, and the Commission on Worship of the Consultation on Church Union.[64]

In 1968, the Commission on Worship and the Consultation on Church Union joined to form the Consultation on Common Texts.

> This group endeavored to arrive at agreed-on versions of liturgical elements in general use in Christian church services: the Our Father, the creeds, the canticles, the chants of the Mass. Its texts

---

[61] Lindemann, 7.
[62] Lindemann, 32–33.
[63] Lindemann, 32–33.
[64] Lindemann, 32–33.

> of the Our Father and the creeds have been used both in the Consultation on Church Union liturgy and in the *Worship Supplement*; the other items were not complete before the publication of these books.[65]

Soon, yet another more inclusive group known as the International Consultation on English Texts would come into prominence. It published its results in the pamphlet *Texts We Have in Common* (1970). The demand for further revision (especially the "inclusive language" movement) resulted in *Praying Together* by the English Language Liturgical Consultation (Abingdon Press, 1988).

Lindemann also gives credit to the Institute for Liturgical Studies of Valparaiso University for promoting interdenominational activity. In 1966, Institute director Hans Boehringer invited representatives of the Roman Catholic, Lutheran, Episcopal, and one or two Protestant churches for "informal consultation to see what might be done on a practical, continuing, cooperative basis."[66] The result was a series of Ecumenical Day conferences (1967, 1968, 1969) held on the day before the annual "Liturgical Week." Lindemann elucidates:

> Perhaps more importantly, the meeting marked the beginning of conversations and friendships which have been mutually helpful. Documents have been interchanged among official commissions, and there has been a voluminous correspondence among the individuals involved. The resultant meeting of minds has been quite striking.[67]

Lindemann leaves little doubt that the primary impact of the Liturgical Movement centered on the Lord's Supper. He writes, "The most consistent emphasis of the liturgical movement in all effected denominations has been on the Sacrament of the Altar."[68] The changes in emphasis are then summarized by Lindemann:

---

[65] Lindemann, 34.
[66] Lindemann, 35.
[67] Lindemann, 35–36.
[68] Lindemann, 37.

1. More frequent celebrations of Holy Communion; the sacrament should be central and prominent in the devotional life of the church.[69]
2. The faithful should be urged to receive the sacrament more frequently.[70]
3. The mood in the celebration "should be one of praise and thanksgiving; the eucharist note should be loud and clear. Gradually this too has 'caught on,' as the faithful have learned to think of the period of worship as a happy time, a wedding feast, an hour of fulfillment in which God's people rejoice in fellowship with him and with one another."[71]
4. "The meal aspect should be brought into prominence." Where this family emphasis has been discovered by parishes, Lindemann notes that their Eucharist services have become quite informal.[72]

Lindemann admits that much of what he has said about the new mood in worship has centered on externals (customs, techniques, statistics, books, vestments). He applauds the striving for proper expression but questions if the changes have reached down into the interior life of the church. The description on the back of the book makes the claim that Lindemann's "carefully considered view of worship renewal and tradition helps establish a basis for evaluating new forms and experimentation in liturgy." What is the "basis for evaluating new forms"? So far it has been a general appeal for the prominence of the Lord's Supper at the center of worship. Beyond that, one looks to the section titled "The Heart of the Matter." The heart of the matter for Lindemann is arrived at by asking the following questions:

---

[69] Lindemann, 37. Lindemann reports, "In the Lutheran church this repeated emphasis has produced results: weekly celebrations in city churches have become the rule; in others the four-times-a-year practice of the '30s has been increased to once a month."

[70] Lindemann, 38. Lindemann notes an increase in reception from a low of two and one-half times per year in the 1930s to an average of about five and three-fourths in 1969.

[71] Lindemann, 38.

[72] Lindemann, 38.

1. Are people today more skilled worshipers because of these developments, better informed, more intense, more devoted, more transformed?
2. Is the church stronger today because of the Liturgical Movement?[73]

A diagnosis of the way a question is asked reveals whether one is running with the law or the gospel, in the realm of justification or sanctification. The two questions reveal that for the author, the heart of the matter is anthropocentric. The first sentence begins, "Are *people*." He is running with the law, with measurements, and with sanctification in "establishing a basis," or criteria for judging worship. Note the abundance of comparatives: "more skilled," "better informed," "more intense," "more devoted," "more transformed," and "stronger."

Immediately after the two diagnostic questions Lindemann acknowledges, "It is impossible to answer the question with accuracy: the spiritual life of the Christian is not capable of measurement." Acknowledgement yes, concession no. He then continues to focus on the externals ("trends, signs, and symptoms"); however, they are not the *extra nos* word and sacraments. There are better questions. How is the word being preached and the sacraments administered? How are Jesus Christ and his gifts being extolled? Is the doctrine of justification by grace alone through faith the primary criteria for all rite and ceremony? *The New Mood* lacks any mention of the doctrine of justification. There is no law and gospel, no forgiveness of sins, no body and blood, no appreciation for Luther's "evangelical genius."

As Lindemann accedes, it can only be supposed that all the external developments must have had an effect on the clergy and laity. (Here he lists the activity of the Liturgical Society of St. James; enrichment in liturgy, ceremony, and ecclesiastical arts; the broadening "concept of the church"; and widening ecumenical contacts).

Primary attention in the section "The Heart of the Matter," is devoted to the positive expectations for church unity to be realized

[73] Lindemann, 39.

by expanding ecumenical ties. His involvement in the publication of the international, interdenominational journal *Studia Liturgica* and recent formation of *Societas Liturgica* has revealed that there are "lines of thought converging among liturgiologists in various branches of the western church." With the failure of theological dialogues in breaking down doctrinal disagreements, the liturgical approach to church unity looked very promising in the early 1970s. Lindemann underscores this:

> We have come to see that the possibilities of meeting on this level are much more promising than on the ground of minutely particularized doctrinal agreement. So, as we have learned from one another through repeated personal contact, the thing we have suspected from the beginning has become experientially clear: The Church is one, and the closer its people get to the Lord, the closer they get to one another .... There may be "diversities of operations and differences of administrations," but it is the same Spirit who works in all of God's children.[74]

This paragraph is very revealing as to the nature of the "new mood." The impression is given that church unity is referenced with the Lord. On closer examination, however, the referent remains anthropocentric. In the sentence "The church is one, and the *closer its people get to the Lord* [emphasis mine], the closer they get to one another," the movement is by the people to God. The means of grace, however, run from God to man. Talking in terms of "closer" is to talk ambiguously. Doctrine is completely ignored yet the work of the Spirit is assured. The Spirit appears to have slipped free from the Word and truth.

The anthropocentric character of worship is seen repeatedly. Particularly revealing is the statement made in the section titled "A Movement of the Whole Person."

> If one thinks of the liturgy as "the people's work," not only the officiating ministers, but all the faithful should be active in worship. Here Kierkegaard's famous illustration of a theater is in

---

[74] Lindemann, 40–41.

> point. He said that for the congregation to think of itself as an audience witnessing the performance of the clergy and listening critically to the music of choir and organ is all wrong. God himself is the audience, watching the performance of his people; as for the ministers and musicians, they are merely the prompters helping the people to do their job well.[75]

The divine liturgy is the work of the Divine One. It is God serving his people who have been gathered to receive his gifts. It is a priesthood of believers, not priesthood of sacrificers. They come to believe, that is, to receive by faith the gifts the Lord is giving out in his divine service to his people. God does not come to be entertained by wretched sinners. He comes to forgive, save, comfort, and strengthen them. The church is neither a theater nor a democratic party meeting. It is the court room of the King. Such is the nature of worship that is built on the criteria of the evangelical doctrine of justification. The Apology of the Augsburg Confession states:

> Thus the service and worship of the Gospel is to receive good things from God, while the worship of the law is to offer and present our goods to God. We cannot offer anything to God unless we have first been reconciled and reborn. The greatest comfort comes from this doctrine that the highest worship in the Gospel is the desire to receive forgiveness of sins, grace, and righteousness.[76]

The New Mood is correct in its insistence that a "full-orbed act of worship calls for expression from the voice, ears, eyes, hands, knees, and feet." Lindemann is right in pointing out that "To confine one's spiritual life to intellectual exercise or unmoving meditation is to stunt one's growth." He undercuts the whole argument, however, by concluding,

> The whole person exists for the service of the Lord, and the church is the place for this to be acknowledged by the surrender of one's

---

[75] Lindemann, 54–55.

[76] *The Book of Concord: The Confessional Writings of the Evangelical Lutheran Church*, trans. & ed. Theodore G. Tappert (Philadelphia: Fortress Press, 1959), 155. Apology of the Augsburg Confession, Article IV, "Justification," 310.

> entire being to the Christ who sacrificed himself completely on the cross and now lives as the Lord of all life.[77]

The church is the place where the Lord exists for the service of his people. It is the location where he promises to give out the gifts he won, once and for all, when he sacrificed himself on the cross. His sacrifice was complete. Man's sacrifice can never be complete. To assume that man is to surrender his entire being to Christ is to assume his entire being is something God wants or finds valuable. This negates God's grace.

Finally, stress on man's action in the man-centered "new mood" in worship is apparent in the recognition of the "four-fold action shape" of the liturgy which puts the stress on man's doing of the liturgy. In promoting the merits of the offertory procession during the offertory canticle, Lindemann writes,

> The bread and wine are also presented before the altar in response to the specific command of Christ, a command which, as our Anglican friends keep reminding us, involves the fourfold action of taking (offertory), blessing (consecration), breaking (fraction), and giving (sharing—the distribution). Unless then the bread and wine are deliberately brought to the altar at the time of the offertory, the liturgical significance of this chant is lost.[78]

The thrust of the Liturgical Movement and its culmination in Vatican II "that all the faithful should be led to that full, conscious, and active participation in liturgical celebrations"[79] has obviously influenced the Inter-Lutheran Commission on Worship. Vatican II themes permeate this paragraph by Lindemann:

> Now consider how participation in congregational worship has paved the way for this experience. Above all else, the overriding concept of the sacrament as a meal has caught hold, so that eat-

---

[77] Lindemann, 57.

[78] Lindemann, 53–54.

[79] James J. Megivern, ed., *Worship and Liturgy* (Wilmington, NC: McGrath Publishing House, 1978), 203. Vatican II, *Sacrosanctum Concilium: Constitution on the Sacred Liturgy*, December 4, 1963, Chap. 1, II, 743.

> ing and drinking in a small room, as a family, does not seem at all strange. Various practices have come to be accepted: laymen reading the lessons and suggesting intercessions, the use of "real" bread, the greeting of peace. Little by little the idea has gained ground that worship is a corporate act, in which other people besides the pastor have parts to play.[80]

Once again, one observes that liturgy is perceived as something we do. Repentance, however, is not mentioned. Nor is the forgiveness of sins. The body and blood of him who both destroys and saves in his divine service is not mentioned. The triumph of the Caselian action theology in the Roman Catholic Church is demonstrated in an article that appeared in the *St. Louis Review*, titled "The Seven Sacraments: Actions That Unite Us To Jesus." Father James T. Telthorst, pastor of St. Louis Cathedral Parish, writes:

> One of the most significant elements of the Catholic Church is its celebration of the seven sacraments . . . nothing so reflects the changes in the Church these last 25 years as these same sacraments . . . . Begin, then by thinking of sacraments as actions, rather than as things.[81]

Before turning to an examination of the provisional liturgical texts themselves (*Worship Supplement*, 1969; *Contemporary Worship* 2, 1970), further insight into the theology behind the new forms may be gained from a review of a major Inter-Lutheran Conference on Worship held in Minneapolis in 1973.[82] The theme of the conference was "Good News in Action," and the eight major addresses were published in a book similarly titled *Worship: Good News in Action.* As pointed out in a critical article written by Oliver Olson,

---

[80] Lindemann, 83.

[81] Editorials, *St. Louis Review: Weekly Newspaper of the Archdiocese of St. Louis*, September 18, 1992, 9.

[82] The conference included lectures by eight leaders in worship renewal: Joseph A. Sittler, Henry H. Horn, James White, Jaroslav Pelikan, Eugene L. Brand, Edward A. Sovik, Daniel B. Stevick, and Wayne E. Staffen. Fifty-two seminars and workshops followed the addresses, plus concerts, dramatic presentations, and six services, three of which were eucharistic.

> Anyone who listened to the speeches at the conference last summer in Minneapolis, arranged to promote the materials of the Inter-Lutheran Commission on Worship, could not fail to notice that the word, "action," was pronounced with extraordinary reverence and frequency.[83]

Olson points in particular to a speech by Pastor Henry E. Horn:

> A good deal of the language of our theologians is in terms of a past when one approached reality through rational discourse, and then applied ideas of generalized truth to particular situations. In many ways the terms *law* and *gospel*, so dear to Lutherans, come to us through this approach. And even though we recognize their truth as ideas, our modern emphasis is to experience reality fully with unobstructed feeling. Encounter groups, transactional analysis experience, almost any foray into feeling is of much more existential value to persons as a way of truth today. . . . So neither liturgical specialists nor theologians serve as authority for us any more. Where has the spotlight shifted? Where shall we discover new authority for our leadership in worship? Where shall we discover the essential integrity of our actions?[84]

Horn acknowledges that the emphasis on action is drawn from the contemporary Liturgical Movement along with other changes. He writes,

> The modern, post Vatican II liturgical movement has brought about great changes: one now talks about worship as action; worship belongs to the whole people of God; leadership is spread among the people; the language and idiom of the people—folk—is the thing; the whole human sensorium is now involved in celebration; human festivity and a theology of play dominate the moods expected.[85]

Twenty-six years later, Henry Horn wrote his retrospective book *Models of Ministry: Afterthoughts on Fifty Years*, in which he

---

[83] Oliver K. Olson, "Liturgy as 'Action,'" *Dialog*, 14, no. 2 (Spring 1975): 108.

[84] Howard E. Horn, "Worship: The Gospel in Action," in *Worship: Good News in Action*, ed. Mandus A. Egge (Minneapolis: Augsburg Publishing House, 1973), 25–26.

[85] Horn, 24.

described being swept into the early phases of the Liturgical Movement, whose aim was to "discern the actions in liturgy." He admits that the "movement received a huge impetus from the findings of Dom Gregory Dix," whose discovery of an early Christian work (ca. A.D. 225) enabled him to deduce the "shape the Christian liturgy took at the earliest age one could discover." Following a succinct description of Dix's view of the last supper as seven actions collapsed to four, Horn makes the astonishing statement:

> Even apart from the words spoken, Christians' actions in imitation of the Lord's were at the center of what these believers did whenever they came together. The eucharistic rite was a strong act of identity. Surely words were used, but the words were to accompany actions that were meaningful in themselves, for worship at its heart is what we do.[86]

Horn goes on to write how in the early years "there was a liberating wind in our leadership. The actions became important: we believed that they should stand out clearly and that all else was secondary." Many of those to whom Horn spoke resisted the new approach. Horn concludes:

> [M]any . . . wanted to conduct the battle in Reformation categories. Until both sides can talk on the basis of what exists in this century—in our tradition and human studies—we will argue the old battles and not meet each other. My experience, however, has taught me that, in trying to open up consideration of the actions of worship, I must not forget that there remains a tremendous importance to the verbal side.[87]

The Inter-Lutheran Commission on Worship came into existence and completed its assignment during the tempestuous 1960s and '70s when tradition and authority were being questioned and jettisoned. Since neither liturgical specialists nor theologians serve as authority for us any more, Horn asks the question, "Where shall we

[86] Henry E. Horn, *Models of Ministry: Afterthoughts on Fifty Years* (Minneapolis: Fortress Press, 1989), 57.

[87] Horn, *Models*, 58.

discover new authority for our leadership in worship?" The way in which the question is framed betrays a radical shift in theological methodology. The biblical and Christian understanding of authority is not something which we discover. Authority is that which is given by the one who has the authority to give it. The highest authority is the Lord God. Even the Lord Jesus said, "All authority in heaven and on earth has been given to me, therefore (οὖν) . . . make disciples of all nations, baptizing . . . teaching them to keep everything I have commanded you" (Matt. 28:19–20). Again in Matthew 18:18–19, "Blessed are you Simon . . . for this was not revealed to you by man, but by my Father in heaven . . . I will give you the keys . . ." Also in John 20:20, "As the Father has sent me, I am sending you." When the authority and task is simply received from the Giver, then it will be run by grace. If it is something we obtain, discover, determine, shape, or achieve, it will be run with the law.

Horn's next question is also indicative of a profound shift in theological methodology. "Where shall we discover the essential integrity of our actions?" To focus the search for a new authority on the "essential integrity of our actions" is to locate certainty on that which will always be uncertain. Our actions never have integrity. Nevertheless, Horn is optimistic and boasts, "It is out of the event of worship that new authority can come to the faith and life of the church. Leaders of worship are midwives of that authority."[88]

The rejection of authority may have been the hallmark of the 1960s and '70s, but the objection to The Authority is as old as the killing of the prophets, the allure of baalism, and the foolishness and scandal of the crucified and risen Christ Jesus. The answer is not to look for a new authority, but to stick with the old authority, which is the only authority, the highest authority, and our Lord's authority with which comes the promise of the Spirit.

A decade earlier, Hermann Sasse anticipated the approach toward liturgical reform which favors *lex orandi* over *lex credendi* in the primary place. In the article "The Liturgical Movement: Reformation or Revolution?" Sasse warned:

---

[88] Horn, "Worship," 27.

> The great tragedy of the Liturgical Movement in the Lutheran Churches is its inability to face the doctrinal issues. A restoration of the Reformation must be at the same time doctrinal and liturgical . . . It is the crucial question for your movement in America. Is the dogma still the standard of your liturgical work? It is not a sort of theological rationalism which tries to rule the liturgy with its irrational elements. The dogma of the Church is for us Lutherans the doctrinal content of the Scriptures as the Word of God.[89]

Certainly, as creatures living in space and time certain human actions are required if worship is to take place. We must walk into the church, sit and stand, move our tongues to speak, and swallow to commune. Worship has a location. But it is quite another thing to make our action the primary thing. One finds here a continuation of the tendency already observed in the *mysterientheologie* of depreciating the theology of the Word in favor of a theology of "action." While it is not wrong to talk about worship as action, it must be kept in mind, as Oliver Olson has pointed out, that "action" is a program-word for a massive theological movement which has not challenged the theology of the Word with such force since the Reformation.[90]

Likewise, it is not enough to make our action the secondary thing after God's action. It has already been noted that the "liturgy as action" approach was a product of the Roman Catholic liturgical movement and found its roundabout way into American Lutheranism via the Anglican Church (i.e., Gregory Dix). Oliver Olson observes that the theology of "action" has also been introduced to the Lutheran Church in this country primarily through Peter Brunner's *Worship in the Name of Jesus.* Olson quotes Brunner and comments:

> "Our task is not primarily to expound a text," he says, explaining his method, "but to interpret an action that takes place in our midst." Although in the European discussion of the notion of "reactualization" Brunner is thought to have made an attempt to preserve somehow the Lutheran emphasis on God's initiative, in handling the benefits of it as "application" he too, as all those who experi-

[89] Hermann Sasse, "The Liturgical Movement: Reformation or Revolution?" 18, 21.
[90] Olson, "Liturgy As 'Action,'" 108.

> ment with the notion of eucharist "action" must do, falls victim to the cult-drama pattern and ascribes an effect on God to man's "action" of *anamnesis.* "In the victorious power of Jesus' sacrificial death on the cross the New Testament covenant memorial . . . ascends to God's throne and evokes his active, end-effecting remembering. Holy Communion, too, is not a passive, static 'mystery' given us for 'contemplation,' but a dynamic event. In its earthly administration it releases a heavenly event, a kingdom-of-God movement in the heavens, yes, even in the heart of God." It is strange to read a Lutheran theologian who writes about a human "action" provoking a heavenly "action," but there it is in cold print: "Indeed, act and act, redemptive act of Jesus there and then and act of worship here and now, merge mysteriously in the celebration of Holy Communion by virtue of Jesus' institution."[91]

The influences of the theology of "action" and of Peter Brunner are seen in the address Eugene Brand made to the liturgical conference in Minneapolis. Brand, who served on the ILCW (1966–71) and the Liturgical Text Committee (1967–71), described the new accent of sacrifice in the Eucharist. Brand concluded that "In the name of the Gospel, the Reformation so over-reacted, however, that a proper and biblical sacrificial position became impossible on both sides."[92]

In answer to the typically Lutheran question whether worship is *sacrificium* (our offering to God) or *beneficium* (God's gift to us), Brand answers, "Actually, of course, it's both." He then offers the following definition of worship:

> Ostensibly worship is our obedient response to what God has made us; we do the things he has commanded with words, water, bread and wine. "In, with, and under," these actions of ours God acts upon and through us.[93]

The first sentence might be phrased more evangelically: Divine Liturgy involves God's ordained servant doing the things he commanded with his Word, water, bread and wine; and our receiving of

---

[91] Olson, "Liturgy As 'Action,'" 110–111. Olson's quotes are from pages 57, 192, and 172 of Peter Brunner's *Worship in the Name of Jesus.*

[92] Egge, 82.

[93] Egge, 82.

them in faith and with thanksgiving. The second sentence in the definition puts a not too subtle spin on the conventional formula "in, with, and under the bread and wine." It becomes "In, with, and under these actions of ours God acts upon and through us." Our actions displace the body and blood. The sentence might better read: "The very body and blood of our Lord Jesus Christ under the bread and wine is given to us by the pastor and we receive the forgiveness of sins, life, and salvation." Forgiveness of sins comes from Christ Jesus through his word and his sacraments, not thorough our actions. In commenting on his definition of worship, Brand writes, "God's action and our action dare not be confused, but neither can they be separated."[94] Brand, however, confuses our works with God's work and has our action subtly contributing to salvation. There is a noticeable absence of any reference to the body and blood and forgiveness of sins. If the body and blood are there forgiving sins, the whole issue of our action becomes irrelevant.

Brand then says that the Eucharist can be called sacrifice in two senses: (1) "The sacrifice of praise which we make as we proclaim the gospel and share the meal is our obedient response through which God in Christ is present and active among us."[95] Instead of a sacrifice of thanksgiving and praise in response to our hearing and believing the gospel which has been proclaimed to us (and where it is proclaimed, there God is giving out his gifts), sacrifice is defined by Brand as our proclaiming, that is, giving out the gifts. Likewise the receiving of the gifts of the body and blood in faith is described in law terminology as "our obedient response."[96] (2) "Sharing the bread and wine proclaimed to be Christ's body *given* and his blood *shed*, is sharing in the benefits of his sacrifice." As he continues, Brand acknowledges his reliance on Peter Brunner: "As Peter Brunner has pointed out, we should not limit our concept of Jesus' self-offering to the cross, though that is where it climaxes . . . . Jesus' sacrifice encompasses his whole life of service to the Father which he offered freely for us."[97] Brand concludes

---

[94] Egge, 82.
[95] Egge, 83.
[96] Egge, 83.
[97] Egge, 83. Brand quotes Peter Brunner's *Worship in the Name of Jesus*, 175.

with the vague comment, "All this we receive as we receive his body and blood, as we share in his sacrifice."[98]

An examination of the writings of American Lutheran liturgical leaders reveals that they readily acknowledged a dependence upon ideas of the contemporary Liturgical Movement. Many were very impressed by and "taken with" Rome's reforms. To a lesser degree the Anglican influences were acknowledged (e.g., Gregory Dix). The movement quickly crossed denominational lines and adopted a strong ecumenical character.

Some of the common themes were:

1. An emphasis on the frequent celebration and reception of Holy Communion.
2. The shift to talking about liturgy and the Lord's Supper in action rather than in spacial or word categories.
3. The attraction of Odo Casel and "re-presentation" language.
4. A return to the ancient liturgies of the early church and the inclination to disparage Martin Luther's liturgical reforms.
5. The enthusiasm for composing eucharistic prayers for inclusion in the liturgy.
6. The active participation of the laity ("people of God") in the liturgy (lay readers, communion servers). "Liturgy is the work of the people." Worship belongs to all the people and leadership should be spread among the people.
7. A host of external changes in form: freestanding altar, table language preferred over altar, three-year pericopes, simplifying of ceremony, and so on.

The few voices who offered thoughtful criticism of the "new mood of worship" (e.g., Sasse, Olson, Vajta) were given little serious consideration. Given the long standing, deep-seated dislike and suspicion of things Roman Catholic among large segments of American Lutheranism, it is astonishing to note the speed with which the leadership of the LCA, ALC, and LCMS embraced the ideology of the contemporary Liturgical Movement.

---

[98] Egge, 83.

5

The Influence of the Liturgical Movement on Liturgical Texts

GREAT pressure was put on the Inter-Lutheran Commission on Worship by the cultural demands of the 1960s to produce contemporary, relevant, and "now" worship forms. A great deal of the work of the ILCW would be jettisoned, and in retrospect, this appears quite fatuous. Simultaneously, the ecumenical agenda placed conflicting demands on the ILCW. The attraction of the action theology of Casel and Dix was too tempting to pass up. Going back to the early church with its allegedly simple and primitive shape of worship was extremely attractive to the church in America in the late 1960s.

Return to the Early Church

The *Worship Supplement* (1969) is representative of the direction taken by the Commission on Worship of the Lutheran Church—Missouri Synod. The booklet was offered to the Missouri Synod for "experimental and exploratory" use during the interim between the abandonment of *The Lutheran Hymnal* revision and the expected production of a pan-Lutheran hymnal. The *Worship Supplement* was new for the Missouri Synod in a twofold sense. It consisted of original compositions as well as forms from outside the Lutheran tradition. Included in this "modern experiment" were such historical forms as the expanded Kyrie litany (19–21); singing of the offertory as the monetary offering and the bread and wine are brought forward by the people to the altar (25); and five eucharistic prayers. The appeal of the early church is most apparent in the *Worship Supplement's* appropriation of the so-called primitive shape of Gregory Dix. Holy Eucharist II (59–62) is conspicuously based on Dix's four-shaped theory.

The most thoughtful and persistent critic of the new liturgical trends as embodied in *Worship Supplement* and *Contemporary Worship 2* was Oliver K. Olson. His 1974 article "Contemporary Trends in Liturgy Viewed from the Perspective of Classical Lutheran Theology"[1] documents the phenomenological method of Lietzmann, Casel, and Dix as the basis of the Liturgical Movement. Olson goes to great lengths to show how this new method differed "considerably" from the Lutheran Movement. Olson writes:

> It took only twenty-eight years until the "Four-Action Shape" appeared in an official Lutheran ritual. In the form made popular by J. A. T. Robinson, who in *Liturgy Coming to Life* did for Dix what in *Honest to God* he had done for Tillich, Bonhoeffer, and Bultmann, it turned up in the Missouri Synod's *Worship Supplement* (pp. 60–62).

The "Shape" in Robinson's *Liturgy Coming to Life*	The "Shape" in the Missouri Synod's *Worship Supplement*
1. Taking	1. Taking
2. Blessing	2. Blessing
3. Breaking	3. Breaking
4. Sharing	4. Sharing

Olson includes a footnote under the "Shape" in the Missouri Synod's *Worship Supplement* in which he states concerning the *WS*, Holy Eucharist II, "Oral tradition is that the order was borrowed from the Anglican church of St. Mark's-in-the-Bowery in New York City."[2] The oral tradition was confirmed in the second printing of Gregory Dix's *The Shape of the Liturgy*. Appended to the back are "Additional Notes," written by Paul V. Marshall, which state:

---

[1] Oliver K. Olson, "Contemporary Trends in Liturgy Viewed from the Perspective of Classical Lutheran Theology," *Lutheran Quarterly* 26, no. 2 (May 1974):110–157.

[2] Olson, 118, n. 33.

> Dix's theory of a primitive "shape" rather than a single primitive rite as the goal of liturgiological inquiry has been well received. In decades past it became the model for several new liturgies. For example, the Episcopal "Liturgy of St. Mark's in the Bowery" (subsequently published in the Lutheran *Worship Supplement* [1969]) was expressly designed according to Dix's scheme, and the parts of the eucharistic rite are identified as "taking," "blessing," "breaking," and "sharing."[3]

Next, Oliver Olson documents how the "'Shape' became the structure of *Contemporary Worship 2*."[4]

Dix	*CW 2*
1. The Offertory—bread and wine are "taken" and placed on the table together.	1. Our offering is thus the first action of the supper, corresponding to our Lord's taking of bread and wine (10).
2. The Prayer; the president gives thanks to God over bread and wine together.	2. Our thanksgiving is the second action (12).
3. The Fraction; the bread is broken.	3. After taking bread and wine, and giving thanks, Jesus broke the bread, the third action (18).
4. The Communion; the bread and wine are distributed together.	4. The action culminates as we receive the bread and wine. This is the fourth and final action (18).

What *Worship Supplement* was to the LCMS, *Contemporary Worship* was to the participating Lutheran denominations of the ILCW. It was supplemental and "provisional in nature." The contemporary emphasis was highlighted in the title chosen for the eleven booklets produced between 1969–76. Each bore the title *Contemporary Worship*.[5]

---

3 Gregory Dix, *The Shape of the Liturgy* (New York: Seabury Press, 1982), 769, n. 21.

4 Olson, 119.

5 *Contemporary Worship*, 10 vols. (Minneapolis: Augsburg Publishing House and St. Louis: Concordia Publishing House, 1968–1976).

The *Contemporary Worship* Series:

CW 1:	*Hymns*	(1969)
CW 2:	*The Holy Communion*	(1970)
CW 3:	*The Marriage Service*	(1972)
CW 4:	*Hymns for Baptism and Holy Communion*	(1972)
CW 5:	*Services of the Word*	(1972)
CW 6:	*The Church Year: Calendar and Lectionary*	(1973)
CW 7:	*Holy Baptism*	(1974)
CW 8:	*Affirmation of the Baptismal Covenant*	(1975)
CW 01:	*The Great Thanksgiving*	(1975)
CW 9:	*Daily Prayer of the Church*	(1976)
CW 10:	*Burial of the Dead*	(1976)

The preface in each booklet spoke of the commission's desire

> to produce a new, common liturgy and hymnal for the churches . . . lively in speech and songs for the church of the future . . . liturgical forms and hymns that are contemporary in text and music and contemporary versions of existing worship forms.

The preface also acknowledged the context of the 1970s. "In the face of the growing pluralism of society, the ecumenical movement and new insights into the meaning and uses of liturgy, Christian history and theology, these participating churches voice the need for common expressions of their Christian faith."

On the one hand, there is no question that the work of the members of the ILCW was new, contemporary, original, and creative. A great many new musical settings were composed. The Holy Communion service in *CW 2* was set to no fewer than four musical settings: contemporary, hymnic, chant, and folk. The texts, especially the Eucharistic Prayers in *CW 2* and *01: The Great Thanksgiving,* vacillated continuously between sterile committee compositions and individualistic, idiosyncratic '60- and '70ish poetry.

Simplification of Entrance Rite

The model of the primitive church was reflected in the trend to simplify the entrance rite. This led to extensive tinkering. The *WS* included three services of the "Holy Eucharist." Holy Eucharist I completely eliminated the opening hymn, invocation in the name of the Father, Son, and Holy Spirit, and confession and absolution. According to the rubric, the hymn of praise "may be omitted generally except in festival seasons." This left a simplified entrance rite of entrance song (Introit), Kyrie litany, Salutation, and Collect of the day. In Holy Eucharist II the opening hymn is optional. The service begins with a stunted and nebulous confession of sins. There is no absolution, only a vague request addressed to the Holy Spirit to "speak to us, help us listen," and to "come and fill this moment," followed by silence. The Service of the Word then begins abruptly with the Old Testament "lesson." Holy Eucharist III may begin with an opening hymn. The Trinitarian invocation is required along with the versicle and response ("Our help is in the name of the Lord." "Who made heaven and earth.") and a confession of sins. Again, the absolution is not a real absolution. It reads:

> God has promised forgiveness of sins to those who repent and turn to him. May he keep you in his grace by the Holy Spirit, lead you to greater faith and obedience, and bring you to live with him forever, through Jesus Christ, our Lord.[6]

Theodore Mueller analyzed this non-absolution in his article "Justification: Basic Linguistic Aspects and the Art of Communicating It." Concerning the phrase "There is forgiveness for all who turn to Christ," Mueller writes:

> The relative clause restricts the forgiveness and makes it conditional on something in man. Any absolution which introduces a relative clause to modify the announcement of forgiveness of sins is out of place, because it denies objective justification. Pieper reproves such conditional statements: The absolution cannot be based on one's contrition, repentance or confession. It is based solely on the objective justification and on God's command to announce forgiveness in the name of Christ. The fine balance between objective and subjective justification is to be noted in the

---

[6] *WS*, 63.

traditional absolution on page 16 of *The Lutheran Hymnal.* The first sentence announces God's unconditional justification; the second adds the promise that everyone who trusts these words is God's child. It is a promise, not a condition.[7]

In Holy Eucharist III, the Hymn of Praise is optional, the Prayer of the Day is followed by the readings, and there is no Kyrie or Introit. *Contemporary Worship 2* is even more drastic. The service begins with the Entrance Hymn, Apostolic Greeting by the presiding minister, and the Prayer of the Day by the assisting minister. The Hymn of Praise is optional. Announcements follow and then the service continues with the Service of the Word.[8] Ultimately, the *Lutheran Book of Worship* would contain a very simple yet flexible "entrance rite."

"Shall"	"May"
	Confession and Forgiveness, page 98, may be used before the service.
Entrance Hymn or Psalm is sung.	
Apostolic Greeting by presiding minister.	
	Kyrie (litany) may follow.
	Hymn of Praise may be sung. (Salutation optional)
Prayer of the Day is said (by presiding minister).	

The entrance rite in the *Lutheran Book of Worship* is cut to simply a required hymn, greeting and prayer. The pruning is seen as a return to the simplicity of the early centuries. One year after the publication of *Contemporary Worship 2*, Philip H. Pfatteicher came to its defense.

[7] *Concordia Theological Quarterly* 46 (January 1982): 34.

[8] *Contemporary Worship 01: The Great Thanksgiving* began with a preface titled "ILCW Memorandum," written by Eugene Brand, in which he concedes: "In response to considerable criticism, a revision of *CW 2* is being proposed to the churches with this structure: (Alternate forms for Confession), Entrance Hymn or Psalm, Apostolic Greeting, (Kyrie litany), (Gloria or Worthy is Christ), Prayer of the Day, First Lesson, etc.

> [T]he new liturgy has greatly simplified the entrance rite, allowing for the possibility of simply the apostolic greeting and the collect. The swollen entrance rite as we have it (hymn, confession, introit, Kyrie, Gloria, salutation, collect) had been elaborated over the centuries far beyond its importance. An elaborate entrance is perhaps suitable in a great cathedral service with an extended procession but scarcely in a small parish church. The new service gets down to business—reading the Bible—with decent dispatch.[9]

The Lutheran Church—Missouri Synod, however, withdrew from the pan-Lutheran hymnal and published *Lutheran Worship.* The compilers of *LW* chose to restore the entrance rite. In Divine Service I, the confession of sins and absolution was clearly placed within the Divine Service yet designated under the sub-category "The Preparation." In the pew edition there is no suggestion that the Divine Service should or may omit "The Preparation" (i.e., Trinitarian invocation, confession of sins, and holy absolution). The *Lutheran Worship Altar Book*, however, does state:

> While it is neither theologically nor liturgically necessary that this congregational act always precede the Holy Communion, custom and pastoral discernment may dictate the need for such a practice most of the time.[10]

Thus the entrance rite takes the following form:

"Shall"	"May"
	Hymn of Invocation
Trinitarian Invocation	
Confession and Absolution	
Introit, Psalm, or Entrance Hymn is sung	
Kyrie is sung (DSI)	Kyrie may follow (DSII)
Gloria in Excelsis is sung	
Collect of the Day is chanted	

[9] Philip H. Pfatteicher, "The New Holy Communion Rite—II: Seven Clear Achievements," *Lutheran Forum* 5, no. 4 (1971):14.

[10] *Lutheran Worship: Altar Book* (St. Louis: Concordia Publishing House, 1982), 26.

Divine Service II in *Lutheran Worship* with its two musical settings follows the same expanded entrance rite as Divine Service I with two exceptions: The Kyrie follows the more ancient litany form and the Gloria in Excelsis may be replaced with a second hymn of praise ("This Is the Feast").

Elimination of Confession and Absolution

The ILCW also appealed to the early church to justify the elimination of confession and absolution from the Holy Communion service. The precedent was set already in the *Worship Supplement.* The Holy Eucharist I eliminated the confession altogether. As noted above, The Holy Eucharist II included a brief and inane confession, but no absolution. The Holy Eucharist III included a lengthy confession and declaration of forgiveness. In *Contemporary Worship 2*, the ILCW cut the confession and absolution from the beginning and experimented with an "Act of Reconciliation" located at the end of the Service of the Word. Notes on the liturgy for the leader offer this rationale:

> Confession. The confession is the first half of the act of reconciliation, calling for the "peace" as its logical concomitant. This act has been relocated both because of its appropriateness at this point and because it provides an experimental option to traditional Lutheran practice of including it in the preparation.[11]

The notes then suggest that the "assisting minister might offer biddings such as these: Our blindness to the needs of families within the shadow of this building we confess to the Lord . . . . Our weak response to the request for help in the after-school study program we confess . . . . Our failure to understand and help our sister, ___________, who took her life . . ." [12] Thus *CW 2* introduces the practice of confessing specific sins with the general/plural pronoun. This is inappropriate for corporate worship and is more properly done in private confession and absolution. Such liturgical practice

---

[11] *CW 2*, xv.
[12] *CW 2*, xv.

assumes all worshipers are guilty of the latest sin to come from the lips of the creative, relevant pastor. It puts an impossible and unfair burden on the penitent which will only cause frustration, guilt, and resentment. Eventually the penitent will come to despise confession as at best a game, or at worst a burden. He must listen intently, interpret the nature of the specific sin the assisting minister is attempting to communicate, and instantaneously determine if and how he is guilty. The plural "we confess" provides a not too subtle coercion to join the group and "fess up." The "meaningful" confession of specific sins is best carried out in private confession and absolution. Of the many abuses rejected by the evangelical fathers, the endless enumeration of sins was of particular concern. The Apology of the Augsburg Confession observes, "How much effort is devoted to the endless enumeration of sins, most of them against human traditions!"[13] Luther's instruction in the Small Catechism on "How Plain People Are to Be Taught to Confess" asks the question, "What sins should we confess?" The answer includes the following: "Before the confessor, however, we should confess only those sins of which we have knowledge and which trouble us."[14] Which sins are these? The confessor does not tell the penitent which sins to confess; rather, the penitent is told: "Reflect on your condition in the light of the Ten Commandments," and then articulate how he or she has specifically broken them. The penitent initiates the confession. The confessor listens. The penitent is to articulate the sins. The confessor is to articulate the forgiveness of sins. The misdirected attempt to make confession more meaningful was included in *LBW* but omitted in the revised *LW*.[15] Ironically, the practice has flourished in many congregations in the Missouri Synod. Many pastors have adopted the practice that the new hymnal is too difficult for visitors and thus an impediment to evange-

---

[13] *The Book of Concord: The Confessional Writings of the Evangelical Lutheran Church*, trans. & ed. Theodore G. Tappert (Philadelphia: Fortress Press, 1959), 184. Article XII, Penitence.

[14] Tappert, 350. The Small Catechism, Part V, "Confession and Absolution."

[15] *Lutheran Book of Worship* (Minneapolis: Augsburg Publishing House and Philadelphia: Board of Publication, Lutheran Church in America), 65. Included in the numerous rubrics under "The Prayers" is the following: "Prayers of confession may be included if the Brief Order for Confession and Forgiveness has not been used earlier."

lism.[16] The popularity of the Church Growth movement in the 1980s, Concordia Publishing House's *Creative Worship,* and the propensity of many churches to borrow contemporary Christian music and liturgical practices from American Protestant groups have led to the influx of much liturgical innovation and change, often with little or no theological or liturgical criticism.

It is not surprising that both liturgical commissions and local pastors feel constrained to innovate. When the sacrament of individual confession and holy absolution disappears, the church attempts to compensate with endless mutations and surrogates. The void created by the absence of the individual confession and personal application of the forgiveness of sins as part of ordinary pastoral care becomes intolerable. The answer, however, does not lie in attempting to accomplish individual confession and absolution with general confession and absolution. The answer lies in the recovery of private confession.

CW 2 does acknowledge that "There is no liturgical necessity for connecting confession with the eucharist celebration."[17] It adds that confession does not make one worthy to receive the Lord's body and blood and therefore it is not necessary always to include confession and absolution before every service of Holy Communion.[18] What therefore is the connection between confession, the liturgical life of the church, and the individual Christian? *CW 2* does not answer this question. Martin Luther does. In the Small and Large Catechisms Luther anchors Holy Absolution in Holy Baptism. In the Large Catechism, under part four on "Baptism," Luther states:

> Here you see that Baptism, both by its power and by its signification, comprehends also the third sacrament, formerly called Penance, which is really nothing else than Baptism . . . . If you live in repentance, therefore, you are walking in Baptism . . . . Repentance, therefore, is nothing else than a return and approach to Baptism, to resume and practice what had earlier been begun but abandoned.[19]

---

16 See chapter 3, n. 39.

17 *CW 2*, xvi.

18 *CW 2*, 8.

19 Tappert, 445–446. Large Catechism, Part IV: "Baptism (Infant Baptism)."

Confession and absolution is connected to and anchored in Holy Baptism. This is also obvious in Luther's Small Catechism. Part V, "Confession and Absolution," is placed immediately after Part IV, "Baptism." The last question in the baptismal section serves as a theological bridge to Holy Absolution.

> What does such baptizing with water signify?
> Answer: It signifies that the old Adam in us, together with all sins and evil lusts, should be drowned by daily sorrow and repentance and be put to death, and that the new man should come forth daily and rise up, cleansed and righteous, to live forever in God's presence.[20]

The liturgical connection of confession is to baptism and the Name. The daily liturgical life is addressed in Part VII of the Small Catechism. "The head of the family is to teach his household to say morning and evening prayers which begin with the sign of the cross and in the Name of God, the Father, the Son and the Holy Spirit." The Apostles' Creed is to be confessed. It is the baptismal creed. The Creed is Gospel. Next comes the Lord's Prayer, which includes the request for forgiveness.

The Large Catechism ends with "A Brief Exhortation to Confession." After discussing the private confession and absolution with the pastor, Luther discusses other methods of confession and how the Lord's Prayer fits in.

> To begin with, I have said that in addition to the confession which we are discussing here there are two other kinds, which have an even greater right to be called the Christians' common confession. I refer to the practice of confession to God alone or to our neighbor alone, begging for forgiveness. These two kinds are expressed in the Lord's Prayer when we say, "Forgive us our debts, as we forgive our debtors," etc. Indeed the whole Lord's Prayer is nothing else than such a confession. For what is our prayer but a confession that we neither have nor do what we ought and a plea for grace and a happy conscience? This kind of confession should and must take place

---

[20] Tappert, 349. Small Catechism, Part IV, "The Sacrament of Holy Baptism."

> incessantly as long as we live. For this is the essence of a genuinely Christian life, to acknowledge that we are sinners and to pray for grace. Similarly the second confession, which each Christian makes toward his neighbor, is included in the Lord's Prayer. We are to confess our guilt before one another and forgive one another before we come into God's presence to beg for forgiveness.[21]

In the morning prayer which follows the Lord's Prayer, the baptized priest asks to be kept this day "from all sin and evil . . . in all my thoughts, words, and deeds." The evening prayer then states, "I beseech Thee to forgive all my sin and the wrong which I have done."

The lifelong drowning of the old Adam through daily sorrow and repentance is a theological undertaking which gives confession and absolution a daily liturgical rhythm. Anchored on baptism and the Name, the prayer for forgiveness includes: the sinner alone before God; the sinner with his family before God; the sinner with the one he has offended before God; the sinner before his pastor whose lips speak the voice of the Shepherd. This is the man (*Amt*) whose hands were once used by God to apply water with the Word. Forgiveness of sins was won in time and space by the incarnate God-man. It is distributed in time and space by the man who stands in the stead and by the command of Christ. Through baptism he bestows our Lord's forgiveness of sins and new life. If and when the church wishes to include a general confession and absolution in the Divine Service, a theological rationale should determine the nature of the rite and its location in the liturgy. Whereas the theological anchor of Holy Absolution is baptism in the name of the Father, Son, and Holy Spirit, the decision to place it at the beginning of the service and connect it to the Invocation is appropriate.[22] We dare come into his presence and make confession because we are baptized and thus are confident of receiving Holy Absolution. Because we are baptized, we dare come to our Lord's Holy Liturgy and partake of his very body and blood.

---

[21] Tappert, 458.

[22] The first official agenda of The Lutheran Church—Missouri Synod appeared in 1856 (*Kirchen-Agende für Evangelisch-Lutherische ungeanderter Augsburgischer Confession*). The confession and absolution followed the sermon and preceded the prayers.

The experimental moving of the confession and absolution to the end of the Service of the Word (immediately prior to the Prayers) and titling it an "Act of Reconciliation" appears to be an attempt to connect it to the historical sharing of the peace (i.e., kiss of peace). In effect this confuses the Pax, which has a completely different origin from that of binding and loosing sin in Holy Absolution.

In *CW 2* the Act of Reconciliation is run primarily by the assisting minister. If the assisting minister is a representative of the people, then the peace is something which is being run by the people and originates from the pew. Historically it came from the Lord and was brought from his altar to his people by the steward of the Lord's mysteries. *LBW* moved confession and absolution to a preparatory rite prior and separate from the Service of the Word. The rubrics for the prayers, however, do indicate that "Prayers of confession may be included if the Brief Order for Confession and Forgiveness has not been used earlier." The *LBW* also retained the sharing of the peace at the end of the prayers. It is, however, given to the Presiding Minister to do. The rubric reads, "The PEACE is shared at this time or after the Lord's Prayer, prior to the distribution." No rubric for the Pax is included after the consecration, betraying *LBW's* preference for the Byzantine interpretation of the Peace (based on Matthew 5:23–24) as reconciliation with one's neighbor rather than the Roman rite (based on John 20:19–23), which flows from Christ who bestows his gift of peace.

Both Divine Service I and II in *LW* place the Pax immediately after the Words of Institution. The historical and theological rationale is explained by Norman Nagel in *Lutheran Worship: History and Practice:*

> In the early liturgies all who received and gave the kiss of peace (Pax) received the "holy things," the body and blood of Christ. The kiss of peace then came after the dismissal of the catechumens, prior to the communion section of the service and so-called Service of Holy Communion in Divine Service I. That it comes after the consecration and before the distribution is a consequence of the Roman usage, which, along with much else, included the Lord's Prayer at this point. Then the Pax echoed "as we forgive" in the Lord's Prayer when coming to the altar (Matt. 5:23) as well as

pointing up the "holy things" and the "holy ones"—and so Holy Communion.[23]

Yet whether by kiss or handshake or words, the Pax is given and received. It comes from the Lord and we receive and embrace it together with our Amen. It is his gift, not something we set going. Lamentable is the disintegration of the liturgy at this point into lots of separate heartinesses. The one so-called Pax, from the Lord, was beautifully expressed by the usage with a piece of wood, metal, or ivory upon which a Calvary was carved. It came from the altar and was kissed by the presiding minister, and then in turn by all the communicants.[24]

An unfortunate innovation, however, was made in Divine Service II which blunts the "sacramental" character. Divine Service I retained the historic form. The pastor says, "The peace of the Lord be with you always." The people respond, "Amen" (151). In Divine Service II the new response is, "And also with you" (171). This mutates the peace from a distinct sacramental blessing (to which the people respond, "Amen," i.e., faith receiving the gift) into a salutation. The rubric above the exchange titles it "The PEACE" nevertheless, the response shows that it is to be understood as a salutation. Martin Luther's explanation of The Peace indicates an understanding of the Pax as pure Gospel.

But immediately after the Lord's Prayer shall be said, "The peace of the Lord," etc., which is, so to speak, a public absolution of the sins of the communicants, the true voice of the gospel announcing remission of sins, and therefore the one and most worthy preparation for the Lord's Table, if faith holds to these words as coming from the mouth of Christ himself. On this account I would like to have it pronounced facing the people, as the bishops are accustomed to do, which is the only custom of the ancient bishops that is left among our bishops.[25]

---

[23] Norman Nagel, "Holy Communion in *Lutheran Worship: History and Practice*, ed. Fred L. Precht (St. Louis: Concordia Publishing House, 1993), 307. In the footnote, Nagel refers the reader to Jungmann's *Mass of the Roman Rite*, 2:321, and for a brief history of the Pax and an overview of the literature, Robert F. Taft's *The Great Entrance* (Rome: Institutum Studiorum Orientalium, 1975), 375–78.

[24] Precht, 307–308.

[25] Martin Luther, *Formula Missae*, AE, 53:28–29.

The altered Peace obscures the distinctiveness of the pastoral office from that of the office of the priesthood of all believers. It operates more with an understanding of liturgy as "the work of the people." This blurring is also found in the salutations used in many, but not all, of the services in *Lutheran Worship*. In *LW* the traditional response "And with your Spirit" is found in Divine Service I, Matins, and Vespers. The altered response "And also with you" is found in Divine Service II, Evening Prayer, and Responsive Prayers I and II. *Lutheran Book of Worship* uses the new response, "And also with you," in the Holy Communion services for the Peace, salutations, and in the opening blessing: "The grace of our Lord Jesus Christ, the love of God, and the communion of the Holy Spirit be with you all." The congregation responds, "And also with you." The new response is also used in the salutations found in Holy Baptism (122, 124), Service of the Word (128), Evening Prayer (144), Responsive Prayer I (163), and Responsive Prayer II (166).

It is inferior liturgical practice to offer two different responses to the Peace and to salutations. It produces confusion, uncertainty, and lack of confidence among the people. They will never feel at home in the liturgy. The congregation will be required to interact primarily with the printed text rather then with the oral word and its pastor. The nature of the Pax and salutation suggests a direct interaction between pastor and congregation.

The move toward equalizing the congregational response blurs the distinctive role of the pastor, who speaks in the stead and by the command of the incarnate, crucified, risen, and present Lord Jesus Christ. The "spirit" is in reference to Holy Spirit and our Lord's words of institution of the Holy Ministry. "And with that he breathed on them and said, 'Receive the Holy Spirit. If you forgive anyone his sins, they are forgiven; if you do not forgive them, they are not forgiven'" (John 20:22–23). The new response forfeits the important distinction between the Holy Ministry and the Church. "The Lord be with you" is spoken by the one sent by God to "provide the Gospel and the sacraments."[26] The Augsburg Confession continues, "Through these,

[26] Tappert, 31. The Augsburg Confession, Article V. "The Office of the Ministry" (German).

as through means, he gives the Holy Spirit, who works faith, when and where he pleases, in those who hear the Gospel." Thus the Holy Spirit is present where the pastor preaches the Gospel, forgives and retains sins, and administers the sacraments. "He breathed on them and said, 'Receive the Holy Spirit.'" Thus in acknowledgement of this, the congregation responds, "And with your spirit." (This will be discussed more fully later in the chapter.)

The Unification of the Rites of Initiation

During the production of *LBW* and *LW* most attention focused on the changes in the Divine Service, especially the Service of Holy Communion. This corresponded with the priority given to the reform of the Eucharist at the Second Vatican Council. Aidan Kavanagh, however, refers to the reform of baptism as the

> "sleeper" among the sacramental and liturgical issues addressed by the Council; that is, the one which would emerge as perhaps that of most fundamental importance for the renewal of the Church as it gradually modulated into a new key after the Council completed its work in 1965.[27]

Following Vatican II, a subcommission was given the responsibility of reforming the rites of initiation. Under the leadership of Balthasar Fischer of Trier a series of wide consultations were convened, involving theologians, liturgical scholars, catechists, missionaries, and pastors from 1967 through 1970. The findings resulted in the production of three documents: the rite of baptism of children (1969), confirmation (1971), and of greatest significance, the *Rite of Christian Initiation of Adults* (1972). The intent of the subcommission was not merely to produce new liturgical rites or even to prepare rites which reflect the unity of baptism, confirmation, and the Eucharist (though this was definitely a primary goal).

> Its intent was to be a preparation not merely for the final sacramental *rites* (baptism-confirmation-eucharist), but for a *life of faith* in which asceticism, good works, and a sacramental engagement

---

[27] Aidan Kavanagh, *The Shape of Baptism: The Rite of Christian Initiation* (New York: Pueblo Publishing Company, 1978), 103.

> could blend in a robust whole rather than languish as mere options before the idiosyncrasies of personal taste and piety.[28]

Kavanagh identifies a fundamental shift in Roman Catholic baptismal reform:

> [T]he document's purpose is less to give liturgical recipes than to shift the Church's initiatory polity from one conventional norm centering on infant baptism to the more traditional norm centering on adults.[29]

The Disintegration of Christian Initiation

One of the marks of the modern Liturgical Movement is its preference for looking to the patristic age for the "classical pattern" of liturgy. Frank Senn, author of *Contemporary Worship 8: Affirmation of the Baptismal Covenant,* acknowledged, "The models we need today are to be found before the age of Christendom, perhaps in the breath-taking period of the Church's first 'coming out,' the period roughly between 339 and 461."[30] Recent studies have noted that the original shape of baptism, that is, of initiation into communicant membership in the Christian Church, kept baptism, confirmation, and the Eucharist together as one unified act of entrance into the church.

Senn explains,

> In order to understand the shape and meanings of the provisional ILCW Baptismal Liturgy it is necessary to monitor the Baptismal Liturgy in various stages of its development. This will enable us to see what principles have governed the shape of Christian initiation.[31]

It was Balthasar Fischer and the authors of the Roman Catholic *RCIA* who found in the *Apostolic Tradition* (ascribed to Hippolytus

---

[28] Kavanagh, 105.

[29] Kavanagh, 106.

[30] Frank C. Senn, "The Shape and Content of Christian Initiation: An Exposition of the New Lutheran Liturgy of Holy Baptism," *Dialog* 14 (1975): 98.

[31] Senn, 99.

of Rome, ca. 250) "the chief source of the new rite."[32] This early church manual describes the three-year catechumenate that preceded baptism. It describes the impressive rite of baptism at which the bishop lays his hands on the candidates and pours oil on their head (i.e., "confirmation"). The fourth century brought with it the legalization of the faith and a host of converts. By this time baptism was intimately tied to the paschal celebrations. The great vigil of Easter became the most popular time to be baptized as it coincided with the time of Jesus' dying and rising. The mystagogical catecheses of Cyril of Jerusalem (ca.315–386), Ambrose of Milan (340–397), and John Chrysostom (345–407) offer rich examples of a thorough catechesis in doctrine and life integrated with the awesome entrance of the new converts into the Church through their reception of the mysteries of Holy Baptism and Holy Communion.

Frank Senn describes the steps by which the rite of initiation disintegrated over the centuries. The first stage took place from the late fifth through the seventh centuries with the beginning of the "privatization of baptism." "The catechumenate was removed from the midst of the worshiping assembly and was relocated in a classroom."[33] Naturally, this period also saw the increase in infant baptisms. The second step of disintegration was due to the high infant mortality rate during the early Middle Ages.

> [I]n a situation in which many infants were not expected to survive until the next Easter, it became the practice to baptize and commune them in the event of serious illness with all due haste. This was done by the local presbyter. The sick child would be taken to the bishop later on for "confirmation" if and when it recovered.[34]

Step three resulted as the church expanded into the vast areas of Europe north of the Alps. Bishops maintained their prerogative for confirmation, so it was not uncommon for baptized children to wait years to "complete" the rite of initiation.

---

[32] James White, *A Brief History of Christian Worship* (Nashville: Abingdon Press, 1993), 46.
[33] Senn, 101.
[34] Senn, 101.

> In time, the now-separate rite of Confirmation came to be regarded as a sacrament in its own right and was construed as an "added gift of grace," to help the baptized Christian engage in spiritual combat against the world, the flesh, and the Devil.

Senn asserts that the fourth stage in the disintegration of Christian initiation in the Medieval West was the separation of baptism and first communion.

> Until the third century it was still the practice to complete Baptism with first communion, even if Confirmation was not received at the time of Baptism. Canon Law continued to insist on it as late as the eleventh century . . . . By the time we get to the Reformation . . . [t]he primitive pattern of Christian initiation had completely disintegrated.[35]

The new rites of baptism and confirmation prepared by the ILCW were published in the provisional booklets *Contemporary Worship 7: Holy Baptism* and *Contemporary Worship 8: Affirmation of the Baptismal Covenant. CW 7* reviewed the historical development of baptism, explained the current situation, and then concluded:

> (1) The provisional liturgy presented here is an attempt to set forth the church's fullest, richest baptismal theology. (2) It seeks to speak to the new situation faced by today's congregations with a flexibility more capable of meeting diverse circumstances. (3) It seeks to overcome a questionable dichotomy between the Baptism of infants and the Baptism of adults by providing one baptismal liturgy for use with the candidates of all ages. Elements which were celebrated during the Middle Ages are reunited in order to *restore a unified rite of initiation* [emphasis mine] in which, to be sure, infants cannot participate completely.[36]

The restoration of baptism, confirmation, and the Eucharist into one unified rite of initiation was and remains one of the primary theological and ritual principles re-shaping liturgical life in the

---

[35] Senn, 102.

[36] *CW 7*, 9.

twentieth century. In the section titled "Time and Place," *CW 7* reflects the influence of the wider ecumenical liturgical agenda.

> The baptismal liturgy is normally celebrated at the regular service of the congregation. Usually this will mean Sunday morning Baptism is an act of the whole church . . . . This provisional rite provides for the verbal participation of all the people. That participation is symbolized by special roles provided for by lay leaders. Location of the font is ideally expressive of two concepts: Baptism as *entrance* into the eucharistic community, and Baptism as entrance into the eucharistic *community*.[37]

The popularity of the term "initiation" is due to more than a desire to draw attention to the importance of baptism as the entrance rite into the full fellowship of the church. It reveals the tendency to de-emphasize the language of washing away sins in favor of entrance into the community of faith. Since Vatican II, sacramental theology has "undergone an enormous transformation."[38] Mark Searle explains:

> Undoubtedly the leading indicator if not the cause of this transformation is the abandonment of the questions and vocabulary of Scholasticism in favor of more existentialist and personalist approaches to understanding what the sacraments are and how they function in the Christian life. What began as a recovery of the ecclesial dimension of the sacraments quickly led to further shifts: from *speaking* of sacraments as "means of grace" to speaking of them as encounters with Christ himself; (2) from *thinking* of them primarily as acts of God to thinking of them mainly as celebrations of the faith community; (3) from *seeing* the sacraments as momentary incursions from another world to seeing them as manifestations of the graced character of all human life; (4) from *interpreting* them as remedies for sin and weakness to seeing them as promoting growth in Christ.[39] (emphasis mine)

---

[37] *CW 7*, 13.

[38] Mark Searle, "Infant Baptism Reconsidered," in *Alternative Futures for Worship*, vol. 2, *Baptism and Confirmation* (Collegeville, MN: The Liturgical Press, 1987), 15.

[39] Searle, 15.

This new way of speaking, thinking, seeing, and interpreting represents a profound challenge to Lutherans who desire to remain faithful to the speaking, thinking, seeing, and interpreting of the Lutheran Confessions. Both *LBW* and *LW* were influenced to some degree by these new emphases. That the rites are included in the pew editions enables greater participation by the entire congregation. The rites actually designate many parts for the congregation (Lord's Prayer, Renunciation and Creed, the Amens, and the closing congregational welcome). The theme of being received into the "Lord's family," "the Body of Christ" (i.e., initiation) is clearly present. The dominant theme remains, however, that baptism is an act of God washing away sins.[40] The *LBW Minister's Edition* includes the interesting analysis,

> The Service of Baptism has several parts which together constitute the fullness of the sacrament of initiation into the community of faith: presentation, thanksgiving, renunciation and profession of faith, baptism with water, laying on of hands and signation, welcome into the congregation.[41]

Hans Boehringer has observed,

> Now that is not quite what the ILCW said earlier in *CW 7*. There the emphasis on the unity of the rite was somewhat more broadly stated. The fullness of Christian initiation was described as baptism with water, laying on of hands, and the eucharist.[42]

Boehringer credits the change to the fact that the Lutheran Churches were "not ready to accept the classic understanding of the rites of Christian initiation." Frank Senn (following Gregory Dix) pushed

---

[40] It is revealing to examine the language of new baptismal rites. *The United Methodist Hymnal* (1989) is a good example. Timing and openness on the part of its authors resulted in extensive influences from contemporary liturgical scholarship. Three of the four optional rites begin ". . . Through the Sacrament of Baptism we are initiated into Christ's holy Church." Each service contains only one statement that baptism forgives sins.

[41] *Lutheran Book of Worship: Minister's Edition*, 30.

[42] Hans Boehringer, "Baptism, Confirmation and First Communion: Christian Initiation in the Contemporary Church," *Institute of Liturgical Studies Occasional Papers*, ed. D. Brockopp, D. Helge, D. Truemper (Valparaiso, IN: Institute of Liturgical Studies, 1981), 75.

for confirmation as a completion of the baptismal rite. "Dix suggested that those who are baptized but not confirmed have not received the indwelling Spirit . . . and should not be admitted to the Eucharist prior to confirmation."[43] Senn adds (with Louis Bouyer), "Ideally [confirmation] should be the conclusion of the baptismal liturgy, the rite of transition into the Eucharist fellowship."[44] What then is the purpose of *CW 8* and the subsequent Affirmation of Baptism found in *LBW*? Senn explains:

> The ILCW has provided us with a baptismal rite which restores the laying on of hands and anointing. But since most Lutherans apparently favor some kind of rite to mark the completion of the post-baptismal catechesis, [the commission recommends] a rite which is not construed as a completion of baptism or as a sacrament of the Church, because the form and matter which have been historically associated with confirmation have now been restored to the Liturgy of Holy Baptism . . . We have no need of a rite of admission to the eucharist fellowship.[45]

Since there were such confusing and contradicting views of confirmation operative among Lutherans, the ILCW determined to avoid the word altogether in favor of affirmation. It was hoped that this would better communicate the meaning of confirmation as a "public identification with one's baptism." But has the full unity of the rite been realized? If the question is asked in ritual terms and in view of the historic "golden age," then the answer is no. That would demand either the communion of infants or the delay of baptism. An attempt to go with the Eastern practice was made in the Anglican provisional booklet *Worship Supplement 8*, but was not accepted by the Anglican communion. There is some indication that the decision to postpone baptism will increase. The popularity of the RCIA not only continues to grow among Roman Catholics in America (along with the Easter Vigil), but also among Episcopalians and Lutherans who now have access to modified RCIA "programs"

---

[43] Frank Senn, "An End for Confirmation?" *Currents in Theology and Mission* 3 (1976): 45.
[44] Senn, 49.
[45] Senn, 51–52.

from their own traditions. Leonel L. Mitchell chaired a subcommittee which produced the Episcopalian rite "Preparation of Adults for Holy Baptism" for inclusion in the 1979 *Book of Occasional Services.* The ELCA has at its disposal the *Occasional Services: A Companion to the Lutheran Book of Worship.* It contains a brief rite titled "Enrollment of Candidates for Baptism." The rite includes "Note on the Service" describing the stages a candidate goes through in preparation for the "baptismal incorporation into the body of Christ."[46] The rite is an early digest of the RCIA In 1992, the Evangelical Lutheran Church in Canada produced *Living Witness: The Adult Catechumenate: Preparing Adults for Baptism and Ministry in the Church,* which explains in detail the stages and rites of the Catechumenate. Again, the RCIA. served as the model.

If a denomination buys into the Roman Catholic Rite of Christian Initiation of Adults, is it buying into a rejection of infant baptism? The answer is yes and no. Lutherans need to be very certain about what they are getting in the bargain. Few explain the fine print better than the eloquent Aidan Kavanagh, who describes infant baptism as a "benign abnormality."

> The norm of baptism was stated by the Council in a more diffused form than that of the eucharist, but no less definitely, to be a solemn sacramental initiation done especially at the paschal vigil and preceded by a catechumenate of serious content and considerable duration. This implies strongly, even if it does not require, that the initiate be an adult or at least a child well advanced in years. The conciliar emphasis is clearly on the adult nature of the norm of Christian initiation, deriving as it does from the New Testament and conversion. Although there is nowhere in the acts of the Council the slightest denigration of infant baptism, there is also no suggestion that the baptism of infants represents the norm of Catholic tradition. Equally, the Council nowhere suggests that the initiation of adults should be regarded either as exceptional or abnormal.[47]

---

[46] *Occasional Services* (Minneapolis: Augsburg Publishing House and Philadelphia: Board of Publication, LCA, 1982), 13–15.

[47] Kavanagh, 109.

Kavanagh acknowledges that "the notion that infant baptism must be regarded as something less than normal cannot set easily with many Catholics." Nor does it set well with most Lutherans, Anglicans, and Eastern Orthodox. Baptists would of course have a more favorable response. However, the new emphasis does not deny the validity of infant baptism. Kavanagh carefully states that the abnormality of infant baptism "does not require one to conclude that it is illegitimate: tradition clearly seems to know the baptism from the beginning."[48] The point Kavanagh is attempting to make is that yes, infant baptism has always occurred, but it is not "the normal manner in which one becomes a Catholic Christian."

> Tradition's witness to the baptism of adults as the norm throws infant baptism into the perspective as a benign abnormality so long as it is practiced with prudence as an unavoidable pastoral necessity—in situations such as the frail health of the infant . . . . At the same time, tradition's witness to adult baptism as the norm provides a solid counterbalance against infant baptism's becoming a malign abnormality due to pastoral malfeasance, theological obsession, or the decline of faith among Christian parents into some degree of merely social conformity.[49]

In summary, Kavanagh states that

> The Council's concern was to reiterate that the Church continually comes into existence in and through the full rhythm of Christian initiation, the normal scope of which is to be seen in the *Rite of Christian Initiation of Adults* [note the word *adults*].[50]

The need to develop the RCIA was due largely to the alarming recognition that the message of the Christian Church was becoming less and less credible to society in the twentieth century. Searle explains,

> Among Roman Catholics the legitimacy and validity of infant baptism was never called into question, but in the de-Christianized conditions of postwar Europe, the Catholic Church faces the prob-

---

[48] Kavanagh, 109.
[49] Kavanagh, 109–110.
[50] Kavanagh, 109–110.

> lems of a vast nominal membership and few deeply committed Catholics. Moves to curtail indiscriminate baptism were accompanied on the one hand by a recovery of the patristic teachings on sacramental initiation and on the other hand by the first steps toward a restoration of the ancient catechumenate.[51]

Pastoral concern over the indiscriminate practice of baptizing infants of delinquent parents along with a serious attempt to restore a thorough adult catechumenate "has served to raise new theological problems about what we are doing in baptizing children."[52] In a day when six-week pastoral information classes and Evangelical-entertainment-style worship are growing in number, Lutheran churches should take note of what the RCIA is attempting to do, and may or may not choose to produce a modified Lutheran Rite of Christian Initiation for Adults. The Lutheran Church, however, already has a unified doctrine and practice of the Word and Sacraments. What unifies the proclamation of the Word and the administration of the Sacraments is that where the Lord's Word of truth and his Sacraments are administered according to his command, there is the Spirit, and the Lord himself delivering his gifts. The unity of the Sacraments of Holy Baptism and Holy Communion is achieved through catechesis, baptism, and Holy Communion in which teaching, administration, extolling, and thanksgiving are consistent with the proper distinction of the law and gospel. Such unity of the word and sacraments is far more important than the unification of rites. Nagel writes in *Lutheran Worship: History and Practice*,

> When Baptism is a culminating part, and not the whole, then there may also be succeeding parts that "complete" Baptism. When Baptism is not the entire gift, then man may have his parts to do; and when man does the doing, there is never enough. "To be baptized in God's name is to be baptized not by man but by God himself. Although it is performed by men's hands, it is nevertheless truly God's own act . . . . Here the devil sets to work to blind us with false appearances and lead us away from God's work to our own."[53]

---

[51] Searle, 26.
[52] Searle, 26–27.
[53] Nagel, 269. Nagel here quotes the *Large Catechism*, IV, 10–11.

Mark Searle writes,

> Process is a key term in this whole project of exploring *Alternative Futures for Worship*, and no single sacrament is as calculated to demonstrate the importance of process in the Christian life as is the sacrament of baptism.

He also points out that in understanding baptism as a process, "In the very nature of things, no process is ever complete unless it be taken up into some further process."[54] A lot of work needs to be done in Lutheran churches in the area of evangelism and catechesis. As the following quote from *Lutheran Worship: History and Practice* aptly demonstrates, however, any so-called Evangelical Rite of Christian Initiation will be profoundly different from the RCIA.

> When Baptism came to be regarded as partial—an initiation, part of a process, a beginning with subsequent quantitative stages and accompanying gifts that brought one to final perfection, and so to fitness to be loved by God—then grace, gifts, and Holy Spirit were quantified and fractionalized. Then the whole lot is not given in Baptism. The Gospel is the whole lot; the Law measures and quantifies.[55]

Presiding Minister, Assisting Ministers, and Liturgy as the "Work of the People"

Among the significant changes to appear in the Divine Services of *Lutheran Worship* is the designation of the *minister* (*TLH*) as president or presiding minister and the addition of assisting ministers. The terms themselves never appear in the pew edition. They appear simply as the symbols Ⓟ and Ⓐ. Two brief explanations of the change in terminology are found in the "Notes on the Liturgy" in the *Lutheran Worship Altar Book*. The note on rubric 11 states:

> Symbols are used to designate those participating in the services. Portions reserved for pastors are marked Ⓟ = presiding minister.

---

[54] Nagel, 13.
[55] Nagel, 269.

> Portions appropriate for those either ordained or non-ordained are marked Ⓐ for assisting minister. Portions for the entire congregation are marked Ⓒ. Portions that do not require a pastor are marked Ⓛ for leader. This is the symbol used in the services of Daily Prayer . . . . If non-ordained assisting ministers or leaders are considered either necessary or desirable or both (in some situations pastors, ordained professors, or seminary students are available to serve in this capacity), the congregations are urged to exercise good judgment in their selection. Prior instruction and practice are necessary, lest the service be disturbed.[56]

Rubric 25 states:

> The liturgy is the celebration of all who gather. Together with the pastor who presides, the entire congregation is involved. It is appropriate, therefore, that where it is considered necessary or desirable or both, lay persons fulfill certain functions within the service.[57]

The use of president (or presiding minister) reflects the early church preference of the contemporary Liturgical Movement. "There is some evidence to suggest that in the early church the celebrant was called 'the president.'"[58] The influence of Gregory Dix can again be seen in his discussion of the Jewish *chaburah*. Following Lietzmann, Dix believes that the Christian Eucharist is "by origin and in essence a '*chabûrah* rite.'" The corporate nature of the two rites sets the stage for an emphasis on participation by all present. Dix points out that the Jewish *chaburah* was lead by a president, and he adds, "conversely, the Christian Justin in the second century refers to the bishop who 'eucharistises' the bread and wine as 'the president' (*prokathemenos*) without further description."[59]

But Jesus was not celebrating a community *chaburah*. He was celebrating the Passover and simultaneously instituting the Lord's Supper. Gregory Dix rejects this and theorizes:

---

[56] *Lutheran Worship: Altar Book*, 11.

[57] *LW: Altar Book*, 11.

[58] P. Hinchliff, "Celebrant," in *The New Westminster Dictionary of Liturgy and Worship*, ed. J. G. Davies (Philadelphia: The Westminster Press, 1986), 155.

[59] Dix, 60.

> The origin of the eucharist as essentially a "*chabûrah*" rite also affords what seems a sufficient answer to the theory that whatever our Lord may have done at the last supper (which can hardly, on this theory, be described as "instituting the eucharist," since there was in His mind no thought of a future rite) was concerned only with the breaking of bread, while the sacramental use of the cup is an addition by S. Paul upon the model of hellenistic mysteries.[60]

For Dix, the Eucharist is something the people "do" as the Body of Christ. The individual Christian

> effectively fulfills himself in this world as a living member of Christ above all by discharging personally his own proper function in the Body of Christ, his proper "liturgy" (as bishop, cleric, or layman) whose climax is his share in the "doing" of the great corporate action of that Body prescribed by our Lord.[61]

The church which confesses the belief that it was Jesus himself who instituted the Lord's Supper as a sacrament, a means of grace dispensing the forgiveness of sins and eternal life, may want to designate the one who stands in the place of Christ in a way that denotes him a mediator of God's grace to people. The title minister would be preferred to president or presiding minister. President stresses his leadership function, whereas the minister is the one who administers ("serves") God's gifts to the people.

The terminology chosen by the writers of the Augsburg Confession reveals an understanding of the Office of the Holy Ministry that is thoroughly evangelical and gift-focused. Article V bears the title "Of the Ministry." In the German text, *ministry* is a translation of *Predigtamt*, office of preacher. The emphasis is on the preaching of the Gospel. The Latin title is *De Ministerio Ecclesiastico* ("Of the Ministry of the Church"). The text refers to the institution of the *ministerium docendi evangelii et porrigendi sacramenta*, that is, the ministry of teaching. The emphasis is not on presiding over actions of a celebrating assembly, rather on the serving out of the *Evan-*

---

[60] Dix, 60–61.
[61] Dix, 268.

gelium und Sacramente/evangelii et . . . sacramenta to the congregation.[62] Adding the modifier "presiding" to minister does not clarify, but contributes to the confusion in an age when "everyone is a minister." Minister, pastor, and officiant stand on their own. Officiant (*officians*) is the one who performs (*officiare*) the duties of the office (*officium*; in German, *Amt*). Celebrant and priest are inferior. The reason for avoiding the term celebrant is explained by Fred L. Precht in *Lutheran Worship: History and Practice.*

> In the past, the pastor who officiated at the Eucharist was often called the "celebrant." Recent understanding, however, of the corporate nature of both the church and its worship considers the congregation as the celebrant, and the priest or pastor as the presider, or presiding minister, not one who celebrates on behalf of or apart from the faithful. Thus, in neither *Lutheran Worship* (1982), *Lutheran Worship: Altar Book* (1982), *Lutheran Worship: Agenda* (1984), nor in *Lutheran Worship: Little Agenda* (1985) does the term celebrant appear.[63]

Presiding minister is defined over against assisting minister(s). The threefold designation raises the question: What is the relationship of the assisting minister to the clergy and congregation? Is it an attempt to restore a type of early church structure similar to bishop, deacon, and laity?

One of the few documents available at the time *LW* was published which offers some historical and theological explanation for the innovations was the *Guide to Introducing Lutheran Worship.*

> The congregation has its service, its liturgy, its offering of prayer, praise, and thanksgiving to do. No one can take that liturgy from the people of God. The presiding minister (pastor) has his liturgy, or service to render. He is called to preach the Gospel, absolve, and celebrate the sacraments. That ministry is from God himself, and the pastor acts as the representative of Christ in the midst of the people of God as the sacraments are celebrated and the Gospel is preached.

---

[62] *Concordia Triglotta* (St. Louis: Concordia Publishing House, 1921), 44–45.

[63] Fred L. Precht, "The Preparation: Part 2," in *Lutheran Worship: History and Practice*, 406.

> The assisting ministers reestablish the important diaconal ministry. They represent the people; as the assisting ministers they lead in prayer, their essential task, and assist in the reading of the Word of God and in the distribution of the chalice at the Communion.[64]

The Lutheran Church—Missouri Synod published no official text explaining the theology of worship which gave shape to *Lutheran Worship* until eleven years after the introduction of the new hymnal. The long-awaited *Lutheran Worship History and Practice* finally appeared in 1993. Chapter 6 offers limited insight concerning the Notes on the Liturgy in the *Lutheran Worship: Altar Book.* Commenting on the statement that "where it is considered necessary or desirable or both, lay persons fulfill certain functions within the service," *Lutheran Worship: History and Practice* states:

> The rationale for using laymen in this way is, in one sense, to restore the ancient office of deacon to the liturgy. The deacons in the New Testament period served as assistants to the bishops (1 Tim. 3:8–13) with the primary responsibility for the care of the needy in the Christian community (Acts 6:1–7). There is no evi-

---

[64] *Guide to Introducing Lutheran Worship* (St. Louis: Concordia Publishing House, 1981), 22–23 offers this historical rationale for the introduction of presiding and assisting ministers: "At the time of the Reformation the low mass or the 'missa Cantata' (a sung low mass) was the normal pattern of worship in Western Europe. It was the mass that the Reformers knew and used for their model. This low mass was led by the celebrant, and the responses were said by the congregation, or in most cases by a single server. To have a single minister at the altar was the normal way the service was done. The Reformers of course understood that the congregation was not to consist of mere passive spectators. They encouraged participation by the people and understood worship to be a corporate action. But the low mass model with which they worked called for a single minister at the altar, and the congregation.

"The corporate quality of worship is a concept that *Lutheran Worship* attempts to expand with the use of assisting ministers. Most Lutheran parishes have only one ordained pastor; therefore, the assisting minister role cannot be limited to ordained clergy. Most congregations would not be able to use the assisting minister sections if they were limited to ordained assistant pastors. Laymen are encouraged to assume the assisting minister role.

"*Lutheran Worship* uses the model of the solemn high celebration of the Eucharist with, to continue in the same idiom, a deacon and a subdeacon. The model is not to be found in the shared leadership of many American Protestant denominations. The assisting minister role is not to give the people of the congregation a chance to 'play pastor,' as if that were the really important part. Nor is the goal of *Lutheran Worship* a clericalization of worship by having more and more ministers, with less and less to do for the congregations. Rather, the rationale behind the use of assisting minister is that we understand that each order (German: "Stand") in the church has its office ("Amt") to perform."

dence prior to the second century to indicate that deacons had any special liturgical responsibilities in the church.[65]

Lutheran Worship: History and Practice identifies the deacon as an assistant to the bishop. This is inconsistent with the view promoted in *Guide to Introducing Lutheran Worship,* which stated, "The assisting ministers reestablish the important diaconal ministry . . . . They represent the people."[66] *Lutheran Worship: History and Practice* concludes:

> As the office of deacon developed in post-New Testament times, several functions were attached to this office, including the reading of Scripture, certain prayers in the liturgy, and the distribution of the cup in the Holy Communion. Thus, the office of deacon represented the link between the altar and the world. In *Lutheran Worship,* the role of the assisting minister is a continuation of this tradition.[67]

The influence of the Roman Catholic liturgical movement is reflected in the adoption of the "high mass" model with many liturgical leaders; in the borrowing of the "president" terminology (which was used in the Vatican II Constitution on Sacred Liturgy,[68] and has since come to dominate in Roman Catholic liturgical language); in encouraging the active participation of the people through expanded leadership roles which include the use of deacons and sub-deacons. In Roman Catholic polity,

---

[65] John Pless, "The Leaders of Worship," in *Lutheran Worship: History and Practice,* 235.

[66] *Guide to Introducing Lutheran Worship,* 24.

[67] Pless, 235–36.

[68] A. G. Martimort, "Structure and Laws of the Liturgical Celebration," Section II, *The Church At Prayer.* vol.1, *Principles of the Liturgy,* ed. A. G. Martimort (Collegeville, MN: The Liturgical Press, 1983), 102–103. Commenting on a quote from the Vatican II Constitution of the Sacred Liturgy, Martimort writes: "The celebrant, who is a bishop or a priest, 'presides over the assembly in the person of Christ.' This formula of Vatican II sums up the three traditional statements: (a) A liturgical action has a president who is in effective charge of the assembly and leads its prayer. (b) This president is the celebrant; in other words, it is he who prays, performs the sacred actions, and breaks both the bread of God's Word and the Eucharist bread for the people. He is therefore by no means just someone who sees to good order. (c) He is the president and celebrant not by appointment of the assembly or because of his human qualities, but because by ordination he has the priestly character proper to bishop or presbyter. In virtue of this character, he plays the part of Christ (he acts "*in persona Christi*"), he is the sign that the community does not gather by simple spontaneous agreement but is called together by the Lord in order to receive his Word and his gifts."

> Deacons are the Church's ministers "par excellence," as their very name *diakonoi*, "servants," indicates. They are primarily servants of the bishop, but they also serve priests in the liturgical celebration; in addition, especially in the Eastern tradition, they are assigned to lead the people in their participation by telling them, through proclamations, what attitudes, external and internal, to adopt, and by suggesting prayer intentions in the form of litanies. They come and go from celebrant to people. Deacons prepare the gifts for the Eucharist . . . help in distributing Communion . . . in particular . . . the chalice. Finally at an early date, deacons were assigned to certain readings . . . at Rome, from the time of St. Gregory the Great on . . . the gospel.[69]

It is quite clear from the liturgical writings accompanying the implementation of *LBW* that the American Lutheran churches interpreted "the active participation of the people" in the liturgy to mean "active leadership." In the *Lutheran Book of Worship: Manual on the Liturgy*, Philip Pfatteicher explains:

> The leadership role is expanded in modern liturgies. In the absence of clergy, lay people are encouraged to lead the daily prayer services—Morning and Evening Prayer, Prayer at the Close of the Day. In the Holy Communion the leadership ought to be shared by several people.[70]

This innovation was retained by the Commission on Worship of the Missouri Synod when it revised the *Lutheran Book of Worship* under the title *Lutheran Worship*. Initially, the symbols Ⓟ (presiding minister) and Ⓐ (assisting minister) went virtually unnoticed and received little if any public attention in the LCMS. They would, however, lead to ambiguity, confusion, and discord in liturgical practice. The LCMS introduced *LW* with little historical, theological, and practical guidance for the new structure. The *Guide to Introducing Lutheran Worship* claimed that "assisting ministers reestablish the important diaconal ministry"; however, the LCMS had established

---

69 Martimort, 105.

70 Philip H. Pfatteicher and Carlos R. Messerli, *Manual on the Liturgy: Lutheran Book of Worship* (Minneapolis: Augsburg Publishing House, 1979), 10.

no such "important" order. Neither the ILCW nor the LCMS Commission on Worship were given the mandate to reestablish new ministries. As seen above, the *Guide* claims the assisting ministers/deacons to be representatives of the people while *LW: History and Practice* presents them as representatives of the pastor/bishop. This discrepancy is the result of the long-standing division in American Lutheranism over the doctrine of church and ministry. To adopt a diaconal "idiom" from the Roman Catholic liturgical movement is not quite as simple and neat is it may seem on the surface. The Roman Catholic Church remains quite hierarchical in spite of the radical post-Vatican II changes. The Eastern Church with its deacons and sub-deacons also has a high view of the office of the ministry inconsistent with "Waltherian Lutheranism."

Vatican II stressed both the hierarchic and communal nature of the liturgy. Liturgical services "are celebrations of the Church . . . a holy people united and organized under their bishops."[71] Vatican II stated:

> In liturgical celebrations, whether as a minister or as one of the faithful, each person should perform his role by doing solely and totally what the nature of things and liturgical norms require of him. Servers, lectors, commentators, and members of the choir also exercise a genuine liturgical ministry.[72]

For the most part, pastors and congregations would be dependent upon the companion reference materials of *LBW* for insight. In *LBW*, the assisting minister is unequivocally a leadership role inclusive of women. The *Manual on the Liturgy* states:

---

[71] "Constitution on the Sacred Liturgy," *The Documents of Vatican II*, Walter M. Abbott, ed. (New York: Guild Press, 1966), 147.

[72] Abbott, 148. Originally the "commentator" was a minister whose task it was to explain the meaning of the Latin liturgy to those who did not speak Latin. The value of the office of commentator is still recognized today in preparing the people to understand and participate in the liturgy. See Constitution on the Sacred Liturgy, 35.3, and also General Instructions of the Roman Missal 68a. "In this activity, however, the commentator is simply a substitute for the deacon." A. G. Martimort, p. 108. The General Instructions of the Roman Missal 68b discuss the historic Order of Porter and restore the position (comparable to modern ushers) to laypersons.

> Lay people—women as well as men—ought to be encouraged to share in the assisting roles as their abilities allow, in addition to the clergy of the parish. They are not just helpers in the absence of ordained people; they have their own rightful role to fulfill. A parish with five pastors, for example, ought not let that deter them from the use of lay leadership. All five pastors and lay people as well should be involved in the service. Lay people ought to be given roles in the service as a matter of principle to show the broadened understanding of leading worship.[73]

In 1978 the Board of Publication of the Lutheran Church in America produced an eight-session course for the laity to acquaint them with *LBW*. Session one identifies three distinctive characteristics of Lutheran worship: (1) It is liturgical, (2) it stresses the balance between Word and sacraments, (3) Lutheran worship involves a great deal of participation by the people.[74] Noticeably absent from the list is *the* distinctive characteristic of Lutheran worship, namely, the doctrine of justification. The doctrine of justification by grace through faith is the central Lutheran criterion of the liturgy. The course goes beyond the traditional Lutheran understanding of the participation of the congregation by insisting: "Not only do the people participate through singing and kneeling—they are also involved as leaders of the services . . . . Worship leadership is clearly not restricted to ordained professionals."[75] The theology driving an inclusive laity as liturgical leaders is explicitly expressed in the *Assisting Ministers Handbook*: "As priests, all participate fully in the service. These are priests who have convened to do their liturgy, not to watch it being done by others for them."[76] This appears to be more a reiteration of Vatican II concerns within the Roman Catholic Church than a legitimate analysis of the state of affairs within Lutheran churches. The *Handbook* continues with an explanation that shows very strong Caselian influences.

---

[73] Pfatteicher, *Manual on the Liturgy*, 11.

[74] S. Anita Stauffer, *Lutherans at Worship* (Minneapolis: Augsburg Publishing House, 1978), 8–9.

[75] Stauffer, 9.

[76] Ralph R. Van Loon, *Assisting Ministers Handbook*, ed. S. Anita Stauffer (Philadelphia: Parish Life Press, 1986), 5.

> As priests, all worshipers are fully attentive and fully involved as the church's liturgy re-presents salvation history and directs the prayers and praises of the priesthood to God through Christ.[77]

Casel repeatedly emphasized the active participation of the laity in the liturgy. All the laity become conjoined to Christ in the mystical body through the sacraments of baptism and confirmation and thus are to share in the liturgical action in a necessary and real sense. At Vatican II the Roman Catholic Church fully embraced this baptismal-participation emphasis. The Evangelical Lutheran Church never had a liturgical theology (nor an ecclesiology) based on the mystical Body of Christ; nevertheless, the scholarship pushing the work of the ILCW enthusiastically, wholeheartedly, and freely adopted this innovation with little if any discretion. The expanded use of the laity in leadership roles based on their baptism would become one of the most important goals guiding the ILCW in their liturgical revision. In the Introduction to *LBW*, it is stated that an examination of the contents of the hymnal reveals several goals toward which the Inter-Lutheran Commission on Worship worked in liturgy:

> [T]o restore to Holy Baptism the liturgical rank and dignity implied by Lutheran theology, and to draw out the baptismal motifs in such acts as the confession of sin and the burial of the dead; to continue to move into the larger ecumenical heritage of liturgy while, at the same time, enhancing Lutheran convictions about the Gospel; to involve the lay persons as assisting ministers who share the leadership of corporate worship.[78]

This trend appeared already in the *Worship Supplement* of the Missouri Synod. Under "Suggestions for the Worshiper" it advises,

---

[77] Van Loon, 5.

[78] *Lutheran Book of Worship* (Minneapolis: Augsburg Publishing House, 1978), 8. See also Hermann Sasse, "Liturgy and Lutheranism," *Una Sancta* 8, no. 3 (1948): 7. "The liturgical movement which flourished in German Roman Catholic circles, partly as a result of the Church music reforms of Pius X, partly as a consequence of the scientific liturgical research of the Benedictines of Maria Laach, notably Ildefons Herwegen and Odo Casel, ultimately sought to answer the vital question, 'What is the Church?' The same is true of the parallel, though not particularly significant, 'High Church' movements in German Protestantism and even among the Reformed Churches of Switzerland and Scotland."

> Think of yourself as a priest of God, functioning as such in the great priesthood of all believers, rejoicing in the privileges of your baptism, and bringing an offering of praise and thanksgiving through Jesus Christ and in the Holy Spirit.[79]

The liturgical texts of the *WS* adopt a variety of designations. The Holy Eucharist II and III follow the twofold designation of "minister" and "people." "Minister" is carried over from *The Lutheran Hymnal*, while "people" is an innovation which echoes the "people of God" language of Vatican II. Holy Eucharist I appears to be a careless composition which uses mainly ℣ and ℟ (versicle and response), but includes the one-time reference to celebrant before the Preface. The Salutation uses ℣ and ℟, while the Collect of the Day, Eucharistic Prayer, and Aaronic Benediction have no title associated with them. One might reasonably make the assumption that in the 1960s both congregation and pastor knew what part was assigned to them. Not so in the 1980s and '90s. Hints of the expanded use of leaders can be seen in the "Rubrics for Minister," where an early allusion to the terminology "assisting ministers" is seen in the statement: "as the celebrant (with his assistants) enters the church" (49); "Before the Intercessions, the celebrant or his assistant may make mention of any special Petitions . . . ." (52); Again in the rubrics: "The Lesson, the Epistle, and the Gospel may be read by laymen" (51); In the Greeting of Peace, immediately after the Pax, the celebrant extends "both his hands to the right hand of his assistant . . ." (52). The rubrics included in The Holy Eucharist II suggest, "Finally someone from the congregation, acting as deacon, may bid the Prayers and intercessions of the assembly" (59). The notes on the Responsories for An Evening Service (Vespers) make reference to the "cantor's parts" (95). No explanation is given of exactly what a deacon or cantor is in the Lutheran Church.

A year after the *Worship Supplement* was published, the ILCW released *Contemporary Worship 2: Services—The Holy Communion* (1970) in which the new practice of multiple leadership by ordained

---

[79] *WS*, 15.

and non-ordained "ministers" was adopted in full. The designations were spelled out as presiding minister, assisting minister, people, and all. This new direction was succinctly explained in the introductory instructions "For the Leadership of Worship."

> The service should never be led by one minister alone. The presiding minister is always ordained, but he should be assisted by others both clergy and laymen. Otherwise the symbolism of a truly corporate action is blurred. The core of the presiding minister's role is the Great Thanksgiving.
>
> Two roles are differentiated in the rubrics. Those parts usually reserved to the presiding minister are marked "Presiding Minister." Other parts marked "Assisting Minister" are done either by a layman or another clergyman.
>
> The assistant's role might also be divided between two people. If the parish has two pastors, one will assume some of the assistant's role. But in no case should this preclude lay participation. As a minimum, laymen should read the first and second lessons.[80]

A helpful feature in *CW 2* is a commentary that runs throughout the entire length of the service and is conveniently located on the pages immediately opposite the liturgical text. The opening commentary describes worship as an exchange between God and his people and states that this action of fellowship is "known as the church, the community each of us entered at baptism."[81] Building on baptism, the commentary continues:

> Worship is the action of us all, the formal expression of the ministry of the entire congregation. The nature of the action requires that some assume roles of leadership. Normally, the presiding minister is an ordained clergyman. He shares leadership with one or more assisting ministers. These people need not be ordained. In fact, laymen should be involved in the service this way.[82]

The ILCW is very dogmatic in its assertion that the "nature of the actions *requires*" that some of the laity *should* be involved in

---

[80] *CW 2*, x.
[81] *CW 2*, 2.
[82] *CW 2*, 2.

leadership roles. The basis for this claim is in understanding the nature of the liturgy as primarily the "work of the people," or as the commentary says, "the action of us all." Herbert F. Lindemann's comments on *CW 2* are enlightening:

> Significantly, the presiding minister is not called "Celebrant," since the entire congregation is thought of as celebrating the eucharistic feast. Various people from the congregation are enlisted for specific tasks: serving at the altar, reading the lessons, offering the bread and wine etc. The thrust is away from a "one man show" toward the idea of a community meal.[83]

The expanded leadership role of the laity is a modern innovation that has triumphed in the production of *LBW* as it has in the practice of post-Vatican II Roman Catholic parishes. The *LBW* adopted the presiding and assisting minister format. The theology behind this change along with how it was to be implemented has been thoroughly expanded through a series of books, booklets, and manuals for clergy and laity.[84] With these books, the pastors, lay leaders, worship committees (and eventually the entire congregation, *lex orandi, lex credendi*) are able to make the adjustment to a new "style" of worship and be given at least a limited rationale and justification for the change. Chapter 1, "The Lutheran Tradition," in the *Manual on the Liturgy* includes a section titled "The Work of the People." This section explains the rationale behind the use of assisting ministers. The opening sentence references worship anthropocentrically. "Liturgy means 'work of the people,' but too often in the past the liturgy gave the impression that it was the work of the pastor." The manual then adds:

[83] Herbert F. Lindemann, "*CW-2* Passes in Review," *The Lutheran Quarterly* 26, no. 2 (1974): 221. Herbert Lindemann (LCMS) served on the ILCW (1966–1969) and ILCW Liturgical Text Committee (1967–78).

[84] *Ministers Desk Edition* (1978); *Manual on the Liturgy* (1979), by Philip H. Pfatteicher and Carlos R. Messerli; *Lutherans at Worship* (1978), Leaders and Study Guide, by S. Anita Stauffer; *Holy Communion Narrative for Adults* (1978); *Commentary on the Occasional Services* (1983), by Philip H. Pfatteicher; *Commentary on the Lutheran Book of Worship* (1990), by Philip H. Pfatteicher; *Worship Handbook* (1990), by Ralph R. Van Loon.

> This tradition that recognized that the presiding pastor was not the only leader has been embraced not only by other Lutheran bodies in North America but by other denominations as well. One feature of contemporary worship is the emphasis on shared leadership to indicate that the service is not something that the pastor does while the people watch but is something which is an action shared by all who assemble to worship and over which one is called to preside.[85]

If the liturgy is understood to be "the work of the people," then the next logical step is to consider it the property of the people.

> Moreover, the restriction depends on an understanding of the sacraments as the God-given property of the church, which are to be guarded against abuse. The church controls the "right use" of the sacraments by committing them to its ministers, who are under the authority of the church organization-congregation and synod or district, who are trained by the church and pledged at ordination to the Scriptures and Confessions. The clergy are not only representatives of the denomination but of the ministry of the whole Christian church, and the presidency of the liturgy is given to those who are in communion with the whole church. Thus the local community is in contact with the larger Christian community. An inevitable tension results: The need to maintain this ecumenical communion is balanced by the necessity of avoiding a clergy-dominated liturgy. To these specially commissioned servants of the people of God the church entrusts the preaching of the Gospel and the celebration of the sacraments, and these ministers are accountable to the church which ordained them for fulfilling their responsibility. Those who preside, therefore, must do so not only with fidelity to the traditions but also with attention to people, and this requires warmth and grace.[86]

The above extensive quote is to be commended for its emphasis on the ecumenical, catholic character of the liturgy in a time when many Lutheran churches are following a go-it-alone, do-your-own, Protestant, even sectarian approach to liturgical theol-

---

[85] Pfatteicher and Messerli, *Manual on the Liturgy*, 9.
[86] Pfatteicher and Messerli, *Manual on the Liturgy*, 10.

ogy and practice. The primary problem, however, is not the emphasis on the agenda of the modern ecumenical movement or the "need to avoid a clergy-dominated liturgy." The primary challenge is to maintain a theology and practice of worship in which the liturgy is understood as belonging to God, not the local or ecumenical Christian community. The local community exercises its freedom best when it guards against false doctrine which destroys the evangelical sacraments and evangelical proclamation of the word in the sermons, hymns, prayers, litanies, and so forth. The primary need is not to balance ecumenical concerns with the "necessity of avoiding a clergy-dominated liturgy," but avoiding heterodox liturgy.

A footnote at the end of the above quote from *LBW Manual* refers the reader, without comment, to Augsburg Confession, Articles V and XIV. Unfortunately, Pfatteicher references the ministry to the church rather than the church to the ministry as the confessions do. Article IV on Justification is linked to Article V (German: The Office of the Ministry; Latin: The Ministry of the Church). The opening words of Article V make this connection quite clear:

> To obtain such faith God instituted the office of the ministry, that is, provided the Gospel and the sacraments. Through these, as through means, he gives the Holy Spirit, who works faith, when and where be pleases, in those who hear the Gospel.

The church does not create or own the gospel and the sacraments. God creates the church through the gospel and sacraments, "when and where he pleases" (AC V). The liturgy is God's working through his ministers. His liturgy is none other than Holy Baptism and the ongoing preaching of "all that I have commanded," namely, Holy Absolution and Holy Communion (AC XXVIII, 5–10). When all are the Lord's things and the Lord's work, then there is certainty (*extra nos*). The adjective "holy" indicates that it belongs to God (not to the Church) and is a ministry done by God to man; thus Holy Ministry, Holy Gospel, Holy Liturgy (*Gottesdienst*, not *Menschendienst*), Holy Baptism, Holy Absolution, Holy Communion, Holy Church.

A fundamental question in resolving the identities of the presiding minister and assisting ministers remains: Is there a clearly distinguishable *Amt* or *Stand* (office or function to be performed) of assisting minister/deacon in the LCMS? For example, are they to lead in prayers? If so, why? Are assisting ministers to assist the congregation in distinguishing between the "sacramental and sacrificial" parts of the liturgy? Are they to lead the people in assuming their sacrificial worship (singing, choir, organist, musicians, ushers, etc.) and demonstrate the role of the laity in sacramental elements, that is, bowing, kneeling, saying "amen"? If so, this is not consistent with the role of assisting minister as included in *LW*. In *LW* the assisting minister does sacramental functions such as reading Scriptures and distributing the Blood.

Is the assisting minister a representative of the sacrificial aspects of the congregation's worship? If so, why? Why should, ought, or must there be an "assisting minister" representing all the congregation? Among the reasons why extra ministers ought to be included in the leadership of worship are the following:

1. To imitate Rome and the East.
2. Ceremonialism—namely, subjective/aesthetic preference.
3. Variety of voice and talent. A talented assisting minister might be able to read and chant in such a way that the communication of the Word is enhanced.
4. To distinguish the uniquely pastoral/sacramental character of the "presiding minister." For example, in the eastern liturgy, only the priest uses the "Gospel" main door to the altar. The deacons use the "deacon's" doors. The deacons' robes are different from the priests'. This serves to heighten the sacramental role of the priest.

The Greeting and Response

The second half of the twentieth century has witnessed many churches' discarding the traditional wording of the response to the salutation when embarking on the revision of their liturgical texts. Historically, the pastor said, "The Lord be with you." The congregation responded, "And with thy spirit." The new response is "And also with you." Both *LBW* and *Christian Worship*[87] are consistent in using this response throughout all their services. *LW* uses both the ancient and contemporary response. The seemingly minor alteration from "spirit" to "you" was barely noticed when the new hymnals were introduced. A look at the origin and development of the salutation, however, reveals the original meaning carried rich theological freight that has now been lost.

Early Church Liturgical Documents

The Greeting "The Lord be with you" is found in Scripture: Judges 6:12, "The Lord is with you" (יהוה עִמְּךָ; LXX, Κύριος μετὰ σοῦ); Ruth 2:4, "The Lord be with You" (יהוה עִמָּכֶם; LXX, Κύριος μεθ' ὑμῶν); Luke 1:28, "The Lord is with you" (ὁ Κύριος μετὰ σοῦ). "And with your Spirit" is not found in Scripture as a response to a greeting. In the liturgical usage of the church, it has remained constant (in both the East and West) as the response of the congregation to a greeting from the pastor. The greeting, however, is found in a variety of forms which were redacted from both the Gospels and Pauline Epistles (John 19:20; Luke 24:36; 1 Cor. 16:23; 2 Tim. 4:22; Gal. 6:18; Phil. 4:23).

What has yet to be explained is how these diverse greetings came to be included in the liturgy. The earliest surviving text of the Eucharist Prayer with a full tripartite dialogue is found in the *Apostolic Tradition,* which has been attributed to Hippolytus. Extant in Latin, Coptic, Arabic, and Ethiopic versions, this liturgy has been dated around 215 and possibly as early as 165.[88] The original Greek is largely lost, but the Latin reads:

---

[87] *Christian Worship: A Lutheran Hymnal* was published by the Wisconsin Evangelical Lutheran Synod in 1993.

With two exceptions the *WS* (1969) used "And with your spirit." The dialogue in The Holy Eucharist II (60) eliminated the salutation and response. The Holy Eucharist III offered the interesting variation "And with you, his servant" (64, 65). *CW 2* (1970) and *TGT* (1975) consistently used "And also with you."

[88] Robert Taft, "The Dialogue before the Anaphora in the Byzantine Eucharistic Liturgy. I: The Opening Greeting," *Orientalia Christiana Periodica* 52 (1988), 299–324. Taft notes: "Given Hippolytus' pretenses at representing tradition, scholars feel safe in supposing that this mid-fourth-century Latin text preserved in fifth-century palimpsest folia of codex *Verona LV* (53) is a version of the Greek original of the preanaphoral dialogue certainly in

Dominus vobiscum.	The Lord be with you.
Et cum spiritu tuo.	And with your spirit.
Su(r)sum corda.	Up with your hearts.
Habemus ad dominum.	We have (them) with the Lord.
Gratias agamus domino.	Let us give thanks to the Lord.
Dignum et justum est.	It is fitting and right.

With minor variations, the second parts of the three-part dialogue (*Sursum corda* to the end) are the same in all liturgical traditions—East and West. The opening greeting and response, however, is divided into "two broad traditions": (1) The single-member Roman-Egyptian greeting. (2) The trinitarian greeting based on 2 Corinthians 13:13.[89] The more simple form (The Lord be with you / And with your spirit) is found in the Roman texts, and its derivative (The Lord be with you all) is found in the Alexandrian Greek Liturgy of St. Mark and the Coptic Cyril. The preanaphoral dialogue in the Byzantine and other non-Alexandrian eastern eucharists fall into the second tradition:

> the Churches to the North and East within the Antiochene sphere of liturgical influence seem never to have known "The Lord (be) with you" as a greeting in the preanaphoral dialogue or, for that matter, elsewhere. "Peace to all" is the normal short greeting throughout the east, and one or another form of greeting based on 2 Cor. 13:13 can be found in the preanaphoral dialogue from the second half of the 4th century, first in Antioch. This is the earliest evidence extant for the liturgies of the west beyond Egypt.[90]

use at Rome around 215, and undoubtedly earlier too, since from comparative liturgy it is obvious that Hippolytus did not invent it. Furthermore, the Sahidic version of *ApTrad* witnesses to the dialogue in the same form, changed but slightly (variants in italics) to conform, undoubtedly, to the local usage familiar to the Coptic redactor:

Ho Kurios meta panton humon.
Meta tou pneumatos sou.
Ano humon tas kardias.
Exomen pros ton kurion.
Euxaristiersomen ton Kurion.
Axion kai dikaion." (305–306)

[89] Taft, 306.

[90] Taft, 309.

The oldest known church manual is *The Teaching of the Twelve Apostles* or the *Didache* for short. It predates even the *Apostolic Tradition.* Some elements of this manual may date from the first century, possibly as early as 60 A.D.[91] The *Didache* contains eucharistic instructions (chapter 9) and a eucharistic prayer (chapter 10). The earliest section is often referred to as "The Two Ways" (chapters 1–5). These chapters reveal that the so-called primitive church possessed a very profound understanding of the presence and power of Christ in the Holy Ministry of the Word and Sacraments. Chapter 4 begins:

> My child, you shall remember night and day him who speaks to you the word of God, and honor him as the Lord; for where that which pertains to the Lord is spoken, there the Lord is.[92]

The Eucharistic Prayer in the *Didache* contains neither dialogue nor *Verba,* but it does conclude with thoughts similar to the later tripartite dialogue.

> Let grace come and let this world pass away. Hosanna to the son of David. If any is holy let him come; if any be not, let him repent. *Maranatha. Amen.*[93]

One would not expect to find the greeting "The Lord be with you" in the Syrian[94] *Didache.* The "Churches of the North and East within the Antiochene sphere of liturgical influence seem never to have known 'The Lord (be) with you' as a greeting in the preanaphoral

---

[91] R. C. D. Jasper and G. J. Cuming, *Prayers of the Eucharist: Early and Reformed, 3d rev. ed.* (New York: Pueblo Publishing Company, 1987). "English and American scholars at first tended to assign it to the second century, but it is now generally accepted as most probably having been written in the first century in Syria. P. J. Audet suggested that, when the *Didache* quotes sayings of Jesus, its version is earlier than that given in Matthew's gospel, which implies a date around A.D. 60," 20.

[92] Roswell D. Hitchcock and Francis Brown, ed., *Didache ton Dodeka Apostolon: Teaching of the Twelve Apostles* (New York: Charles Scribner's Sons, 1885), 8.

[93] Hitchcock and Brown, 18 & 20.

[94] Some scholars suggest Egypt as a possible provenance. For a detailed history of the theories of dating and provenance see Clayton N. Jefford, *The Sayings of Jesus in the Teaching of the Twelve Apostles* (New York: E. J. Brill, 1989).

dialogue or, for that matter, elsewhere."[95] The East preferred either the brief "Peace to all," which may appear in numerous places in the liturgy, or a longer greeting based on 2 Corinthians 13:14, "The grace of the Lord Jesus Christ and the love of God and the communion of the Holy Spirit be with you all." The biblical and theological meaning of the greeting "The Lord be with you" is located in the expression *Maranatha*. Jasper and Cuming point out:

> The Aramaic words *Marana tha* were interpreted by the early Fathers as meaning "The Lord has come," but they should probably be translated "Come, Lord," as in the parallel passages at the end of 1 Corinthians 16:22 and Revelation 22:20. In all three passages prayer is made for the grace of Christ, and it is possible that a liturgical closing formula is behind all three.[96]

The words *Lord, peace,* and *grace* say the same thing yet in different ways. Each adds a different element to the full gift which is always more than words can express. The intimate connection of the pastor with the giving out of the grace and peace of the Lord, and of the Lord himself, has already been seen in the quotes from chapter 4 of the *Didache*. Now in the text immediately following the Eucharistic Prayer the same emphasis is found again. Chapter 11 begins:

> Therefore, whoever comes and teaches you all these things of which were previously spoken, receive him; but if the teacher himself turn aside and teach another teaching, so as to overthrow this, do not listen to him; but if he teaches so as to promote righteousness and knowledge of the Lord, *receive him as the Lord* [emphasis mine].[97]

The *Didache* places great emphasis on the presence of the Spirit in the prophets who teach the things of the Lord. One way to check whether or not the prophet has the Spirit is to look at his life. If he behaves in a way morally incompatible with the ethics of The Two Ways, he manifests himself to be a false prophet and thus void of the Spirit. Chapter 11 continues:

---

[95] Taft, 309.
[96] Jasper and Cuming, 21.
[97] Hitchcock and Brown, 20.

> Now concerning the apostles and prophets, [deal with them] according to the ordinances of the Gospel. Every apostle who comes to you, let him be received as the Lord . . . [the text then alerts them to false prophets who will attempt to get financial/material benefits from the people]. And every prophet who speaks in the *Spirit* you shall try or judge; for every sin shall be forgiven, but this sin shall not be forgiven. But not everyone that speaks in the *Spirit* is a prophet, but only if he have the sayings of the Lord.[98]

The earliest surviving full text of the dialogue representing the Roman-Egyptian form with a eucharistic prayer is in the *Apostolic Tradition* (ca. 215). The *Apostolic Tradition* actually describes two eucharistic prayers; the first in connection with the ordination of a bishop and the second after a baptism. As it was in the *Didache*, so began the *Apostolic Tradition.* The early church believed it to be of great importance that her pastors-teachers were faithfully passing on the doctrines of the apostles and thus passing on Christ—present with his grace and peace. Even the choice of titles given to these church orders emphasized this: The Teaching of the *Twelve Apostles, Apostolic* Tradition, *Apostolic* Constitution, *Apostolic* Church Order, and Didascalia *Apostolorum.* The opening paragraph of the *Apostolic Tradition* established the importance of the Holy Spirit in the office and work of the bishop. "Since the Holy Spirit bestows perfect grace on those who believe rightly," it was very important that "those who preside over the Church should hand down and guard all things."

Chapter 2 describes the selection of the bishop ("chosen by all the people") and the laying on of hands (by the Presbytery) and then the prayer:

> And all shall keep silence, praying in their hearts for *the descent of the Spirit* [emphasis mine], after which one of the bishops . . . shall lay his hand on him who is being ordained bishop, and pray thus:[99]

The prayer which follows asks that the "God and Father of our Lord Jesus Christ" would bestow upon the bishop being ordained

---

[98] Hitchcock and Brown, 20.

[99] Geoffrey J. Cuming, *Hippolytus: A Text for Students with Introductions, Translations, Commentary and Notes* (Bramcote Notts, England: Grove Books, 1976), 8.

the same "princely Spirit" given to the Old Testament priests and the New Testament apostles.

> You foreordained from the beginning a race of righteous men from Abraham; you appointed princes and priests, and did not leave your sanctuary without a ministry . . . now pour forth that power which is from you, of the *princely Spirit*[100] [emphasis mine] which you granted through your beloved Son Jesus Christ to your holy apostles who established the Church in every place as your sanctuary, to the unceasing glory of your name.
>
> You who know the hearts of all, bestow upon this your servant, whom you have chosen for the episcopate, to feed our holy flock and to exercise the high-priesthood . . . and by the *spirit of the high-priesthood* to have the power to *forgive sins according to your command*. . . . [emphasis mine][101]

At the conclusion of the prayer, "all shall offer him the kiss of peace, greeting him," after which he begins the celebration of the Eucharist with the greeting, "The Lord be with you." The congregation responds, "And with your Spirit." Should *spiritu/pneumatos* be translated Spirit or spirit? Is it in reference to the Holy Spirit, the "princely Spirit," bestowed on the man ordained into the holy ministry, or is it simply referring to his spirit or soul? The former is certainly consistent with the thrust of the prayer and flows naturally from it. It allows the laity repeatedly to acknowledge and confess the doctrine of the holy ministry through a concrete and personal liturgical exchange with their pastor/bishop. It allows the people to receive and acknowledge the holy ministry as a gift from the Holy Spirit.

Chrysostom, Theodore, and Narsai

The use of *spirit* in the dialogue is both ancient and universal. That the Fathers understood *pneumatos* in its fuller Spirit-filled sense is demonstrated by the explanations offered by Chrysostom, Theodore of Mopsuestia, and Narsai of Nisibis. In a sermon preached in the presence of Bishop Flavian of Antioch, Chrysostom

---

[100] LXX, Psalm 50(51):14, *pneumati hegemonikoi*. English translations follow the Hebrew of 51:14 וְרוּחַ נְדִיבָה "steadfast" or "willing spirit."

[101] Cuming, *Hippolytus*, 9.

(ca. 345–407) explained "that if there were no Holy Spirit there would be no pastors or teachers, who became so only through the Spirit." He then continues:

> If the Holy Spirit were not in this common father or teacher [Bishop Flavian] when he *gave the peace* to all shortly before ascending to his holy sanctuary, you would not have *replied to him all together, "And to your Spirit." This is why you reply with this expression* not only when he ascends to the sanctuary, nor when he preaches to you, nor when he prays for you, but when he stands at this holy altar, when he is about to offer this awesome sacrifice. You don't first partake of the offerings until he has prayed for you the grace from the Lord, and you have answered him, *"And with your spirit,"* reminding yourselves by this reply that he who is here does nothing of his own power, nor are the offered gifts the work of human nature, but it is *the grace of the Spirit present and hovering over all things which prepared that mystic sacrifice.*[102] (emphasis mine)

The statement "when he gave the peace" refers to the opening greeting in the East, "Peace be with you." It is noteworthy that the peace is not "wished upon" or "acknowledged," but "given."[103] Theodore of Mopsuestia (ca. 350–428) clearly expresses a similar understanding in a sermon.

> But it is *not the soul* they are referring to by this "And with your spirit," but it is the *grace of the Holy Spirit* by which those con-

---

[102] *De sancta Pentecoste hom.* 1,4. *PG* 62, 659.

[103] Writing in 1976, Johannes H. Emminghaus speaks of the greeting as proclamation. "The congregation's answer is literally 'And with your Spirit.' From a purely philogical standpoint, the phrase is simply a Semitic expression of 'And also with you.' 'And also with you' is the translation that has been adopted by the official English Missal. When the German Missal was being redacted, it was frequently suggested that this simpler everyday form be used, but it was finally decided not to use it on the grounds that it would impoverish the meaning of the greeting. Just as the president's greeting is not simply an expression of his personal good will and readiness to communicate with the congregation, but is a proclamation of salvation in the name of Christ, so too the congregation is not responding to an individual person with a human function but to a minister who is a 'servant of Christ and steward of the mysteries of God' (1 Cor. 4:1). The greeting and response help form a human community, but this community itself is oriented toward 'the presence of the Lord to his assembled community' (GI, no. 28)." J. Emminghaus, *The Eucharist: Essence, Form, Celebration*, trans. Matthew J. O'Connell from *Die Messe: Wesen-Gestalt-Vollzug*, 1978 (Collegeville: The Liturgical Press, 1988), 114–115.

> fided to his [the bishop's] care believe he had access to the priesthood.[104] (emphasis mine)

Narsai of Nisibis (d.ca. 502) indicates that "spirit" was understood as pertaining to the Spirit received by those in the Holy Ministry. He writes,

> The people answer the priest lovingly and say: "With thee, O priest, and with that priestly spirit of thine." They call "spirit," not that soul which is in the priest, but the Spirit which the priest has received by the laying on of hands. By the laying on of hands the priest receives the power of the Spirit, that thereby he may be able to perform the divine Mysteries. That grace the people call the "Spirit" of the priest, and they pray that he may attain peace with it, and it with him. This makes known that even the priest stands in need of prayer, and it is necessary that the whole church should intercede for him. Therefore she (the Church) cries out that he may gain peace with his Spirit, that through his peace the peace of all her children may be increased; for by his virtue he greatly benefits the whole Church, and by his depravity he greatly harms the whole community . . .[105]

Contemporary English Translations

Should *spiritu/pneumatos* be translated *Spirit* or *spirit?* Is it in reference to the Holy Spirit promised to the ordained minister or is it simply referring to his spirit or soul? The early liturgies and Fathers opt for the former. Contemporary English revisions, however, go with the latter interpretation of spirit. The result is twofold: (1) the episcopal greeting is emptied of any freight pointing to the uniqueness of the office of the holy ministry in the word and sacrament liturgical life of the Church; (2) the word (S)spirit is replaced with the pronoun *you.* Again, the uniformity of address blurs the distinction between the role of the pastor who speaks in the stead and by the command of the

---

104 Theodore of Mopsuestia, *Hom.* 15, 37.

105 Narsi, *"Homilae et Carmina," An Exposition of the Mysteries* (Hom. 17), 277. English Translation in R. H. Connolly, ed., *The Liturgical Homilies of Narsai* (London: Cambridge University Press, 1909), 8–9. See also Kent A. Heimbigner, "The Relation of the Celebration of the Lord's Supper to the Office of the Holy Ministry" (S.T.M. thesis, Concordia Seminary, St. Louis, 1991).

incarnate, crucified, risen and present Lord Jesus Christ. The pastor cannot do this without the gift of the Holy Spirit. Such is recognized by the Prayer for the Ordination of a Bishop in the Apostolic Tradition—that God would now pour forth the same power "of the *princely Spirit*," which he granted to his holy apostles "to establish the Church in every place as our sanctuary." The prayer for the spirit of high-priesthood is prayed in order that the bishop would be able

> to have the power to forgive sins according to your command, to confer orders according to your bidding, to loose every bond according to the power which you gave to the apostles.[106]

There is little doubt that "your command" is in reference to John 20. The Lord's Word's of Institution of the Office of the Holy Ministry in John 20:19–23, though brief, contain the chief and necessary elements: the risen Lord, the giving of peace with God, the risen lord truly present in his flesh, the sending by the Lord, the receiving of the Holy Spirit from Jesus, and the power to forgive and retain sins. On these elements the Church was and continues to be built (cf. Matthew 16:13–20).

The decision to translate (or paraphrase) *et cum spiritu tuo* as "And also with you" has often been justified on the basis that the original expression was a Semitism. This view was repeated by such scholars as Adrian Fortescue, Joseph Jungmann, and Pius Parsch.[107] Theodore Klauser's influential book helped to foster the view in English-speaking circles.[108] As late as 1990, the *Commentary on the Lutheran Book of Worship* perpetuated this interpretation with the brief notation, "Most [scholars] understand it as a Semitism meaning simply the person, 'you.'"[109] Even if it

---

[106] Cuming, 9.

[107] Adrian Fortescue, *The Mass: A Study of the Roman Liturgy* (London: Longmans, Green and Co, 1st ed. 1912, 11th ed. 1955), 246. Joseph Jungmann, *The Mass of the Roman Rite: Its Origins and Development*, vol. 1 (New York: Benziger Brothers, Inc. 1950) trans. Francis A. Brunner, 19. Pius Parsch, *The Liturgy of the Mass* (London: B. Herder, 3d ed., 1957), trans. & adapted by H. E. Winstons, 122.

[108] Theodor Klauser, *A Short History of the Western Liturgy*, trans. John Halliburton, (Oxford: Oxford University Press, 1979), 6.

[109] Philip P. Pfatteicher, *Commentary on* LBW, 158.

were true that the original Hebrew expression simply carried the meaning of the person "you," the fact remains that it took on new theological and liturgical meaning for the early Christians when they gathered for the Eucharist around their bishop in Jesus' name. Jesus began with just another celebration of the Passover meal, but the Lord of the Sabbath made of it a new meal, a new testament. Similarly, nothing remains the same when incorporated into the Lord's meal. "And with your Spirit" may come in as an everyday greeting, but it is transformed by its usage in a meal that is unlike any other meal.

Still, the question remains: Is *Et cum spiritu tuo* simply a Semitism? Robert Taft takes deadly aim at this popular opinion.

> Today it is taken to be no more than a Semitism for "And also with you." But there is no philological basis for this demonstrable misconception. In Semitic texts it is soul *(nephes,* Syriac *naphso = psuche*), not spirit (*ruah,* Syriac *ruho = pneuma*), that bears this meaning. Agreement on this point among both biblical and knowledgeable liturgical commentators is universal. [Taft quotes van Unnik, Botte, Ashworth, and P.-M Gy.] Furthermore, the Semites themselves whom one might expect to recognize a Semitism when they see it, did not take it to be one. [Taft quotes Botte's *Dominus vobiscum,* p. 37.] The Liturgy of Addai and Mari, oldest and most Semitic of the Semitic liturgies, has the response: "with you and with your spirit." That would be ridiculously tautological if both meant the same thing. So what we have here is not a Semitism but a "Paulinism" that has become a "Christianism," as Botte put it. [Botte, *Dominus vobiscum,* 34 ff.][110]

In the East Syrian tradition the *Dominus vobiscum* took the form of *pax vobiscum* and the congregational response was "And with you and your spirit." This full pre-anaphoral dialogue in Addai and Mari finds corroboration in the fifth-century sermon of Narsai on the liturgy.[111] Narsai interprets the meaning of the Addai and Mari

---

[110] Taft, 320–321.

[111] Bryan Spinks, *Addai and Mari: The Anaphora of the Apostles: A Text for Students,* Grove Liturgical Study 24 (Bramcote Notts, England: Grove Books, 1980). See also L. Edward Phillips, "The Kiss of Peace and the Opening Greeting of the Pre-Anaphoral Dialogue," *Studia Liturgica* 23, no. 2 (1993), 183.

response as follows: "They [the people] call 'spirit,' not that soul which is in the priest, but the Spirit which the priest has received by the laying on of hands."[112] No tautology here.

All of this is not to suggest that only those ordained into the Holy Ministry possess the Holy Spirit or that they receive more of him. The Holy Spirit is not a liquid that can be measured out. To have the Spirit is to have the whole Spirit. The Holy Spirit, however, is given to the ordained with the special promise that when they preach repentance and forgiveness and loose sins in Holy Absolution, he is there accomplishing that of which his Word speaks. Whether or not the Spirit dwells in all Christians is not the question. He does (Rom. 8:9–11). The questions are: Does *pneumatos* refer to more than simply a person's selfhood? Does it in the case of those ordained into the Holy Ministry refer to the Spirit-filled spirit, reflecting John 20:22?

The Biblical Meaning of the "Lord Being With a Person"

In short, what does the greeting mean? Robert Taft observes that "Several authorities, most thoroughly W. C. van Unnik, have examined its pristine biblical and Roman-Egyptian liturgical form, '(The) Lord with you (thee).'"[113] It is ironic that Taft would find the most thorough biblical resource from a Dutch Reformed scholar. Van Unnik's exegetical study was precipitated by the new service book of the Dutch Reformed Church, which introduced the ancient dialogue ("The Lord be with you," "And with thy Spirit." "Let us pray.") as an introduction to prayer. Van Unnik writes:

> To Roman Catholic, Anglican and Lutheran Christians it is a familiar part of the liturgy, because it belongs to the age-old heritage of Latin Christianity. As such it was taken over by the committee which prepared the revision of the Dutch Reformed Liturgy.[114]

---

[112] Quoted from Norman Nagel, "Holy Communion," 316, n. 7. I am indebted to Norman Nagel whose commentary on the response "And with your Spirit" in this companion volume to *Lutheran Worship* alerted me to the richness of the ancient usage of "Spirit." See pages 291–292.

[113] Taft, 316. Taft is referring to van Unnik's article "Dominus vobiscum: The Background of the Liturgical Formula," in *Sparsa Collecta: The Collected Essays of W. C. van Unnik*, Part III Supplements *Novum Testamentum*, 31 (Leiden: E. J. Brill, 1983), 362–391.

[114] Van Unnik, 362.

> [Van Unnik explains] I have consulted many books and various experts, but did not receive a satisfactory answer; it seemed as though this formula is so customary and revered that nobody asks for its proper meaning.[115]

Van Unnik notes that the phrasing of the salutation raises many important questions, the most crucial being, "What is contained in this 'to be with somebody,' when said of the Lord?"[116] Van Unnik does not limit himself to an examination of the small number of texts usually quoted in which "the Lord with you" is used in the context of a greeting from Judges or Ruth, or even from an apostolic greeting. He begins with the dominical promise in Matthew 28. He acknowledges that

> It goes without saying that the Bible and the Christian Church firmly believe in God's transcendence. God is in heaven and Jesus who was once on earth is now at the right hand of the Father in heaven (Eph. 1:20). But what did Jesus promise to His disciples when he said, "And lo, I *am with you* always, even unto the end of the world" (Matt. 28:20)?[117]

Καὶ ἰδοὺ always alerts the hearer that "something extraordinary and unexpected" is to follow. A promise is then given to the eleven disciples (see 28:16). It is common to jump immediately to the church "as the locus of the presence of Christ during the interval between his resurrection and *parousia*."[118] Broadly speaking, it is true that the promise is given to the church; however, van Unnik's exegetical treatment is more precise. He asks,

> But is it not, I dare ask, *loose* thinking? Are we to credit the early Christians who so clearly knew about Jesus' separation from the earth and His glorification in heaven, with such a conflicting view? On the other hand, Jesus does not speak to the church (a word Matthew knows), but to the apostles as missionaries. The

---

[115] Van Unnik, 364.
[116] Van Unnik, 364.
[117] Van Unnik, 365.
[118] Van Unnik, 365.

use of the word "locus" suggests a static presence while, as will appear from the following pages, Jesus' "being with them" has quite different associations.[119]

A study of the meaning of "God being with a person" in Peter's speech (Acts 10:38), Stephen's sermon (Acts 7:9ff.) and Nicodemus's visit with Jesus (John 3:2), demonstrates that this "being with" is: (1) located in a person, (2) an active, not static presence, and (3) connected with the Holy Spirit. A study of the phrase (that God or the Lord is with a person) in the Old Testament reveals the same understanding. Van Unnik locates no less than 102 Old Testament references,[120] from which he makes ten "remarkable observations." The list includes:

> (2) The verb "to be" is sometimes used, sometimes left out. It is deployed in all three tenses . . . The Lord's help was there in the past, is experienced in the present and will be there in the future. In past present it can be seen. As to future it is not always formulated as a wish, but *mostly as a definite declaration.* [emphasis mine]
> (3) Frequent though the expression is, it occurs only twice in greetings viz. Judges 6:12 and Ruth 2:4, the usual greeting-form being: "Peace." . . .
> (6) In some places the term is given in the form of a wish. [Yet, in its usage i]t is important to see that this note of certainty about the future help and blessing is far stronger than the subjective forms of wish and possibility. . . .
>
> (9) . . . In the large majority of texts the term is used of *individuals*, and even where the people is meant it is sometimes individualized. . . . The line does not go from the people as a whole to the individual, but rather the other way. It is not applied to every pious man in general, but to very *special persons*. . . . It is often mentioned in connection with a special divine task, in which the particular man is assured of God's assistance . . . the man is afraid to accept the task, because he has no strength in himself. . . .
> (10) Here we come to a point that is of vital importance for the exact and full understanding of the expression. *Most of the individ-*

[119] Van Unnik, 365.
[120] Van Unnik, 388, n. 37 lists all 102 references.

> *uals of whom it is declared that "God was with them" were specially endowed with the Spirit of God.*[121] [emphasis van Unnik's]

Van Unnik then turns his attention to numerous New Testament texts and concludes:

> In reviewing these texts from the NT we discover that in light of the OT usage they receive their full force. The phrase is like a short-hand note. At face value it does not seem of great importance and is therefore passed over in the commentaries. On closer inspection, however, it turns out that the NT authors themselves would understand it as well. They did not use an outworn phrase, but wrote it down as expressing a self-evident truth. There is a marked difference here from later Judaism. In its humble wording it contains the fullness and certitude of the Christian faith.[122]

Apostolic Greetings

Paul ends his letter to the Galatians with the greeting "The grace of our Lord Jesus Christ be with your spirit, brethren. Amen." (Ἡ χάρις . . . . μετὰ τοῦ πνεύματος ὑμῶν). For Paul the word *spirit* means more than simply *you.* Taft concludes:

> Paul does not define spirit, but sets it opposition to the letter (Rom. 2:29, 7:6; 2 Cor. 3:6, 8), the flesh (Gal. 3:3, 6:8; Rom. 8:4–6, 9, 13; 2 Cor. 7:1; Col. 2:5), the body (Rom. 8:10–11; 1 Cor. 5:3–5, 7:34) human wisdom (1 Cor. 2:13). So it seems difficult to deny a special Pauline nuance to "And with your spirit," a reference not just to oneself but to one's better, Christian, Spirit-filled self.[123]

Et cum spiritu tuo not a Semitism

A recent publication prepared by the International Commission on English in the Liturgy acknowledges that it is now "generally accepted that [*Et cum spiritu tuo*] is not a Semitism but a Christian-

---

121 Van Unnik, 371–373.

122 Van Unnik, 381.

123 Taft, 318. Taft is quoting B. Eager, "The Lord Is with You," *Scripture* 12 (1960), 48–54.

ism based on the Pauline use of *pneuma* where the spirit is [to quote Bernard Botte] '*la partie spirituelle de l'homme le plus apparentée à Dieu, object immediat des actions et des influences divines. . . .*'"[124]

The replacing of the response "And with your Spirit" with "And also with you" came at a time of unprecedented liturgical revision within the Lutheran and Anglican communions and even greater change within the Roman Catholic Church. In 1970 the International Consultation on English Texts (ICET) suggested the appropriate translation of the greeting and response would be: "The Spirit of the Lord be with you," "And also with you."[125] Thomas Krosnicki explains:

> The reason ICET did not translate *spiritu* in the people's response was given; "If 'Spirit' is used in the greeting, it need not be used in the response." In light of the comments that resulted from the use of the initial ICET translation of the greeting, in 1972 the English was changed to: "The Lord be with you." It should be noted, however, that the people's response remained unchanged (without explicit reference to the spirit) although the original argument for its omission by ICET was no longer valid. The 1975 ICET translation follows the 1972 text without additional comment or explanation.[126]

The new ICET response found its way into the English liturgies of the Roman Catholic, Lutheran, and Anglican churches during the 1970s and 1980s. The Inter-Lutheran Commission on Worship accepted the new ICET text, and thus it found its way into the *Lutheran Book of Worship* and *Lutheran Worship*. *Lutheran Worship* and the new Episcopal *Common Book of Prayer* included both forms.

The introduction of van Unnik's essay "*Dominus Vobiscum*" included a tender quotation from the German liturgical reformer Wilhelm Löhe, who wrote (1853), "sich jedesmal der Knoten der Liebe und Eintracht zwischen Pfarrer und Gemeinde aufs Neue

---

[124] Thomas A. Krosnicki, "Grace and Peace: Greeting the Assembly," *Shaping English Liturgy: Studies in Honor of Archbishop Denis Hurley*, ed. Peter C. Finn and James M. Schellman (Washington, D.C: The Pastoral Press, 1990). The quote is originally attributed to C. Spicq, *Les epitres pastorales* (Paris: 1947), 397.

[125] Krosnicki, 98.

[126] Krosnicki, 98. The reader is referred to the International Consultation on English Texts, *Prayers We Have in Common* (Philadelphia: Fortress Press, 1970, 1972, 1975).

schürzt" (Every time [the greeting and response is exchanged] the knot of love and unity between the pastor and congregation is tied anew). Mere Semitic greetings do not elicit such profound and intimate descriptions of the church and ministry.

The ambiguity of the words "Spirit," "spirit," and "Lord," plus the variety of greetings, "The Lord be with you," "Peace be with you," and "Grace and peace be with you all," simply serve to compound the richness of its meaning. Norman Nagel writes:

> The terms Lord, grace, and peace are all interchangeable, and yet not equitable. Each says the same thing, and something more that is its special freight. "Peace be with you" confesses the risen Lord as the one who is among us. "Grace" tells of God's favor where Jesus is welcomed and confessed as Lord. "This world passes away" [Didache] echoes Matthew 24:35, "Heaven and earth will pass away, but my words will never pass away."[127]

It is remarkable that this change could take place with hardly a whimper of objection. The dialogue with the greeting and response is among the oldest parts of the liturgy, yet old age and continual use offer no guarantee that a text will be understood or appreciated today.

Without question, the major objections to the liturgical reforms centered on the addition of eucharistic prayers to the liturgical texts of the pew and minister's editions. An examination of eucharistic prayer deserves fuller treatment. Chapter 6 will deal exclusively with this topic.

---

[127] Nagel, 316, n. 4.

6

The Eucharistic Prayer

INCONGRUITY between worship as God's work and the work of the people became most evident with the introduction of the Eucharist Prayer by the ILCW. These inverse theologies of worship have been recognized by those preparing *Lutheran Worship: History and Practice.*

> Ceremonies must be viewed in light of their integral relationship to the doctrine of worship (*Gottesdienst*). This immediately exposes the conflict that exists between the theology of worship held by Luther and confessed in the Lutheran Confessions and that theology articulated by the many adherents of the contemporary Liturgical Movement.[1]

Author John Pless continues:

> A number of voices within recent history of American Lutheranism have called for a liturgical theology that not only supersedes the position of Luther and the Lutheran Confessions but stands in contradiction to them. . . . the Lutheran Confessions take great pains to distinguish man's actions from God's action in the liturgy.[2]

---

[1] John Pless, "The Leaders of Worship," in *Lutheran Worship: History and Practice*, ed. Fred L. Precht (St. Louis: Concordia Publishing House, 1993), 228. The quote includes a footnote which reads: "for examples of this theology within American Lutheranism see Eugene Brand, *The Rite Thing* (Minneapolis: Augsburg Publishing House, 1970), and Frank Senn, *The Pastor as Worship Leader* (Minneapolis: Augsburg Publishing House, 1977). For a well-argued critique see Oliver Olson, 'Contemporary Trends in Liturgy Viewed from the Perspective of Classical Lutheran Theology,' *The Lutheran Quarterly* XXVI/2 (May 1974): 110–157."

[2] Pless, 228. Reference is made to The Apology of the Augsburg Confession, Article IV, paragraphs 154 and 310; Martin Luther's "Admonition Concerning the Sacrament," *Luther's*

Pless observes that this conflict is a result of viewing worship as man's work rather than God's work. He quotes "a key spokesman for contemporary liturgical scholarship within American Lutheranism," who writes:

> Liturgical renewal among Lutherans shares goals similar to those of other communions: restoration of significant practices of mainstream Western Catholicism, expressing the interrelation of worship and mission, recovering the spirit of joy and celebration in the Eucharist, *grasping the mystery that God's work and man's work are indistinguishable*."[3] (emphasis Pless's)

Pless points to the Eucharist Prayer and offertory procession in the *Lutheran Book of Worship* as prime examples of this difference.

> This seems to have ritual expression in the *Lutheran Book of Worship* where, in the Sacrament of the Altar, the Words of Institution become part of the prayers of the gathered congregation. The actions of the congregation cannot be easily distinguished from the testamental Word of the Lord who is himself host at the supper. The Lutheran emphasis on the receptivity of faith is masked by the action of the believer as the presiding minister prays: "Therefore, gracious Father, with this bread and cup we remember the life our Lord offered for us."[4]

The fusion of God's work with man's work is consistent with post-Vatican II Roman Catholic liturgical theology, which puts a new spin on the old description of sacraments as "outward signs that give grace."

> Remember, however, that these "signs" are not just items such as water, bread and wine, but the actions we do with such items. We pour or enter into the water, share the bread, drink wine, anoint

Works, American Edition (AE) (St. Louis: Concordia Publishing House and Philadelphia: Fortress Press, 1957–86), 38: 106–107; the Formula of Concord's use of *actio* in Bjarne W. Teigen's, *The Lord's Supper in the Theology of Martin Chemnitz* (Brewster, MA: Trinity Lutheran Press, 1986), 182–184.

[3] Pless, 228, quoting Eugene Brand, "Lutheran Worship," in *The Westminster Dictionary of Worship*, 251.

[4] Pless, 228. Pless draws the quote from *LBW*, page 70.

> with oil. It is these actions, experienced reverently by a people of faith, that reveal the divine presence of God with us and for us . . . . They are not simply actions of a heavenly or invisible Jesus, but actions of his mystical body called the Church. It might be helpful to think of the Church as the first of all sacraments.[5]

Concerning the underlying premise of *LBW,* Pless writes:

> Having the premise that the liturgy is the Church's action, the formulators of the *Lutheran Book of Worship*, not surprisingly, reinstituted two ceremonies specifically rejected by Luther and the Lutheran Confessions: an offertory procession where the bread and wine are ritually offered at the altar, and a Prayer of Great Thanksgiving which incorporates the Verba.[6]

Pless then offers the following prescient quote from Luther:

> We must sharply distinguish the testament and sacrament itself from the prayers which we offer at the same time. Not only this, but we must also bear in mind that the prayers avail utterly nothing, either to him who offers them or to those for whom they are offered, unless the testament is first received in faith, so that it will be faith that offers the prayers; for faith alone is heard, as James teaches in his first chapter (James 1:6). There is therefore a great difference between prayer and the mass. Prayer may be extended to as many persons as one desires, while the mass is received only by the person who believes for himself, and only to the extent that he believes. It cannot be given either to God or to men. Rather it is God alone who through the ministration of the priest gives it to men, and men receive it by faith alone without any works or merits. Nor would anyone dare to be so foolish as to assert that a ragged beggar does a good work when he comes to receive a gift from a rich man. But the mass (as I have said) is a gift of divine promise, proffered to all men by the hand of the priest.[7]

The inclusion of the Eucharistic Prayer in the liturgical texts of American Lutheranism began with the *Service Book and Hymnal*

---

[5] James T. Telthorst, "Actions That Unite Us to Jesus," *St. Lewis Review: Weekly Newspaper of the Archdiocese of St. Louis.* (September 18, 1992), 10.

[6] Pless, 228.

[7] AE 36:50–51.

(1958). Eucharistic prayers of various types (containing praise, anamnesis, and epiclesis, but not the Verba) appeared in the Lutheran sphere as early as 1522 in the German liturgy of Kantz, the Strasbourg Order (1525), and Pfalz Neuburg (1543).

> The Agenda of the Lutheran Church in Bavaria, 1879, provided three such prayers, one of which was to be used following the preface and sanctus and before the Words of Institution. A similar procedure was followed in the "Massbok" of the Church of Sweden, 1942.[8]

It would not be until 1936 that the first eucharist prayer would be composed in which the Verba were contained within the prayer context. This text was "originally proposed by Paul Z. Strodach, and was later adopted, with some changes," in the *Book of Worship* of the Lutheran Churches in India.[9]

Lutheran Worship includes two prayers of thanksgiving. The prayer in Divine Service I is based on the Pre- and Post-Verba prayers in *Agenda I* (1957) of the United Evangelical Lutheran Church of Germany (VELKD). The prayer in Divine Service II is adapted from the prayer from the Swedish *Kyrko-Handboken* (1942).[10] Neither of the prayers contain a specific prayer of anamnesis or epiclesis. In both cases, the prayers are placed immediately prior to the Lord's Prayer and are clearly separated from the Verba. As early as 1979, Armand J. Boehme made the observation:

> Though there was a struggle over the adoption of the Eucharistic Prayer in the *Service Book and Hymnal*, the real theological struggle concerning Eucharist Prayers did not begin in American Lutheranism until the work of the Inter-Lutheran Commission of Worship (ILCW), which produced the *Lutheran Book of Worship* (*LBW*). Arguments began in earnest in 1970 after Contemporary Worship II . . . was issued by the ILCW. From 1970 to 1975 only ALC and LCA theologians seemed concerned about the dangers to

---

[8] Frank C. Senn, ed., *New Eucharistic Prayers: An Ecumenical Study of Their Development and Structure* (New York: Paulist Press, 1987), 3–4.

[9] Luther D. Reed, *The Lutheran Liturgy*, Revised Edition (Philadelphia: Fortress Press, 1959), 756.

[10] Charles J. Evanson, "The Service of the Sacrament," in *LW: History and Practice*, 425.

> grace and justification brought about by the liturgical innovations of the ILCW. In 1973, three LCA/ALC seminary faculties formally objected to the doctrinal changes present in the ILCW Communion liturgy. Since 1975, LCMS theologians have also begun to write about the ILCW/*LBW* liturgies.[11]

The liturgical scholars of The Lutheran Church—Missouri Synod and the Synod of Evangelical Lutheran Churches were also moving toward the adoption of eucharistic prayers. The *Worship Supplement* (1969) included five eucharistic prayers.[12] The contents of the *WS* reflect the work of the Missouri Synod and SELC in revising *The Lutheran Hymnal* of 1941. It would receive limited experimental use in some congregations and on college and seminary campuses. With the formation of the Inter-Lutheran Commission on Worship in 1966, the experimental *Contemporary Worship* series would quickly overshadow the *WS*. In 1970, the ILCW published *Contemporary Worship 2*. The booklet included a eucharistic prayer which would be revised and eventually find its way into the *Lutheran Book of Worship* pew edition as option I.

The ILCW would ultimately provide four eucharistic prayers for use with *LBW*; however, optional prayers II, III, and IV would only appear in *LBW Altar Book* and *Ministers Desk Edition*. Only option I would appear in the pew edition, and thus become the most popular prayer. *CW 2* offered only one eucharistic prayer with no option for using only the Verba. This was reluctantly granted in *LBW Pew Edition* with the further option to use the bare Verba or to use a brief prayer from the Swedish Massbook (1942) to which the con-

---

[11] Armand J. Boehme, "Sing A New Song: The Doctrine of Justification and the *Lutheran Book of Worship* Sacramental Liturgies," *Concordia Theological Quarterly* 43, no. 2 (1979):97. For further information on the struggle over the inclusion of the Eucharist Prayer in the *SBH*, Boehme refers the reader to the Minutes of the 16th Biennial Convention of the ULC (1948), 444, and the Minutes of the Central Pennsylvania Synod for May 25, 1949. "The three seminaries were Luther Theological Seminary, St. Paul, Minn. (ALC), whose faculty wrote the formal objections; Southern Theological Seminary (LCA), Columbia, S.C.; and Lutheran Theological Seminary (Mt. Airy—LCA), Philadelphia, Pa.," 104, n. 14. For an extensive list of the ALC/LCA articles on the Eucharist Prayer prior to 1975 and those of the LCMS after 1975 see 104–106, notes 13 and 15.

[12] The *Worship Supplement* identified the source of three of the Eucharistic Prayers: "El Culto Christiano" (45), "Cambridge" (46), and "Hippolytus" (46–47).

Chart of Origins and Development of Eucharistic Prayers

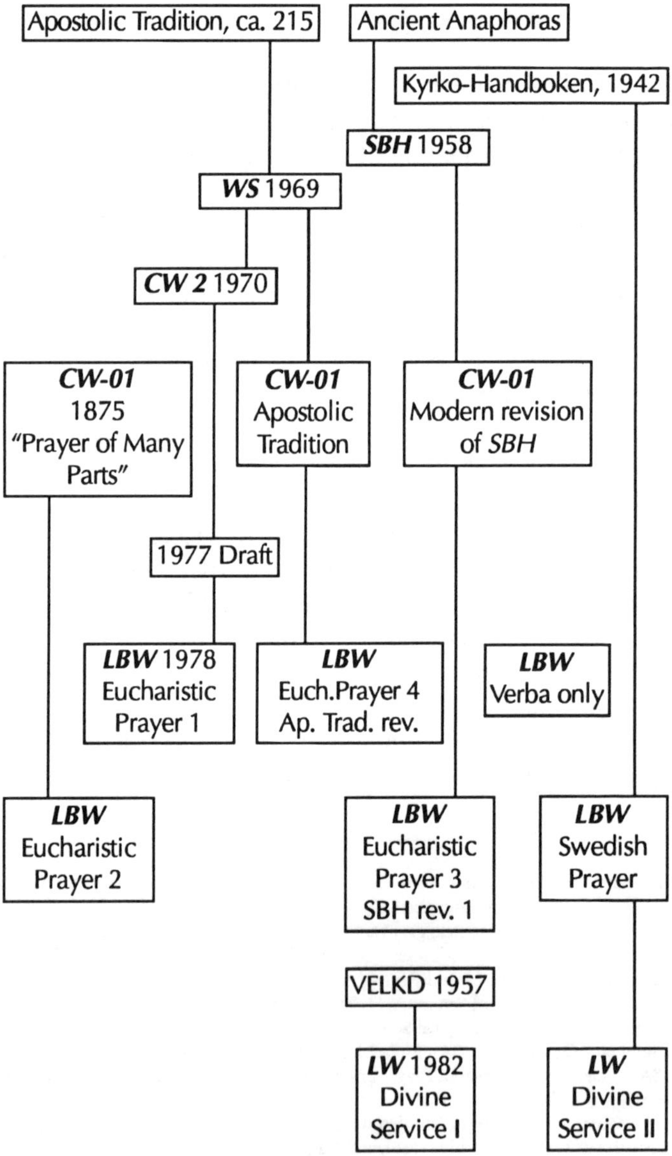

gregation responds, "Amen, Come, Lord Jesus." Then follow the Verba, which are clearly distinguished from the preceding prayer by the congregational response.

For over 1,500 years the Roman rite had only one anaphora and only in later years a small number of prefaces. One of the most significant results of Vatican II was "the expansion of the corpus of prefaces to well over eighty and the addition of three general eucharistic prayers, three eucharistic prayers for children, and two eucharistic prayers on the theme of reconciliation."[13] A comparison of the structure of the Roman Catholic Eucharistic Prayer II with that of Eucharist Prayer option I in *LBW* reveals that they are identical except for one difference. The Roman rite has two epiclesis prayers.

> One before the Institution Narrative which asks that through the action of the Holy Spirit the bread and wine may become the body and blood of Christ, and the other after the *anamnesis* which asks the Spirit to transform those who share in the body and blood of the Lord. The first epiclesis is consecratory and the second sanctificatory.[14]

Contemporary Worship 2 included a double epiclesis; however, they are placed together and come immediately after the congregational response, "Amen, Come, Lord Jesus." The text and rubric in *CW 2* read: Send the power of your Holy Spirit upon us (He extends his hands over the bread and wine) and upon this bread and wine . . . [15] The *LBW* revision of this anaphora eliminated the offensive epiclesis of consecration and retained the sanctificatory epiclesis on the people immediately after the anamnesis. However, optional prayers III and IV include the double epiclesis.[16]

---

[13] Alan F. Detscher, "The Eucharistic Prayers of the Roman Catholic Church," in *New Eucharistic Prayers: An Ecumenical Study of their Development and Structure*, ed. Frank C. Senn (New York: Paulist Press, 1987), 15.

[14] Detsher, 29–30.

[15] *Contemporary Worship 2*, 17.

[16] *LBW*, 225–226. Option III reads: ". . . we implore you . . . with your Word and Holy Spirit, to bless us, your servants, and these your own gifts of bread and wine . . . ." Option IV reads: "And we ask you: Send your Spirit upon these gifts of our Church . . . fill us with your Holy Spirit . . . ."

Structure of Roman Catholic Eucharistic Prayer II
Compared with
***Lutheran Book of Worship*, Optional Prayer I**

Eucharistic Prayer II	***LBW* Optional Prayer I**
Dialogue	Dialogue
Preface	Preface
Sanctus	Sanctus
Post-Sanctus	Post-Sanctus
(Epiclesis I)	
Institution Narrative	Institution Narrative
Memorial Acclamation	Memorial Acclamation
Anamnesis	Anamnesis
Epiclesis II	Epiclesis
Intercessions	Intercessions
Doxology	Doxology

In *LBW*, the Sanctus has rendered "Lord, God of Sabaoth" with "Lord, God of power and might." Lost is the reference to the awesome heavenly angels that surround the throne in the prophet's commissioning (Isaiah 6). Rendering "Sabaoth" with "power and might" is "not a false idea, but one which loses entirely the personal vividness of the original."[17] Both the Roman Catholic Eucharist Prayer II and *LBW* option I continue with the Post-Sanctus, which echoes the theme of the Sanctus and leads into the "ritual thanksgiving of the institution narrative and the actions with the bread and cup."[18] The text of *LBW* option 1 appears as follows (Post-Sanctus through Doxology):

[17] Horace D. Hummel, "Angels: Especially in the Old Testament," *The Bride of Christ* 15, no. 4 (1991): 6. Hummel observes that the spelling "Sabaoth" is often confused by the uninstructed with "Sabbath." "If 'Sebaoth' is retained (and understood!) it is one of our explicit liturgical reminders that the Christian community understands itself in union and continuity with also the faithful of the Old Testament," 6.

[18] *LBW*, 162. See also Detscher, 29.

Post-Sanctus

Ⓟ Holy God, mighty Lord,
gracious Father:
Endless is your mercy
and eternal your reign.

You have filled all creation
with light and life;
heaven and earth
are full of your glory.

Through Abraham you promised
to bless all nations.
You rescued Israel,
your chosen people.

Through the prophets
you renewed your promise;
and, at this end of all the ages,
you sent your Son,
who in words and deeds
proclaimed your kingdom
and was obedient to your will,
even to giving his life.

Institution Narrative

In the night
in which he was betrayed,
our Lord Jesus took bread,
and gave thanks; broke it,
and gave it to his disciples,
saying: Take and eat;
this is my body, given for you.
Do this for the remembrance of me.
Again, after supper,
he took the cup, gave thanks,
and gave it for all to drink,
saying: This cup is
the new covenant in my blood,
shed for you and for all people
for the forgiveness of sin.
Do this for the remembrance of me.
For as often as we eat
of this bread
and drink from this cup,
we proclaim the Lord's death,
until he comes.

Memorial Acclamation

C Christ has died. Christ is risen.
Christ will come again.

Anamnesis

P Therefore, gracious Father,
with this bread and cup
we remember the life
our Lord offered for us.

And, believing the witness
of his resurrection,
we await his coming in power
to share with us
the great and promised feast.
C **Amen. Come, Lord Jesus.**

Epiclesis

P Send now, we pray,
your Holy Spirit,
the spirit of our Lord
and of his resurrection,
that we who receive
the Lord's body and blood
may live to the praise
of your glory
and receive our inheritance
with all your saints in light.
C **Amen. Come, Lord Jesus.**

Intercessions

P Join our prayer
with those of your servants
of every time and every place,
and unite them with the ceaseless petitions
of our great high priest
until he comes
as victorious Lord of all.

Doxology (sung)

C **Through him, with him, in him, in the unity of the Holy Spirit, all honor and glory is yours, almighty Father, now and forever. Amen.**

Then follows the Lord's Prayer, after which the congregation sits. At this point rubric 34 (71) reads: "The COMMUNION follows. The bread may be broken for distribution." Then rubric 35 (71) immediately follows, which reads:

> The presiding minister and the assisting ministers receive the bread and wine and then give them to those who come to receive. As the ministers give the bread and wine, they say these words to each communicant: The body of Christ, given for you. The blood of Christ, shed for you.

The *Lutheran Worship* revision of the *Lutheran Book of Worship* is more precise. Rubric 29 (151) reads:

> The DISTRIBUTION. The minister and those who assist him receive the body and blood of Christ first and then distribute them to those who come to receive, saying: Take eat, this is the true body of our Lord and Savior Jesus Christ, given into death for your sins. Take drink; this is the true blood of our Lord and Savior Jesus Christ, shed for the forgiveness of your sins. (or) Take, eat, this is the very body of Christ, given for you. Take drink; this is the very blood of Christ, shed for you."

The *Lutheran Book of Worship* rubric gives bread and wine, and references the body and blood to the communicant. *Lutheran Worship* references the body and blood outside of the communicant, which is consistent with the doctrine of the *manducatio indignorum. Lutheran Worship* says, "true/very body and blood," versus simply "body and blood" in the *Lutheran Book of Worship.* In *LW* the title *Christ* is solidified with the name Jesus and is thus clearly historical and truly sacramental. The reference "for the forgiveness of your sins" keeps the "for me" benefits of the Lord's Supper where Christ put them, namely, on the distribution of the forgiveness of sins.

The institution Narrative is a poor translation of the Holy Scriptures. The justification is undoubtedly that it is not meant to be a translation. It is questionable practice to assume to improve on what was "received from the Lord" (παρέλαβον ἀπὸ τοῦ κυρίου). The line "and gave it for all to drink" is found in none of the accounts and contributes nothing. The apostolic explanation "For whenever you eat this bread and drink this cup, you proclaim the Lord's death until he comes" (1 Cor. 11:26) is changed from "you eat and drink" (ἐσθίητε and πίνητε, second person plural, present active subjunctive) and "you proclaim" (καταγγέλλετε, second person, plural, present, active indicative) to the first person plural "we eat-drink-proclaim." If this Pauline addition is to be added to the Verba (it is not in any of the Gospels or the conflation) it is best to keep it in the original. The ὁσάκις γὰρ ἐάν references the interpretive appendix to Paul and the situation in Corinth. We do not determine the nature of the proclamation. We merely eat and drink in faithful obedience to our Lord's mandate. Unworthy participation is explained to us by the Apostle in his words to the Corinthians.

Roman Catholic influences also determined the addition of a sung doxology. In line with the directive of Vatican II to achieve the "full, conscious, active participation of the people," the "words of institution are followed by the memorial acclamation which was introduced into the Roman Canon," to introduce anamnesis and provide "additional congregational participation in the Eucharistic Prayer."[19]

The *LBW* also chose to include the memorial acclamation: "Christ has died. Christ is risen. Christ will come again." Alan Detscher explains this Roman Catholic innovation as follows: "The doxology of Eucharistic Prayer II is not that of Hippolytus; rather it is that which concluded the Roman Canon. The reason for abandoning the distinctive doxology of Hippolytus was not theological, but merely practical. The text of the Roman Canon was chosen because it was more easily sung to the traditional chant."[20] The *LBW* is designed to allow for the singing of the doxology by the congregation following Eucharistic Prayer options I and II.

As the various optional eucharistic prayers attest, the texts may vary and the order of the various sections may be altered or

---

[19] Frank Senn, *New Eucharistic Prayers*, 30.
[20] Ibid., 31.

omitted entirely. The Eucharist Prayers of the *Worship Supplement, Contemporary Worship 2, The Great Thanksgiving,* and *LBW* pre-publication *Draft of Liturgical Texts* received a great deal of criticism over a broad range of issues.[21] But the most controversial and debated issue was the placing of the Verba within the context of prayer. The most vigorous attempt to address the "new mood" and new direction of the ILCW was the critique in the booklet titled *The Great Thanksgiving of the Inter-Lutheran Commission on Worship: It Is the Christians' Supper and Not the Lord's Supper*, by Gottfried G. Krodel, professor of church history at Valparaiso University.

Krodel undertakes a serious examination of the texts of the Great Thanksgiving in the ILCW booklet *CW 01* (1975). His critique is driven by two primary questions: "What kind of theology is the basis of *TGT*? What does one have to say about *TGT* if it is measured in terms of Luther's theology?"

---

[21] In some cases the new texts were simply contemporary poetry reflecting idiosyncratic, '60- and '70-ish relevant lingo. In *The Great Thanksgiving*, the variable prefaces included such expressions as "Therefore, with all the choir of shining spirits" (16); "for Christ our Lord has loved us to the end, yet lives with death behind him, that fear may yield to godly sorrow, and despair to joy of new beginning" (11); ". . . God, Holy Father, through Christ our Lord; whose love will be the Spirit's final gift, that we now may trust the will from which we come, and live embraced in time by love three times repeated . . ." (12). In the praise section of *TGT* one reads: "We praise your holiness that calls all things from nothingness to take the chance of life" (14). In other places *TGT* was theologically vague. One epiclesis began, ". . . the Spirit of our Lord. . . . Let him be the Spirit of our eating and drinking"; and in another, "Let him [Spirit] bless and vivify this bread and cup . . ." (18). In the Words of Institution of *CW 2* "our Lord Jesus took some bread in his hands . . . and he gave it to his friends." The first prayer in *TGT* underwent extensive editing by Frank Senn and eventually became Option 2 in *LBW Altar Book*. The Eucharist Prayer in *CW 2* also underwent a great deal of editing before it became the primary option in *LBW*. In this case, the key issue was theological. Gail Ramshaw-Schmidt explains: "This final prayer was expanded from its original by a committee [which was] under considerable pressure to obtain the convention's imprimaturs by eliminating all possible controvertible phrases. The committee hoped that were this first option acceptable to all, *LBW* could forego offering as options the naked verba and the short detached prayer. Unfortunately the committee lost to popular prejudice and ended up with both a minimalist prayer and the no-eucharistic-prayer options as the ones printed in the pew edition. One criticism must be directed especially at Lutherans. Granting agreements reached in the Lutheran-Roman Catholic dialogues on the eucharist, and granting current scholarship on the metaphoric use of the word 'sacrifice' in the Christian tradition, it is no longer defensible for Lutherans to continue their eccentric refusal to speak the language of offering and sacrifice in the eucharist." See Senn's *New Eucharistic Prayers*, 77–78.

In the first half of the paper, Krodel's critique centers on the Word's of Institution[22] and on three premises which give justification for treating the Lord's Supper as a memorial thanksgiving.[23] Krodel identifies premise (a) as being "central to the whole argumentation" of the authors of *TGT*. He writes: "It is wishful thinking on the part of the authors when they expect us to accept as gospel truth the idea that 'Do this in remembrance of me' must be connected with 'and when he had given thanks' the way they connect it."[24] Krodel also points out:

---

[22] Gottfried G. Krodel, "The Great Thanksgiving of the Inter-Lutheran Commission on Worship: It Is the Christian's Supper and Not the Lord's Supper," in *The Cresset Occasional Paper I*, ed. Kenneth F. Korby (Valparaiso, IN: Valparaiso University Press, 1976), 5. Krodel says, "[O]ne is struck by the license which the authors take with what is supposedly to be the central text of the Lord's Supper, the Words of Institution." He critiques the text on page 15 of *Contemporary Worship 01: The Great Thanksgiving.* The text is as follows: "Who in the night he surrendered to betrayal and death, took bread, and gave thanks, broke it, and gave it to his disciples saying: Take and eat; this is my body, given for you. Do this for my remembrance. Again, after supper, he took the cup, gave thanks, and gave it for all to drink, saying: This cup is the new covenant sealed by my blood, shed for you and for all people, for the forgiveness of sin. Do this for my remembrance. As often as you eat this bread and drink from this cup, you confess the Lord's death, and proclaim that he is risen and lives, until he comes." In the second half of the paper, Krodel raises four theological issues. (1) "Marginals vs. centrals." The failure of TGT to adequately address the radical nature of the Lord's Supper as God's action toward us and not our action (which is merely to respond by hearing, receiving, and believing— or by rejecting) result in a liturgical approach to revision and structure in which the words of Jesus (the central thing) are overgrown by our thanksgiving and telling of the story (the secondary and marginal things). (2) "Narrative vs. Proclamation." Here Krodel marshals extensive quotations from Luther in which he demonstrates that "For Luther the Lord's Supper is Christ's action by which what he accomplished on the cross is distributed to me for my assurance, not recalled, or re-enacted, or represented." (3) "Remembrance vs. Real Presence." (4) "Our actions vs. Christ's action."

[23] Premise (a) is that we are commanded to give thanks as Jesus did; (b) is that Jesus gave thanks in the "matrix" of a Jewish fellowship meal; and (c) is that Jesus used a traditional Jewish thanksgiving (thanking the creator-God for the good and for the saving deeds of God in the history of his people Israel and hence a thanksgiving becomes an act of "remembrance," i.e., a "memorializing") and invocation; "ergo: Jesus recalled to memory the great salvation deeds of the God of Israel and called on God eschatologically to fulfill the salvation for Israel." Krodel shows how two minor premises are built on (a), (b), and (c), and lead to the following conclusion: "The prayer which as a result of this line of arguments we are to make, if we wish to obey Christ's command 'Do this in remembrance of me,' must be modeled according to Jesus' own thanksgiving, i.e., we must imitate what Jesus said; consequently our prayer must contain thanksgiving, remembrance, and invocation. Into these 'verbal acts' of obedience to Christ's commandment are 'inextricably' woven the 'non-verbal acts' (taking, eating, drinking; why not also breaking?) both together make up our obedience to Christ's command, or The Great Thanksgiving (pp. 1, No.1; 2, No. 6)," 8.

[24] Krodel (9) continues: "They are able to maintain this position only because they perform major surgery on the texts. From 1 Cor. 11:25c they drop 'as often as you drink it'; thus

> For "the *immediate antecedent* of *Do this*" [emphasis author's] in 1 Cor. 11:23–26 is not "our Lord's thanksgiving before and after the fellowship meal with his disciples," as the authors tell us in the opening sentence of the next paragraph (1, no.2, italics by the authors); the antecedent is the matter-of-fact statement regarding the bread and the cup, coupled with the appropriate imperatives.[25]

Krodel is not arguing that it is wrong to treat "Do this" as a reference to the "whole previous action." He is merely arguing that "when it comes to the specificity of an *immediate* antecedent for 'Do this' as *content of our obedience we may not roam the whole action* [emphasis author's] and finally find this antecedent in Jesus' own thanksgiving which, in turn, we must imitate."[26] As the title makes clear, "The Great Thanksgiving" makes the giving of thanks the big thing. The great and big thing, however, is not our giving thanks in imitation of our Lord, as the ILCW would have it. *CW 01* states, "The immediate antecedent of 'Do this,' in St. Paul's text, is our Lord's thanksgiving before and after the fellowship meal with his disciples."[27] The booklet admits that both the "particular wording" and "content of Jesus' thanksgiving" is unknown; however, it connects the giving of thanks to the command "Do this." The ILCW also assumes:

> [W]e know what kind of prayer a thanksgiving is, and that indicates what kind of prayer we are to make. Moreover, the scriptural command specified that we are to give thanks "for" my

---

they eliminate the connection of 'Do this' with the previously mentioned command and can therefore connect it with Jesus' thanksgiving. From v. 26 they drop 'For'; thus they destroy the interpretive connection between the previously mentioned doing in Christ's remembrance and the subsequently mentioned proclamation of the Lord's death. By rewriting v.2 6 and eliminating its context, vs.27–32, they eliminate the possibility of the 'manducatio impiorum.' This textual surgery enables the authors to make out of the command, 'Do this in remembrance of me,' a bridge to the Anamnesis, the E-Prayer, which they designate as the goal of our thanksgiving: By doing this 'for my remembrance,' as the authors rephrase vs. 24c and 25a, i.e., by giving thanks as the Lord did and using 'this bread and cup' we 'confess the Lord's death' (16, 17) before God and the world; consequently our thanksgiving ends in a recalling of Christ's sacrifice (E-Prayer) and the invocation of the Holy Spirit (F-Prayer)."

[25] Krodel, 10.

[26] Krodel, 11.

[27] *Contemporary Worship 01: The Great Thanksgiving*, 1.

> "remembrance." As we bring God's saving acts to remembrance, these are to include, and be included in, his one saving act in the Lord Jesus.[28]

TGT interprets "Do this" as a fourfold command: to remember, to pray, to eat, and to drink. It then chooses to give priority to a fifth command: to give thanks. Of the four accounts of the institution of the Lord's Supper, Mark and Paul are the oldest. Later comes Luke, Paul's disciple, who combines Mark and Matthew according to his editorial principles established in Luke 1:1–4.[29] Paul's account in I Corinthians 11:23–26 reflects the liturgical text which Paul acknowledges as that which he "received from the Lord" (παρέλαβον ἀπὸ τοῦ κυρίου).

The main verbs in Mark and Matthew are *took, broke, gave,* and *said.* All these point to the eating and drinking of the body and blood as the big thing in the sacrament. Jesus said, "Take, eat." The imperative λάβετε (take or receive) is the same verb used by Jesus in the Words of Institution of the Holy Ministry in John 20:22. When λάβετε is translated *receive,* it better communicates the point that the divine gifts of the Spirit, the Body and Blood of the Son, and all the saving benefits that come with them, are just that: gifts to be received by faith.

The minor verbs are the participles εὐλογήσας, as used by Mark and Matthew, who adopted the more Hebraic expression "blessing," and εὐχαριστήσας, as used by Luke and Paul, who went with the Greek way of speaking, namely, "thanksgiving." The blessings or thanksgivings at the meal are not the important thing, nor is the celebration of the passover the big thing. The text of the blessings is not recorded. The passover was an annual event. The Lord's Supper is repeated each Lord's Day. The passover drops out of the liturgical text. The liturgy is always concerned with retaining the important things. In the παρέλαβον (the tradition received from the Lord and

---

[28] *Contemporary Worship* 01, 1.

[29] Sasse, *This Is My Body,* 286. Sasse continues, "The slight differences between the four accounts, and especially between the two oldest ones, Paul's and Mark's, are partly due to the fact that they were not originally preserved as historical documents, but as liturgical texts."

passed on by Paul) the big thing is the body and blood which the people are to eat and drink.

"Do this" is not in Mark and Matthew. The emphasis, however, is on the verbs *took, broke* and *gave,* and thus point to the eating and drinking of the Lord's body and blood as the main thing. Again, in Luke and in Paul's liturgical account (which he received from the Lord), the big imperative "Do this" (τοῦτο) is in grammatical agreement with *body* (σῶμά) and *cup* (ποτήριον). Only Luke and Paul includes the anamnesis; however, the "Do this" clearly refers to "as often as you drink it/cup." Neither Paul nor Luke include the Lord's commands "Take, eat" (Mark and Matthew) and "Drink of it" (Matthew). These drop out in the liturgical text and are replaced with "Do this." So also with the expression "for you." The historical accounts of Mark and Matthew state that Jesus gave the bread and cup "to the disciples/to them." This is replaced with "for you" in the 1 Corinthians 11 and Luke 22.

Two years after the release of *The Great Thanksgiving,* the Commission on Worship published the booklet *Draft of Liturgical Texts for Study by LCMS Pastors/Congregations.* It included the Eucharistic Prayer from *Contemporary Worship* 2 with "numerous revisions," plus the liturgical texts for the office and occasional services to be included in *LBW.* The structure and text of the service of Holy Communion is very close to what would ultimately be included in *LBW.* The Eucharistic Prayer is nearly identical to the anaphora in *LBW* pew edition. Page one of the booklet consisted of a "Review of Worship Material" questionnaire. "Of the some 5000 copies sent out, about 285 returns were received."[30]

[30] Inter-Lutheran Commission on Worship, Report From the LCMS: Agenda, Exhibit E. The questionnaire allowed for respondents to evaluate the various orders according to three categories, "Completely Acceptable," "Acceptable but Offer Suggestions Attached," and "Questionable in the Area Noted and Attached." According to Exhibit E, page 1, "Tabulation of responses . . . found overwhelming support for the texts as submitted . . . . There really was no suggested category 'Totally unacceptable' but some seven made such a category of their own devising." The exhibit notes twenty areas in which objections were made. These include: offertory rubrics, Eucharistic Prayer, Verba (version), distribution formula, ritual action in all sections of liturgical corpus, original sin (missed traditional wording in various formularies), prayers for (i.e., for the benefit of) the dead, and others.

Once the ILCW reached the point of producing the final drafts of the various liturgical and hymn texts, it was still faced with a major obstacle. The LCMS had one step in the approval process which the other participating churches did not have, "namely the by-law provision for review of materials for conformity with Scripture and the Lutheran Confessions."[31] Every word of the new hymnal had to undergo doctrinal review. Many items in the new book were questioned as "ambiguous" or "objectional." "Negotiations" ensued, which "In most instances . . . resulted in the reviewer's approving the text. . . . In some cases, however, there has been somewhat of an impasse."[32] Many of the official evaluators appointed by the president of the Missouri Synod expressed serious concerns about the content of the new hymnal and recommended against its adoption in its present form.[33]

---

31 ILCW Report from the LCMS, 2.

32 ILCW Report from the LCMS.

33 F. Samuel Janzow submitted his official evaluation, dated March 23, 1977, to the LCMS Commission on Worship. Janzow ends his three-page evaluation of the texts with the following conclusion: "With a sense of disappointment and reluctance, I now state my evaluation: As they now stand, the liturgical materials for *LBW* are unsuited for use in the Lutheran Church—Missouri Synod." Bornmann's seven-page evaluation includes these comments: "The Words of Institution are paraphrases which distort the word of Jesus . . . as they are proposed, they are not acceptable . . . . The 'Words of Institution' are absolutely unacceptable as they stand. The words in Matthew, Mark, Luke and Paul . . . do not allow for (1) 'for my remembrance,' (2) 'give it for all to drink,' (3) 'New covenant sealed by my blood.'" [Note: The *LBW* retained 1 and 2, but dropped 3.] Bornmann continues, ". . . they are paraphrases which give a theological interpretation which to many of us is unacceptable. The Formula of Concord takes great pains to distinguish between the Word of Christ (identical to the Words of Institution) by which the elements of bread and wine are hallowed or blessed in this holy use . . . . (Tappert, p. 584, 81–82) and the words of men (identical to the prayers of the church spoken by the minister) which do not "effect the true presence of the body and blood of Christ in the supper. (Tappert, p. 583, 74)." James G. Manz concluded, "I don't see how we in the Missouri Synod, as confessional Lutherans, can accept this proposed hymnal as it now stands." He also points out that the time allotted to the pastors and congregations for adequate study and response to the liturgical texts sent for their review was far too short. He received his copy on February 9 and the deadline for the survey was February 15. Evaluator Jane Schatkin Hettrick was opposed to the "massive and penetrating change" in the new hymnal. She noted that "it cannot fail to have a disturbing effect on the worship life of the church, especially on the Missouri Synod. There is no historical precedent for such extensive revision of the liturgy." Schnaible's evaluation centered on the inferiority of the ICET texts as adopting "less natural, inelegant (and on occasion childish) English constructions." He adds, "There were just too many changes for the sake of change without any increase in the clarity of thought." D. C. Appelt's ambivalent evaluation dealt with cosmetic and linguistic concerns. Two evaluators were quite supportive of the new texts. Victor E. Gebauer responded with 36 pages of "Comment(s) on the Liturgical Corpus of

From its inception, the pan-Lutheran hymnal project was conceived as part of the larger ecumenical plan among the leadership of the LCMS to move the Synod toward closer ties with the ALC and LCA. With the schism within the LCMS in the mid-1970s, coupled with extensive criticism of the theology driving much of the "new mood in worship" (most of the criticism came from the scholars of the ALC and LCA), the prospects of a pan-Lutheran hymnal ended as abruptly and surprisingly as they had begun with the "so-called" LCMS invitation of 1965. The Special Hymnal Review Committee forty-three page report to the 1979 LCMS convention recommended that the Missouri Synod adopt the *Lutheran Book of Worship* with certain modifications. The SHRC analysis of the proposed new hymnal identified many examples of theological deficiencies and ambiguity. Unfortunately, given the extreme polarization during those turbulent times, a more thorough and detailed explanation of the theology behind the liturgical reforms would probably have been more useful. The issues shaping "The Great Thanksgiving" were given only scant and superficial treatment. In the end, proponents of the new hymnal saw the report as a "nit-picking" document in support of that faction of Synod opposed to closer ecumenical ties with the ALC and LCA. For those in favor of avoiding further entanglement with the theologically liberal Lutheran synods in America, the SHRC "Blue Ribbon" report presented the needed justification for pulling out of the project. The report did not challenge either side in the controversy to a deeper examination and study of the profound liturgical issues facing American Lutheranism in the mid-twentieth century.

---

the *Lutheran Book of Worship*." He "recommended acceptance" of *LBW* "because of its historic significance for Lutheranism in the USA. The common use of this book could fulfill two centuries of effort to achieve unified service for Lutherans. . . . History itself cannot bind us to a course of action, but never before has Lutheranism been so close to achieving an expression of its true spirit as in *LBW*," 7. Gebauer notes: "The Great Thanksgiving is, of course, at the heart of the issues . . . . it can only be added that these prayers represent the most ancient traditions of the Church, are absolutely no contradiction to Lutheranism's principles, and would help enormously to raise consciousness among us about the fullness of the meanings in the Eucharistic action. In fact, the prayers will help us considerably to become more *Lutheran* [emphasis Gebauer's] and to move away from some of the unfortunate Reformed practices which are now standard in our piety." Frederick W. Kemper's three page evaluation offers numerous literary criticisms, yet he concludes: "I have read through the other liturgical drafts and feel that I can live with all of them," 2.

Summary on the Eucharistic Prayer

It would be improper to insist that Lutheran theology demands either the inclusion or exclusion of a eucharistic prayer. Some anaphoras are good, some are bad. If a eucharistic prayer contains an element(s) of false doctrine (e.g., sacrifice of the mass), the offensive part should be eliminated. Weak or vague theological elements should be strengthened and clarified.

It is not un-Lutheran or anti-Lutheran to include the Words of Institution within the context of a prayer. The framing of any question about the propriety of a eucharistic prayer in the Lutheran liturgy that demands an unequivocal yes or no is prudently avoided. Those in favor of a "Lutheran" eucharistic prayer justify its usage on the basis of biblical and liturgical precedent. Biblical analogies abound. The prayer of Solomon in 1 Kings 8:15–23 and Asaph in Psalm 80 include proclamation.[34] The whole pattern of the sacrificial system in Israel merged man's sacrifice with God's. The people brought the animals. Priests did the sacrificing. Some of the meat went to the work of the church (i.e., the "salary" of the priest). Liturgically and externally, man's actions were required. Theologically, however, the sacrifices were vehicles of God's action upon man, namely, means of grace or sacraments. "There is no reason why you cannot merge God's action with man's action formally, liturgically, or externally without succumbing theologically to synergism or semi-pelagianism."[35]

Lutheran Worship and the *Lutheran Book of Worship* have entered middle age. The debate over the Eucharist Prayer continues, minus the emotional and political intensity of the 1970s. Thoughtful, careful debate cannot be rushed. At the annual Theological Symposium held at Concordia Seminary, St. Louis in 1994, three scholars pre-

[34] In an unpublished seven-page essay/report titled "Lutheran Book of Worship" (1975?) Paul Foelber (LCMS member of ILCW Hymn Texts Committee) wrote: "Some have been disturbed by framing the Verba within the great proclamation of God's saving work through Jesus Christ. They have not been able to understand that proclamation can indeed take the form of prayer. Solomon anemnestically proclaims God's great works in 1 Kings 8:15–23 as does Asaph in Psalm 80. Yet both are offering prayer to God," 6.

[35] Horace Hummel, "Convocation on the Eucharistic Prayer," Concordia Seminary, St. Louis, MO, October 25, 1978 (cassette tape 78-49).

sented thoughtful papers on the Eucharist Prayer. Lee Maxwell and William Weedon co-wrote and delivered "Lutheran Liturgy and Eucharist Prayer: On the Possibility of a Eucharist Prayer."

The paper proposes that the inclusion of the Verba in a prayer "is not of itself wrong, that is, does not change what is God's gift into something we do, and that as a confession of 'gift received!' it may actually be desirable."[36] If, as the Preface states, we are to give thanks *always* and *everywhere*, then surely at the Lord's Supper would be a preeminent time and place to do so.

The paper also points out that Luther did not object to including the words of the Lord's Testament in a prayer. In fact, in his *Formula Missae* (Latin Mass of 1523) the Verba are "built into the introductory words of the Preface by way of a relative clause." The paper also notes:

> What is so utterly significant for our inquiry, however, is that nowhere in this work does Luther criticize the fact that the Words of Institution are included in prayer. What he does ruthlessly sniff out and abominate is the doctrine of sacrifice which was built into the prayer . . . in short, it was the doctrinal content and not the liturgical form that was objectionable.[37]

The paper does not ignore the fact that three years later, in his *Deutsche Messe* of 1526, Luther removed the Words of Institution from prayer and "let them stand alone in splendid isolation."[38] The paper simply points out that these were matters of liturgical form and not doctrine and thus both options were permissible for Luther.

Is a eucharistic prayer possible in the Lutheran Church? The answer is obviously yes—yes theologically, historically, and in current reality. As we have seen, *Lutheran Worship* adopted modified Eucharistic Prayers from Germany and Sweden. Some would object to their inclusion in *LW*. Others would object that these do

---

[36] Lee Maxwell and William Weedon, "Lutheran Liturgy and Eucharist Prayer: On the Possibility of a Eucharist Prayer," Concordia Seminary, Theological Symposium, 1994. Quoted from unpublished manuscript, 3.

[37] Maxwell and Weedon, 14.

[38] Maxwell and Weedon, 15.

not represent full and authentic eucharistic prayers. Robert Clancy addresses this second group in the opening words of his symposium paper "Criteria for the Use of a Eucharistic Prayer: In Luther and the twentieth-century Lutheran Liturgical Movement." Clancy begins, "The modern liturgical movement has not treated Martin Luther kindly."[39] Clancy aptly demonstrates how Luther's "orders did not emerge from a vacuum, fully formed like Athena from Zeus' head," but could be foreseen already in his writings of 1520 and 1521.[40] He points out that Luther's most "vocal detractors come from within the denomination which bears his name," yet one will not find them attacking Luther's theological integrity. At best they can repeat the standard line that Luther was liturgically inept. Clancy, however, pushes past the standard objections to the heart of the issue. He writes:

> Thus, the liturgical reforms of Luther did not do away with eucharist praying, only of the sole eucharistic prayer which was used in the medieval Western church. Luther could not permit the theology of sacrifice, which flies in the face of the gospel, to stand; and he was unwilling to be an innovator, and thus could only adapt and preserve those things in the received liturgy which were contrary to the gospel. Only if one insists that there is a single, standard form for the eucharist prayers against which Luther's and others' attempts at praying eucharistically must be measured can one maintain that Luther did a hatchet job on the liturgy.[41]

The driving motivation behind the unkind treatment of Luther's reforms appears to be the opinion of many modern liturgical reformers who "seem to simply assume that everyone would agree that having a eucharistic prayer is a good thing."[42] A good thing aesthetically, yet more importantly, Clancy observes that Luther Reed's and Frank Senn's

---

[39] Robert A. D. Clancy, Concordia Seminary Theological Symposium, 1994, unpublished manuscript, 1.

[40] "Treatise on the New Testament, That Is, the Holy Mass," AE 35:79–111. "The Babylonian Captivity of the Church," AE 36:11–132. "The Misuse of the Mass," AE 36:133–230.

[41] Clancy, 13–14.

[42] Clancy, 14–15.

> rationale for the inclusion of a eucharistic prayer indicate two criteria which the modern Lutheran liturgical movement have embraced as their own: the historicity of the anaphora, and the ecumenical consensus on its inclusion.[43]

Both the Maxwell-Weedon and Clancy papers acknowledge the ecumenical motivation. Clancy is especially to the point:

> It seems that the contemporary Lutheran liturgical movement is seeking to reverse the relationship which Lutheranism has traditionally insisted between theology and practice. Where, for Luther, his theology, and particularly his confession of the gospel, found expression in his eucharistic practice, today's liturgical movement has a desire for historical and contemporary consensus which will inform their doctrine. There is a vast difference between Luther's criteria for liturgical reform—the gospel of justification by grace, and pastoral concern for the weak of faith—and that of the current liturgical movement—historicity and ecumenicity.[44]

One of the most important contributions of the Maxwell-Weedon presentation is the reminder that Lutheran liturgical renewal and revision ought not ignore the part the Eucharistic Prayer has played in the Lutheran theological heritage.

> Löhe and others of the nineteenth century, for example, in their work of liturgical revision and renewal, looked at historical liturgies of the sixteenth century under the guiding principles of confessional Lutheranism. This work contrasts greatly with what was done by the Liturgical Movement, and to a certain extent the ILCW, under the rubric ecumenism.[45]

The Maxwell-Weedon paper then offers ten helpful confessional principles for liturgical revision and renewal. Five are framed in the positive and five in the negative. A confessional Eucharist Prayer cannot have the following:

---

[43] Clancy, 16.
[44] Clancy, 19.
[45] Maxwell and Weedon, 35–36.

1. The notion of sacrifice.
2. A focus on our actions.
3. An anamnesis with cultic "analogy."
4. An epiclesis suggesting a transformation of the elements.
5. Verbosity obscuring the chief thing of the Sacrament.

A Lutheran Eucharistic Prayer may do the following:

1. Give thanks to God for what He is giving in the Sacrament.
2. Focus on the action of God.
3. Have an anamnesis which points to our salvation in Christ.
4. Include the Verba in a central position both textually and theologically.
5. Locate the Verba in a central position both textually and theologically.

Hermann Sasse reiterates the warning of Theodor Knolle (see *Luther-Jahrbuch* [1928]; *Vom Sakrament des Altars* [1941]), who "raised a warning against the introduction of the Words of Institution again into a *relative clause* between purely human words, even if they are beautiful and venerable human words." The result:

> The forgiveness of sins recedes. It is no longer seen as the great and joyful gift of the Sacrament . . . . the deeper inner connection that exists between absolution and the reception of the Sacrament is no longer understood. It can only be understood when one knows that both *absolution and the Sacrament of the Altar* are two sides of the same thing, that both are the Gospel for sinners.[46]

Sasse's and Knolle's warnings need to be taken seriously. Lee Maxwell and William Weedon are duly cognizant of these concerns, yet they conclude their paper with an excellent example of how a truly Lutheran Eucharist Prayer might look. They are bold enough to resist the pressure of conforming entirely to the so-

[46] Hermann Sasse, "The Lutheran Understanding of the Consecration" (Letters to Lutheran Pastors, no. 26, July 1952) in *We Confess the Sacraments*, trans. Norman Nagel (St. Louis: Concordia Publishing House, 1985), 130–131.

called classical structure of the Eucharistic Prayer and follow instead that of Luther's *Formula Missae.*

According to *The New Westminster Dictionary of Liturgy and Worship,*[47] the possible component parts of a developed anaphora of classical structure are (1) introductory dialogue, (2) preface or first part of the thanksgiving, (3) Sanctus, (4) post-Sanctus or second part of the thanksgiving, (5) preliminary epiclesis (alternative or additional post-Sanctus), (6) narrative of the institution, (7) anamnesis, (8) epiclesis, (9) diptychs or intercessions, which may be divided, (10) concluding doxology.

The structure of the Maxwell-Weedon anaphora (as outlined in the *Formula Missae*) has the following elements: (1) introductory dialogue, (2) with seasonal or common preface, (3) an anamnesis, (4) the Verba, (5) an epiclesis, and (6) Sanctus. Maxwell and Weedon are clear on what they are attempting to accomplish:

> The emphasis throughout is on thanksgiving to God for what He has done for our salvation, particularly as it comes to us now in the Supper of His Son. The Verba are prominent and proclamatory, as indicted by their introductory sentence and the rubric that they be chanted. The climax in the Sanctus points to the Real Presence and the blessing that now comes to us in the Body and Blood.[48]

The following is the Preface and Consecration from the Maxwell-Weedon Divine Service.[49]

Ⓟ The Lord be with you.
Ⓒ And with your spirit.
Ⓟ Lift up your hearts.
Ⓒ We lift them to the Lord.
Ⓟ Let us give thanks to the Lord our God.
Ⓒ It is right to give Him thanks and praise.
Ⓟ It is indeed fitting, right, and salutary that we should at all

---

[47] W. Jardine Grishrooke, "Anaphora" in [*The*] *New Westminster Dictionary of Worship,* ed. J. G. Davis (Philadelphia: The Westminster Press, 1986), 14–15.
[48] Maxwell and Weedon, 37.
[49] Ibid., 38.

times and in all places give thanks to You, O Lord, holy Father, almighty and everlasting God, for all the innumerable blessings You so freely bestow upon us and upon all creation. But above all, we give You thanks for Your boundless love

[The Common Preface follows]

shown to us when You sent Your only-begotten Son Jesus Christ into our flesh and laid upon Him our sin, giving Him into death that we might not die eternally. Even as He is now risen from the dead and lives and reigns forever, so You have ordained that whoever believes in Him shall not perish but have eternal life.

Ⓟ Out of great love with which our Lord Christ loved us, and that the extent of His great mercy might never be forgotten, He established His holy Testament and gave us His Supper, that in the communion of His true body and blood, we might receive forgiveness of sins, life, and salvation. In reverent faith and holy joy, O heavenly Father, we listen now to His certain Word and unfailing Promise.

[The Words of our Lord's Testament: chanted]

Ⓟ Send, O Father, Your Holy Spirit upon us, that we may ever rejoice in the manifold mercies bestowed on us in these holy gifts; and join now our voices with those of the angels and archangels and the whole company of heaven, to laud and magnify Your glorious name, evermore praising You and saying: [The Sanctus is sung]

The Verba are introduced by the words "In reverent faith . . . we listen now to His certain and unfailing Promise." The passive posture of the worshiper during the proclamation of the *Verba Testamenti* is clearly expressed as that of "faith" and "listening." The great passive verbs of faith describe how the faithful receive the "certain Word and unfailing Promise." Such is the way of *Gottesdienst.* Likewise with the anamnesis which appears in the paragraph proceeding the Lord's Testament. The emphasis of the remembering is on the object, namely, that "the great love with which our Lord Christ loved us, and that the extent of His great mercy might never be forgotten." Such phrasing avoids making the anamnesis into something we do in order to make-present-again the saving work of Christ. There is no hint of the Caselian theory in which the remembering is a mystery, that is, a sacred ritual action (*heilige kultische Handlung*) in which the saving deeds of Christ are made present again (*Gegenwärtigsetzung*), and the worshiper by performing the rite ("work of the people") thereby win (*erwirbt*) salvation (see chapter 2).

Although this Eucharist Prayer contains an epiclesis, which is located after the Verba, nevertheless, it is carefully worded so as to avoid any notion of being consecratory. It is unequivocally an epiclesis upon the worshipers: "that we may ever rejoice in the manifold mercies bestowed on us in these holy gifts."

Maxwell and Weedon have offered an excellent model by which to judge future attempts to introduce old, revised, or new eucharistic prayers in Lutheran worship. Their text is theologically thoughtful, evangelically and confessionally precise. The style is economical, reasonably polished, and avoids ambiguity. It is obviously not the product of a committee nor driven by the latest popular social agenda. Its language and content are biblically and theologically shaped.

Liturgy is always interpretation. Biblical and theological clarity is essential in worship. The end of the twentieth century is marked by indifference and outright mistrust of theological distinctions. Simply noting distinctions in theology and practice is not enough. Applying them in practice is a difficult theological art. The line between *adiaphora* and the *Zeit der Bekenntnis* is never static. At times the liturgy needs to be pruned. It may be filled with dead branches (as was the Canon of the Mass in Luther's day) or it may simply be overgrown. Luther may have pruned the Canon down to the bare Verba in the German Mass, but what usually goes unnoticed is that he put the Words of Institution to music (to be chanted according to the Gospel intonation) and then draped the distribution with his theologically rich German Sanctus ("Isaiah, Mighty Seer").[50]

---

[50] AE, 53:80–83.

In the *Formula Missae* Luther retained the Preface, but preferred that a brief pause separate the prayer from the words of Christ (Verba) which are then to be recited "in the same tone in which the Lord's Prayer is chanted."[51] The pause, audible chanting, plus Luther's preference for "the so-called westward position with the priest facing the people" all distinguish the Verba as gospel proclamation rather than prayer.[52]

Today, liturgical tinkering runs rampant among Lutherans. Knowingly or not, Luther's German Mass is the preferred model. The *Sursum Corda* and Preface disappear along with the theologically profound Sanctus. It is not uncommon for Gospel hymns or contemporary praise music to give mood and definition to the distribution.

Many Lutheran churches have bought into the Church Growth, Mega-Church, Meta-Church paradigms. Clearly, the preferred styles of worship are those modeled after the contemporary evangelicalism. In an all-too-typical example from a Lutheran parish, "In the Garden" is used as a distribution hymn. Stanza 1 reads: "I come to the garden alone / While the dew is still on the roses / And the voice I hear, falling on my ear / The Son of God discloses. (Refrain:) And He walks with me, and he talks with me / And He tells me I am his own / And the joy we share as we tarry there / None other has ever known." The service of Holy Communion begins with the Invitatory from the Venite in Matins: ℣ : O, Come, let us worship the Lord. ℟ : For he is our maker. This is followed immediately by the Words of Institution. There is no *Sursum Corde*, Preface, or Sanctus.[53]

The nature of the *status confessionis* is clearly defined by American Evangelicalism. Against this backdrop, the two criteria offered by Daniel Overduin take on added value. Before deciding for or against the appropriateness of the Eucharist Prayer, he suggested asking two questions: (1) Does the Eucharistic Prayer serve the purpose of bringing us to a deeper understanding of what happens during the

---

[51] AE 53:28.

[52] See also: Robin A. Leaver, "'Verba Testamenti' versus Canon: The Radical Nature of Luther's Liturgical Reform," *Churchman: A Journal of Anglican Theology* 97, no. 2 (1983): 123–131.

[53] Printed order of service from St. John's Lutheran Church, Ellisville, Missouri (October 17 & 18, 1992).

celebration of the blessed sacrament? (2) Does the Eucharistic Prayer serve the evangelical and liturgical interpretation of the *Verba Testamenti* in the context of our joyful communion celebration?

In today's "evangelical" context there is a need for liturgy which confesses an understanding of worship that is fully incarnational, sacramental, and escatological. To communicate the full meaning of what takes place in the Lord's Supper it is necessary to draw in all of Scriptures and all of our Lord's saving deeds. All doctrines are found in the Doctrine of the Lord's Supper. The fellowship in Holy Communion includes the saints of the Old Testament. It transcends time and space. A eucharistic prayer that brings the worshiper to a deeper understanding of the meaning of communion with Jesus Christ and all believers of all times may be helpful for those tempted to twist Holy Communion into a solitary, mystical walk in the garden.

Two eucharistic prayers were included in *Lutheran Worship*. In Divine Service I a prayer from the Swedish *Kyrko-Handboken* (1942) was placed between the Sanctus and Lord's Prayer. In Divine Service II the portion of the Eucharistic Prayer of the United Evangelical Lutheran Church in Germany which comes before the Verba was placed between the Sanctus and Lord's Prayer.[54] The proclamation of the Verba is clearly distinguished from the prayer form.

There is no question that the theology driving the transmutation of *Lutheran Worship* takes seriously the theology of remembrance (זָכַר), yet without buying into the whole notion of remembrance as a "making-present-again" the ancient saving action (e.g., Casel). We are to remember what our Lord did for his people then, and his Word delivers salvation to us now. "His Word bestows what it says."[55] There is no sacrifice of the mass and no transubstantiation. Nor is there any notion of "transaction" (not water, bread, wine and action, but water, bread,

---

[54] The portion of the German prayer which comes after the Verba (adapted to read: O Lord, heavenly Father, we here remember the suffering and death of your dear Son . . . .) was placed in Divine Service I as a conclusion to the Prayer of the Church. The next revision of *LW* will have to deal with this innovation and decide whether it is preferable to connect the Eucharistic Prayer structurally and theologically to the Prayer of the Church and/or to the Preface and Sanctus (or to the Verba).

[55] *Lutheran Worship*, 6.

wine, and the Word). "'The anamnesis is Gospel not prayer.' . . . An understanding of *anamnesis* different from that given here seeped in later: a way for us to transcend time . . . . Evidence in Casel, Dix, Brunner."[56]

Certainly Lutherans may have prayer and proclamation going on at the same time. Prayer and proclamation are constantly being woven together throughout the fabric of the service. Good liturgy, however, encourages a careful separation of the two at certain points. The whole debate is over the nature and location of these points. For example, prayers should not become sermons to admonish, educate, and promote the latest denominational program. Sermons should not become prayers. For the sake of good liturgy, churches have chosen to establish rubrics about the appropriate distinctions in numerous areas of worship. Today, great attention is given to aesthetic and anthropological concerns. This is fine, but how much more should the chief theological criteria of the church shape the structure and rubrics. Worship is after all the theological enterprise *par excellence* of the church. An issue usually overlooked in the debate is that the one point in which all traditions are forced by the nature of the sacrament to stop the praying is when the mouth is opened to receive the body and blood. The proclamation of the *Logos* is at its most concrete when His liturgy pauses, nothing is said, and we are left speechless. Eating and drinking is not prayer; it is eating and drinking. We do not talk with our mouths full. Most traditions acknowledge this by humble acts of liturgical piety: taking off the shoes before entering the chancel and covering the mouth with a napkin immediately after reception (Coptic), bowing, kneeling, making the sign of the cross. If words are spoken by the minister during distribution, they will usually be proclamation rather than prayer. This is comparable to the Sacrament of Holy Baptism where the Verba stand in bare isolation from the previous prayers.

Many may lament the fact that Luther pared down the Canon to the bare Verba. Before liturgical committees endeavor to radically

---

[56] Norman Nagel, "Notes on Divine Service," 34. Nagel quotes Volk KD 33, 198; Goppelt, 33, 197, n. 29.

alter orthodox Lutheran practice which has been going on for over four hundred years, however, it is incumbent upon them to demonstrate how these changes represent an improvement in the liturgical expression of the doctrine of justification by grace through faith alone. If those authorized by the church to make such revisions are able to demonstrate the advantage of returning to the eucharistic prayer form, they will discover that some early anaphoras are more suitable models than others.

It can only be speculated on what things would have been like if only Luther had other more "neutral" liturgies to work with. There are early Eastern anaphoras that avoid the offensive references to sacrifice. Bryan Spinks has pointed out that modern liturgical studies are obsessed with fifth-century classic anaphora forms. One factor stimulating the research was the ecumenical possibilities to be reaped from so-called pure extant liturgies from the period prior to the many schisms during the later centuries. A great number of new eucharistic prayers were composed in the 1970s and '80s. Most are modeled on the classic style of the fourth and fifth century West Syrian and Syro-Byzantine anaphoras. These liturgies have unfortunately overshadowed the evidence of earlier anaphora patterns. An investigation of those earlier prayers confirms that the Verba were not always contained within the Eucharistic Prayer. Thus there is good early catholic as well as Reformation precedent for omitting the narrative from a eucharistic prayer. Spinks suggests that Lutherans use the Verba as proclamation and then continue with a prayer of thanksgiving.[57]

Anaphoras worth examination include the Egyptian Anaphora of St. Basil which "has been recognized as one of the earliest surviving eucharistic prayers [late third century], comparable with the *Apostolic Tradition* and *Addai and Mari*." The Holy Spirit is not asked to change the elements but only to "sanctify them and make them holy of holies . . . . The whole epiclesis is reminiscent of the *Apostolic Tradition*, as is the offering of 'this bread and this

[57] Bryan Spinks, "Berakah, Anaphoral Theory and Luther" (Cassette tape of lecture given at Concordia Seminary, St. Louis, 1988. Copy available in Concordia Seminary Library, CASS 88-18, 3536).

cup,' rather than 'this sacrifice.'" Another unusual feature is the introduction to the Institution Narrative: "He left us this great mystery of godliness," a quote from 1 Timothy 3:16. This moves things clearly from narrative and remembrance into the present tense in which the Lord's Supper is a present, for us, for me, sacred act.[58]

If a "new" American Lutheran liturgy is to be written, Spinks offers three recommendations. First, a modern version of the *Formula Missae* might be followed since the *FM* is the authentic sixteenth-century Lutheran common pattern or catholic pattern. The *Deutsche Messe* was specifically aimed at the German culture. Second, perhaps the liturgy could include some common American eucharistic prayer "as a token of acknowledgement of the present ecumenical consensus and a recognition of the catholicity of the earlier forms which antidate the splits of Christendom." Spinks stresses that the advantage of the Syro-Byzantine model over the Latin or Egyptian forms is that in both the latter, the institutional narrative is set within an intercessory context and is consecratory. In the Syro-Byzantine form it is purely an extension of the thanksgiving. To see it as consecratory or sacrificial is to see with sixteenth-century polemical eyes or modern-day Roman Catholic eyes. The Roman Catholics declined the use of an unaltered Coptic-Basil because they knew the narrative was not in the petition form. "A Lutheran version could perhaps emphasize the thanksgiving nature of the Institution Narrative as opposed to the consecratory by introducing it as 'and we also give you thanks for the sacrament of Christ's body and blood, for on the night on which he was betrayed,' and so forth." Third, Spinks encourages Lutherans to feel truly free to use those particular early church models that are consistent with its unique evangelical criterion and create "a number of new American Lutheran prayers experimenting with different structures and drawing on lessons from the past and present." He states:

[58] Jasper and Cuming, *Prayers of the Eucharist: Early and Reformed*, 67–68.

> There would be no necessity to include an institution narrative within these prayers, and as we have seen, this has early precedent. Perhaps some of these prayers might be responsory prayers which reflect the priesthood of all believers. And perhaps these new prayers might work with images of redemption other than those of sacrifice and offering in response to Luther's warning about the problems of these images. Lutherans should be freed from the intimidation of the popular perception of liturgical scholarship which insists that you must have a eucharistic prayer on the fourth- or fifth-century model. [The Lutheran Church] must be free to do its own thing, appealing to an earlier catholic tradition.[59]

Any return to the East, whatever the century, is a trip that cannot be hurried. Both the *Lutheran Book of Worship* and *Lutheran Worship* were rushed. *LW* in particular was produced under unbelievable political pressures and impossible deadlines. It has its flaws. Nevertheless, it represents a last-minute victory for those who desired to cling to an evangelical theology of worship in which the Divine Service is just that, God's present saving work to man. The Evangelical doctrine of justification remained the criteria determining the shape of the liturgy.[60]

The history of *LW* shows that there was a vigorous effort to restore *LW* to a "style and substance" that is fully formed by a truly evangelical and confessional theology of worship. This was not an easy task given the political, social and theological pressures in the Missouri Synod during that volatile era.

Shortly after *LW* was published, Lowell C. Green made an analytical review of the new hymnal. He acknowledges that "The LCMS had every right and privilege to publish a service book meeting its tradition."[61] The article examines the extent to which *LW* succeeded in shedding the influences of the contemporary Liturgical Movement. Green poses the question:

---

59 Spinks, "Berakah, Anaphoral Theory and Luther." In his lecture Spinks later made reference to the influence of Notre Dame on the liturgical developments in American Lutheranism and urged the Lutherans not to be pressured by them.

60 Sasse, "Liturgy and Lutheranism," 10.

61 Lowell C. Green, "*Lutheran Worship:* An Analytical Review-Article on the New Hymnal," *Lutheran Theological Review* 1 (Spring 1983):38.

> Where does *LW* stand in relation to "celebration theology," with its mingling of comparative religions, higher criticism, and the concept of worship as a good work? It takes a mixed position.[62]

Green observes the influence of Dom Odo Casel's "mystery theology."

> The Roman Catholic liturgical innovator, Odo Casel (1886–1948), whose influence spread since Vatican Council II, frankly conceded that the Christian worship was the adaptation of pagan myth and mystery of Christianity. Out of the pagan celebration as re-enactment of the myth of the deity came the modern concept of Christian worship as the "celebration" of the acts of God for our salvation, or the re-enactment (or re-presentation) of them. Regarding Christ's suffering, death, and resurrection, "the liturgy re-enacts these redemptive events" (*LW Altar Book*, p. 7).[63]

On the other hand, Green states that "*LW* is to be congratulated for a number of returns to sound Confessionalism."[64] He points to the use of the name Divine Service in place of Holy Communion; the restoration of the rubric which refers to the pastor distributing the body and blood of Christ (most rubrics in English-language Lutheran service books refer to the bread and wine); and a general "conscious endeavor . . . . to be faithful to the Holy Scriptures and the Lutheran Confessions."[65]

---

[62] Green, 47. Green gives examples of Lutheran Worship's mixed position by referring to the few pamphlets available from the LCMS at the time of publication which offered theological insights. He quotes from the *Guide to Introducing Lutheran Worship*: "The divine services of *LW* are 'celebrations of the victory of our Lord Jesus Christ' (24). This brings us dangerously close to the 'Christus Victor' theology of Aulen which helped shape *LBW*, including the subordination of Good Friday and the atonement to Easter and triumphalism. That concept of natural theology and reason which is called 'worship,' is totally absent in classical Lutheranism, is included in materials for promoting *LW*, i.e., worship as ascribing worth to God (*Guide*, 9). At times *LW* supports the position of Augsburg Confession 14 by which only ordained clergy take part in the Divine Service ('If non-ordained assisting ministers or leaders are considered either necessary or desirable or both . . . .' *LW Altar Book*, 11). At other times, the opposite position is supported. 'The liturgy is the celebration of all who gather . . . . It is appropriate, therefore, that . . . lay persons fulfill certain functions within the service' (Ibid., 25)."

[63] Green, 45–46.

[64] Green, 48.

[65] Green, 48.

The *LBW* followed the "ecumenical" pattern (popularized by Gregory Dix) of a full-scale Offertory procession of money, bread and wine. "This gives the appearance of a transaction between man and God and seems to confuse the gift of God in the sacrament with the good works of man."[66] *LW* retains the pattern. Green opines, "Fortunately, *LW* has avoided the 'Great Thanksgiving' (Eucharist Prayer) of *LBW* in which the Words of Institution were changed into prayer after the model of the Canon of the Mass."[67] The Eucharistic Prayer was probably the most hotly debated and controversial element imported by the ILCW. Traditional Lutheran liturgy follows Luther's reform of the mass in which the Words of Institution are sung as pure proclamation of the Gospel; literally, God's work (thus *Gottesdienst,* God's service).

Green's 1982 article points out that, in general, there was widespread ignorance when it came to "familiarity with the origins of 'celebration theology' and other recent innovations" borrowed from the Liturgical Movement. Nevertheless, his concluding sentence is significant: "However, *LW* is, theologically speaking, an immense improvement over *LBW*."[68]

The difference between the theology shaping *LW* and *LBW* is nowhere in more stark contrast than in the introduction of each book. *LW* conspicuously begins with God, his Word, and his work ("Our Lord speaks and we listen. His Word bestows what it says."). It gives the forgiveness of sin. *LBW* begins with people (the body), and their expressions, and their work ("Corporate worship expresses the unity of the people of God . . . [their] gestures, songs, words by which Christians have identified themselves and each other."). *LBW* makes no mention of God's work, the forgiveness of sins, or the primary evangelical article of faith and *the* criterion for Lutheran worship, that is, justification by grace through faith alone. It does state: "The key to the particularity of Lutheran worship is the Lutheran love of hymns." The introduction to *LW* is concise, yet one of the

---

[66] Green, 48.
[67] Green, 48.
[68] Green, 48.

most eloquent and powerful expositions of the meaning of Divine Service *(Gottesdienst)* to be found anywhere. Divine Service is God's work. Divine Service is the Triune God present, giving out his gifts. At God's liturgy man receives and extols them. The 1960s and '70s were a time of much innovation and change in worship as well as a time of serious attempts at liturgical renewal. For Lutherans who find themselves entrusted with the holy things and the liturgical life of the church, the thoughtful words of Hermann Sasse ring clear and true: "Wherever the pure Gospel comes, there the great Liturgy of the true Church revives. And wherever men seek genuine liturgy they cannot avoid facing the question, 'What is the Gospel?'"[69]

---

[69] Sasse, "Liturgy and Lutheranism," 10.

Conclusion

UPHEAVAL and great social change in America characterized the period during which the *Lutheran Book of Worship* and *Lutheran Worship* were created. It was a generation in search of "new" experiences. The popular slang "mod" (short for modern) epitomized the vacuous demands for the new and trendy. This put tremendous pressure on those responsible for hymnal revision to produce a truly new hymnal. Liturgy is always changing, but it does violence to the integrity of what it means to be liturgical when manifold, creative, new, and rapid changes are demanded and made. Changes are constantly being made, but they are best made an inch at a time. In looking for something new, the Lutheran liturgical scholars in America found the vast resources of the Roman Catholic liturgical reforms impossible to pass up. It was also a time when the attention and energies of American Lutherans were focused on Lutheran unity. The appeal of returning to the early church as a way of avoiding theological problems inherent in the history of the liturgy was duly noted. Whereas doctrinal discussions had not resulted in the unity wished for by the ecumenical movement, there was great hope that a common liturgy would do what a common creed/confession could not. *Lex orandi, lex credendi.*

Lutheran Worship was an attempt to return to a truly evangelical and justification-centered liturgy. Within the context of the *Lutheran Book of Worship*, the result was a fortunate transmutation. *Lutheran Worship* is still somewhat of a confusing hybrid, but according to the criteria of the doctrine of justification, it is a definite improvement.

The impact of the Roman Catholic liturgical movement upon American Lutheranism has been extensive. It can be observed among the liturgical leaders (as seen in their books and articles) and in the many liturgical texts produced since 1960. Major themes were borrowed from the modern Liturgical Movement:

(1) The frequent celebration and reception of Holy Communion.

(2) Return to the early church and the inclination to disparage Martin Luther's liturgical reforms.

(3) Odo Casel and the popularization of the concept of "re-presentation."

(4) Shift to action terminology rather than talking about the liturgy and sacraments in spacial or word categories.

(5) The active participation of the laity ("people of God") in the liturgy as lay readers, and communion servers ("assisting ministers"). Worship belongs to the people and leadership should be spread among the people. The popularization of the expression that "liturgy is the work of the people." This represents an anthropocentric and sanctification-centered understanding of worship.

(6) The shift away from speaking of the sacraments "as 'means of grace' to speaking of them as encounters with Christ himself; from thinking of them primarily as acts of God to thinking of them mainly as celebrations of the faith community; from seeing sacraments as momentary incursions from another world to seeing them as manifestations of the graced character of all human life; from interpreting them as remedies for sin and weakness to seeing them as promoting growth in Christ."[1]

(7) The unification of the rites of initiation and recovery of the paschal mystery.

(8) A host of external changes: freestanding altar, table language preferred over altar language, three-year lectionary, changes in the church year, simplifying of ceremony, early communion, preference for Gregorian chant, introduction of the Easter Vigil, and so forth.

What will be the future of liturgical life for Lutherans in America? One thing seems certain: Lutheran liturgical texts and piety will continue to be influenced by, and to influence, other traditions. This has always been the case, but since the rise of the modern, self-conscious Liturgical Movement (in the mid-nineteenth century), the borrowing has been going on within the context of the concurrent Ecumenical Movement. As has been demonstrated, the liturgical books and rites

---

[1] Searle, "Infant Baptism Reconsidered," 15.

of Lutherans in America have been greatly influenced by this movement and thus by contemporary Roman Catholic developments. The influence has also been felt by many Protestant denominations in America which were historically less liturgical and sacramental.

To what extent will and should Lutherans in America consciously adopt and adapt things from the Roman Catholic confession? Will the Lutheran Church become increasingly interdenominational, pan-denominational, and generic in shape and style? How will this strengthen or weaken the theological substance and confession of the Evangelical Church? What then will be confessed? What faith (*lex credendi*) will be established by the Church's liturgy *(lex orandi)*?

What is both surprising and ironic is that even as *LBW* and *LW* were being introduced into Lutheran congregations in the 1970s and 1980s, an entirely different theology of worship was beginning to be adopted from American Evangelicalism. The "evangelical" style and substance was being incorporated into the worship of many Lutheran congregations who had forsaken the liturgy as not meeting the needs of today's baby boomer "seekers." The standard justification for abandoning Lutheran worship was that it is more important to win souls and fulfill the so-called Great Commission of Matthew 28:19–20 than to be legalistically bound to so-called Germanic (or European) forms of worship. The controversy which once surrounded the ILCW, *LBW*, *LW*, and the Eucharistic Prayer was relatively minor in comparison to the current passions that are ignited among Lutheran pastors, church musicians, and congregations at the very mention of the words worship and liturgy. The 1995 Synodical Convention of the LCMS was inundated by issues of *worship* and *liturgy*. The *Convention Workbook* included a host of memorials from individual congregations, circuit forums, district conventions, and seminary faculty to retain the Commission on Worship as a self-standing entity rather than bury it under a bureaucratic Board for Congregational Services. Extensive memorials were also submitted which expressed deep concern over recent anti-liturgical influences which undermine pure Lutheran liturgical practice.[2]

---

[2] *Convention Workbook*, St. Louis, 1995, 135-144. One overture from St. John, Chester, Illinois, called for the beginning of work on a new [revised] hymnal.

With the advent of affordable personal computers and copy machines, plus the strong influence of Protestant-evangelical worship forms, some are predicting the end of the hymnbook. I will not venture to predict whether they are right or wrong. I would, however, suggest that in this age of incessant change and running after whatever is new and exciting, a *book* of worship is needed more than ever. This is true for at least two reasons. First, many people will eventually grow tired of the adolescent pursuit for the feeling-centered and entertainment-patterned liturgies that change from Sunday to Sunday—almost as quickly as MTV. This is already happening among some adolescents and young adults.

Second, the more Lutheran pastors experiment from week to week, the more important it is to have a standard by which to judge the plethora of "creative," user-friendly, seeker-sensitive liturgies. Individual pastors and congregations may refuse to use the common services in the hymnbook, but at least the books will be in the pews (hopefully) as a constant source of reference for any who desire to look for the liturgical standard shared by the whole church. The liturgical abuses and demands of the Roman Catholic Church in the sixteenth century led Luther and many others to exert their evangelical freedom to reform the received liturgies of the Church. Today, those who are eager to justify their constant tinkering with and abandonment of liturgies that are truly faithful to Lutheran theology often appeal to worship as an adiaphoron. They would do well to heed Luther's admonition which is found in the concluding words of his *Deutsche Messe* (German Mass): "This work is just beginning; not everything has been prepared that is needed. We must arrive at a *common standard to assess and control the profusion of orders*."[3] (emphasis mine)

[3] "The German Mass and Order of Service," 1526. AE, 53: 90. In his introduction to the 1523 *Formula Missae* Luther made the often quoted statement, "We must dare something in the name of Christ." What is too often left off is the next sentence. "For it is right that we should provide at least for the few, lest by our desire to detach ourselves from the frivolous faddism of some people [enthusiasts], we provide for nobody, or by our fear of ultimately offending others [Romanists], we endorse their universally held abominations." And just prior to the statement, Luther wrote, "For I have been hesitant and fearful partly because of the weak in faith, who cannot suddenly exchange an old and accustomed order of service for a new and unusual one, *and more so* [emphasis mine] because of the fickle and fastidious spirits who rush in like unclean

So, what is the future of the hymnal as the repository of the Church's divine liturgies and hymnody? It is a relatively safe assumption that future revision will not be undertaken by those who are anti-liturgical or liturgically ambivalent. If *Lutheran Worship* and the *Lutheran Book of Worship* are to be significantly revised, then it will be done by those who are liturgically informed, and thus the influences of the Liturgical Movement(s) will more likely be felt. Among other things, this means that the Lutheran Church must come to grips with the Eucharistic Prayer. For the Roman Catholic Church and those committed to the modern Liturgical Movement, the heart and center of the mass is the Eucharistic Prayer with anamnesis and epiclesis. It is possible that the reader may have concluded from the historical overview that most of the resistance to the Eucharist Prayer comes from those in the Lutheran Church—Missouri Synod, while those in the Evangelical Lutheran Church in America, by virtue of their liturgical leadership, publications, and hymnal (*LBW*) are unanimously supportive of the Prayer. This is not the case, however. Granted, one of the reasons given by the Missouri Synod's Special Hymnal Review Committee (among many other examples cited) for appealing to the other Lutheran synods involved in the production of *LBW* to postpone its production was the inclusion of "eucharistic prayer forms." (See Appendix C.) Nevertheless, as seen in chapter 3, the vast majority of the written material published in objection to the proposed Eucharistic Prayers was written by scholars of the synods that eventually merged to form the Evangelical Lutheran Church in America (that is, the ALC, LCA, and AELC). Similarly, as seen in chapters 3 and 4, many of the Eucharistic Prayers were, in their initial forms, at their best, products of inept liturgical writing, and at their worst, products of the popular "action" theology.

While the Eucharistic Prayer has been debated within Missouri Synod circles, few congregations use the *Lutheran Book of Worship*, and of those who do, many do not use the optional Eucharistic Prayer. The 1958 *Service Book and Hymnal* of the ALC and LCA contained a Eucharistic Prayer (though surveys have shown that the

swine without faith or reason, and who delight only in novelty and tire of it as quickly, when it has worn off. Such people are a nuisance even in other affairs, but in spiritual matters, they are absolutely unbearable." AE, 53: 19–20.

majority of the pastors used only the Words of Institution). The *LBW* pew edition and altar book contain many optional anaphoras. The Eucharistic Prayer continues to be an issue of debate in the ELCA—if for no other reason than it is present in the liturgical texts. Philip Pfatteicher, writing in the *Lutheran Forum* on the fifteenth anniversary of *LBW*, concludes that there are two large liturgical issues that face the Lutheran Church at this time. One concerns a "required" public confession of sins prior to every celebration of the Lord's Supper. The second large theological issue still before the Lutheran Church in 1993 is put in the form of this question:

> Is it legitimate in the Lutheran context to incorporate the words of institution within the body of a eucharistic prayer of thanksgiving? Lutherans simply do not agree on the answer to these questions, and the answers one gives raises a great number of other issues that go to the heart of the Christian faith.[4]

The Eucharistic Prayer remains an issue in the Evangelical Lutheran Church in America. The service of Holy Communion in *LBW*, as did the *SBH*, included the option of using the bare Verba. Many churches continue to do just that. Ironically, the Missouri Synod's *LW* included modified Eucharistic Prayers in its Divine Services which are not listed as optional.

No one can predict with certainty the future of the Eucharistic Prayer in the Missouri Synod. There are some who believe that it would not be prudent at this time for the Lutheran Church—Missouri Synod to adopt a "more complete" anaphora. Few would go so far as saying that it would be wrong ever to use a proper Eucharistic Prayer; however, they would caution that at this time when the popular emphasis is on "worship as the work of the people" (a notion also heard repeatedly in Lutheran circles) that it would be advisable to forgo its use.

No one can predict with certainty the future of the Eucharistic Prayer among Lutherans in America. Whatever it might be, the crucial point is that it must be a good prayer that gives clear testi-

---

[4] Philip H. Pfatteicher, "Still To Be Tried," *Lutheran Forum* 27, no. 4 (1993): 22.

mony to the Lord's Supper as Gospel—gifts given and received through faith alone with thanksgiving. It should be a prayer of thanksgiving for God's service. If it is not a good prayer in every sense of the word—biblically, theologically, and aesthetically—then it is best to have no Eucharistic Prayer. As the Inter-Lutheran Commission on Worship discovered (see chapter 4), the literary integrity of the Eucharistic Prayer is not something to be written by a committee.

No one can predict with certainty when (or whether) the Lutheran Church—Missouri Synod or the Evangelical Lutheran Church in America will publish a revised *Lutheran Worship* and *Lutheran Book of Worship*. It is not too soon to begin work. Recent revisions have demonstrated that good liturgy and hymnody should not be rushed. If eucharistic prayers are desired, then their composition (or translation/adaptation) should be begun now. Individual liturgical scholar-composers should begin now. They should be theologians who are trained in Lutheran liturgical theology and gifted with literary skills of the highest level. Above all, they must be expert in the exegesis of Holy Scriptures. This excludes most of us, but for those few who are so gifted by God to serve his Church, let them humbly begin now. Let them begin, but they must not go it alone. Before any pastor would write and use a new liturgy, it is both prudent and proper to set the text before peers who are equipped and appointed to offer theological (as well as literary) criticism and oversight.

Future attempts at revision will have to come to grips with many of the complaints being hurled against *LBW* and *LW*. Some of what needs revision has nothing to do with the changes imported from the modern Liturgical Movement. They are, however, revisions that will make an important contribution to liturgical renewal on the congregational level. Valid complaints are numerous and varied: for example, the book is too confusing (why must Divine Service I begin on page 136?); it has too many options; it is too difficult to sing; it weighs too much.

The next hymnal must be a revision, not a "new" hymnal. It must not be rushed. The time to begin is now, in order that the revisions might be done thoughtfully and thoroughly—without any hidden agendas, and in precise, articulate, Lutheran theological language and categories.

One does suspect, however, that much of the resistance to and criticism of the new hymnal stems from those who are of a different theological school, or atheological in things liturgical. Theological education which gives serious and in-depth treatment to "liturgical theology" is desperately needed in the church's seminaries, colleges, and universities. The teacher's and music colleges have the awesome responsibility of training both the musicians of our church and the teachers of our children. It is imperative that the church do much better than the inane ditties and feel-good pap that comprises much of the so-called contemporary praise music being inflicted on the children. Such music is being introduced into the congregation via the official curricula as well as by pastors and musicians who are taken with the style and excitement of today's pan-denominational, "evangelical" music. Seminaries must review where and how "liturgical theology" is related to the traditional divisions of exegetical, historical, systematic, and practical theology. Seminary graduates who have not been taught to approach all theology doxologically and who have not been shaped by a consistent and daily worship life in the campus chapel will be ill-equipped to teach and lead Lutheran congregations. All departments must make their contributions; however, it must be primarily taught as an integral part of systematic theology and grow out of a profound Christology. It is best learned in a way that is given shape by a thorough understanding of the doctrine of Christ, justification, the sacraments, the ministry, and the church. Then it will be truly relevant because it is eternally relevant.

APPENDIX A

Dates of Important Events and Key Publications

1886 Odo Casel born (d. 1948)

1921 (1921–1941) *Jahrbuch für Liturgiewissenschaft* articles by Casel

1941 *The Lutheran Hymnal*

1945 *The Shape of the Liturgy* by Gregory Dix

1958 *Service Book and Hymnal*

1959 *TLH* "revision" approved by Missouri Synod Convention in San Francisco

1960 American Lutheran Church merger

1962 Lutheran Church in America merger

1962 Odo Casel's *The Mystery of Christian Worship*, English translation

1963 Vatican II promulgates Constitution on the Sacred Liturgy

1965 LCMS Convention in Detroit, Resolution 13-01 authorizes pan-Lutheran hymnal

1966 Formation of Inter-Lutheran Commission on Worship

1966 "Ecumenical Days" initiated prior to annual Roman Catholic Liturgical Week

1969	*Worship Supplement* published by the LCMS Commission on Worship
1969	(1969–1976) ILCW publishes ten *Contemporary Worship* booklets
1970	*Contemporary Worship 2*
1973	ILCW Theological Symposium on *Contemporary Worship 2*
1975	*The Great Thanksgiving* published by ILCW
1977	Liturgical Texts—draft of proposed texts for *LBW* sent by LCMS Commission on Worship to pastors for evaluation
1977	LCS Dallas Convention (July 15–22) established a Special Hymnal Review Committee
1978	*Lutheran Book of Worship*
1979	LCMS Anaheim Convention (July 6-12), Resolution 3-01 to adopt a revised *Lutheran Book of Worship*
1982	*Lutheran Worship*

APPENDIX B

Understanding Liturgical Texts in the Vernacular: A Document from the U.S. Bishops' Commission on the Liturgical Apostolate

"This reform in our custom is intended to bring the people into more effective contact with the Sacred Scripture and the holy text of the liturgy, thereby fostering deeper faith, greater knowledge, and more sincere prayer.

"But the worthy objectives will not automatically be achieved by the use of the vernacular. Such prayer and reading will have to be done in a more meaningful and appropriate manner than has, unfortunately, been employed by some priests when reciting the Latin texts. To celebrate the liturgy in a manner that is hasty, matter-of-fact, and without attention to the meaning of the words would, of course, be irreverent and improper no matter what the language; however, when the vernacular is used, there is the greatest possibility of scandal. For this reason the following comments are offered." The document first points out that "there is a basic difference between reading the Word of God and reading other texts.

"All Scripture readings are to be proclamations, not mere recitations . . . . The character of this reading is such that it must convey that special reverence which is due the Sacred Scriptures above all other words.

"It is of fundamental importance that the reader communicate the fullest meaning of the passage. Without exaggerated emphases or affectation, he must convey the particular significance of those words, phrases, clauses, or sentences which constitute the point being made. Careful phrasing and thought are necessary to enable the listener to follow every thought and the relationships among them. Patterns of speech must be avoided, and the pattern of thought in the text must be adhered to. The message in all its meaning must be earnestly communicated.

"The manner of speaking and tone of voice should be clear and firm, never indifferent or uncertain. The reader should not draw attention to himself either by being nervous and awkward or by being obviously conscious of a talent for dramatic reading. It is the message that should be remembered, not the one who reads it. The voice should be reverent without being offensive or overbearing . . .

"By his voice, attitude, and physical bearing, the reader should convey the dignity and sacredness of the occasion. His role is that of a herald of the Word of God; his function to provide a meaningful encounter with that living Word . . .

"When the celebrant leads the people in prayer, or speaks to them, or addresses God in their behalf, his manner of speaking will differ somewhat in each case . . . . [In the dialogue] all participants should speak their parts with meaning. When the priest says, 'The Lord be with you,' for example, he must convey that he is really addressing the people, that he sincerely means the greeting, and that he invites response. . . . At the same time, the dialogue should never become extremely informal . . . .

"When reading the orations, preface, and the like, the priest should speak in a manner befitting his sacerdotal role. His tone of voice should be more formal, more reverent; yet he must remember he is speaking to a person, not merely reciting formulas."

[*Worship and Liturgy: Official Catholic Teachings,* James J. Megivern, ed. Wilmington: McGrath Publishing House, 1978.]

APPENDIX C

To Deal with the Proposed *Lutheran Book of Worship* Resolution 3-04A

Report 3-02 (CW, pp. 58–62); Overtures 3-54, 3-116, 3-201A—3-228 (CW, pp. 85, 103, 125–132)

WHEREAS, The Lutheran Church—Missouri Synod has stated in its Constitution that one condition of membership in the Synod is the "exclusive use of doctrinally pure agenda, hymnbooks, and catechisms, in church and school" (Constitution VI, 40; and

WHEREAS, There has been a desire for an updated Lutheran hymnal by members of the Lutheran Church—Missouri Synod; and

WHEREAS, The Lutheran Church—Missouri Synod in convention at Detroit in 1965 instructed the President of the Synod to invite the other Lutheran church bodies in North America to work with the LCMS in the preparation of common worship materials, and the Synod at Milwaukee in 1971 urged the speedy completion of these materials; and

WHEREAS, The Synod's Commission on Worship has been working diligently with the Inter-Lutheran Commission on Worship for production of common worship materials; and

WHEREAS, Theological questions have been raised by agencies and members of the LCMS (e.g., CTCR [Commission on Theology and Church Relations], faculty members of the two seminaries, worship material reviewers) concerning the proposed *Lutheran Book of Worship* (e.g., commemorations, eucharistic prayer forms, adequacy of expressions, optional use of "he descended to the dead" in the Apostles' Creed, theological implications of hymn text alterations, confirmation promise, fellowship implications); and

WHEREAS, Members of Synod have not had the opportunity to review the final draft of the proposed *Lutheran Book of Worship;* therefore be it

Resolved, That the Synod in convention assembled commend our Commission on Worship for all its work and effort expended on the proposed *Lutheran Book of Worship;* and be it further

Resolved, That in the light of many theological questions (raised in whereas 5) a "blue ribbon" committee of seven be appointed as follows:

1) a representative of the CTCR;

2) a representative of the Commission on Worship;

3) & 4) a representative from each synodical seminary, appointed by the respective seminary presidents;

5) a synodical Vice-President selected by the praesidium;

6) & 7) two members appointed by the synodical President; and be it further

Resolved, That this committee be responsible for conducting a thorough review of the final ILCW draft of the *Lutheran Book of Worship* as it has been reviewed by the doctrinal review process, utilizing the (published) study of the CTCR as well as other sources for the purpose of formulating a recommendation to:

a) adopt the final draft of the *Lutheran Book of Worship,* or

b) adopt the final draft of the *Lutheran Book of Worship* with specified modifications, or

c) reject the *Lutheran Book of Worship* and propose that an alternative new hymnal for the LCMS be developed; and be it further

Resolved, That the Synod's congregations be given the opportunity to review and respond to the final ILCW draft of the Lutheran Book of Worship and the blue-ribbon committee's evaluation of the same; and be it further

Resolved, That the Lutheran Church—Missouri Synod in convention appeal to the ALC, LCA and ELCC to postpone publication of the *Lutheran Book of Worship* until the LCMS has implemented the above process and reached a final determination on the *Lutheran Book of Worship;* and be it further

Resolved, That if the other participating church bodies of the ILCW deem it necessary to proceed unilaterally in the publication of the *Lutheran Book of Worship* or if the blue-ribbon committee determines the *Lutheran Book of Worship* unsuited for use in the LCMS, the Commission on Worship is directed to gather materials for a new hymnal for the LCMS utilizing all available material; and be it further

Resolved, That if a separate hymnal is to be developed by the Commission on Worship, the blue-ribbon committee be directed to review the worship materials after the doctrinal review process; and be it finally

Resolved, That the blue-ribbon committee present its report and recommendation to the next regular synodical convention.

[Adopted at the 52nd Regular Convention of the LCMS, Dallas, Texas, July 15–22, 1977]

SELECTED BIBLIOGRAPHY

Abbott, Walter M., ed. *The Documents of Vatican II.* New York: Herder and Herder Association Press, 1966.

Berger, Teresa. "Liturgy-a Forgotten Subject-Matter of Theology." *Studia Liturgica* 17 (1987): 10–18.

Boehringer, Hans. "Baptism, Confirmation and First Communion: Christian Initiation in the Contemporary Church. *Institute of Liturgical Studies Occasional Papers.* Edited by D. Brockopp, D. Helge, D. Ttuemper.Valparaiso, Indiana: Institute of Liturgical Studies, 1981.

Brand, Eugene L. "The Lutheran Book of Worship at 'Mid-Life.'" *Lutheran Forum* 27 (November, 1993): 18–21.

Brilioth, Yngve. *Eucharistic Faith and Practice, Evangelical and Catholic.* Translated by A. G. Hebert. London: Society for Promoting Christian Knowledge, 1930.

Brown, Edgar S. Jr. *Liturgical Reconnaissance: Papers Presented at the Inter-Lutheran Consultation on Worship.* Philadelphia: Fortress Press, 1968.

Brunner, Peter. *Worship in the Name of Jesus.* Translated by M. H. Bertram. St. Louis: Concordia Publishing House, 1954.

Buszin, Walter E. "Progress Report of the Commission on Worship, Liturgics, and Hymnology." Concordia Historical Institute, St. Louis (111.1K.13, Box 1).

Casel, Odo. *Das Christliche Kultmysterium.* 3d ed. Regensburg: Gregorius-Verlag Vorm. Friedrich Pustet, 1948.

________. *The Mystery of Christian Worship: and Other Writings.* Translation of the fourth German edition of *Das christliche Kultmysterium and of Other Writings* which appeared with it in 1960, ed. Burkhard Neunheuser. Maryland: Westminster , 1962.

Charron Research and Information, Inc. *Lutheran Church— Missouri Synod: A Program of Assessment and Recommendation.* St. Louis, 1977.

Commission on Theology and Church Relations of the Lutheran Church—Missouri Synod. *Theology and Practice of the Lord's Supper.* St. Louis: Concordia Publishing House, May, 1983.

Commission of Worship of The Lutheran Church—Missouri Synod. *Lutheran Worship.* St. Louis: Concordia Publishing House, 1982.

_______. *Lutheran Worship Altar Book.* St. Louis: Concordia Publishing House, 1982.

Commission on Worship of the Lutheran Church—Missouri Synod and Synod of Evangelical Lutheran Churches. *Worship Supplement.* St. Louis: Concordia Publishing House, 1969.

DeLaney, Theodore E. "Response to Judicius, CTQ 1/77." Unpublished article, thirteen pages, single spaced. Copy available at Concordia Historical Institute, St. Louis, Missouri. See file: 111.1B, "Commission on Worship."

Dietz, Paul T. "The Transition from German to English in the Missouri Synod from 1910 to 1947." *Concordia Historical Institute Quarterly*, 22 (1949): 97–127.

Dix, Gregory. *The Shape of the Liturgy.* Additional notes by Paul V. Marshall. New York: Seabury Press, 1982.

Evanson, Charles J. "Lutheran Worship at 'Midlife.'" *Lutheran Forum*, 27 (November 1993) 25–27.

Fuchs, John M. "From *The Lutheran Hymnal* to *Lutheran Worship:* A Paradigm of Lutheran Church—Missouri Synod History." *Concordia Journal* 20 (April 1994):130–146.

Green, Lowell C. "Lutheran Worship: An Analytical Review-Article on the New Hymnal." *Lutheran Theological Review* 1 (1983): 37–48.

Horn, Henry E. *Models of Ministry: Afterthoughts on Fifty Years.* Minneapolis: Fortress Press, 1989.

Inter-Lutheran Commission on Worship. *Contemporary Worship 01: The Great Thanksgiving.* St. Louis: Concordia Publishing House, 1975.

_______. *Contemporary Worship 1: Hymns.* St. Louis: Concordia Publishing House, 1969.

_______. *Contemporary Worship 2: The Holy Communion.* St. Louis: Concordia Publishing House, 1970.

_______. *Contemporary Worship 3: The Marriage Service.* St. Louis: Concordia Publishing House, 1972.

_______. *Contemporary Worship 4: Hymns for Baptism and Holy Communion.* St. Louis: Concordia Publishing House, 1972.

_______. *Contemporary Worship 5: Services of the Word.* St. Louis: Concordia Publishing House, 1972.

_______. *Contemporary Worship 6: The Church Year: Calendar and Lectionary.* St. Louis: Concordia Publishing House, 1973.

_______. *Contemporary Worship 7: Holy Baptism.* St. Louis: Concordia Publishing House, 1974.

_______. *Contemporary Worship 8: Affirmation of the Baptismal Covenant.* St. Louis: Concordia Publishing House, 1975.

_______. *Contemporary Worship 9: Daily Prayer of the Church.* St. Louis: Concordia Publishing House, 1976.

_______. *Contemporary Worship 10: Burial of the Dead.* St. Louis: Concordia Publishing House, 1976.

_______. *Lutheran Book of Worship.* Minneapolis: Augsburg Publishing House and Philadelphia: Board of Publication, Lutheran Church in America, 1978.

Jounel, Pierre. "From the Council of Trent to Vatican Council II." In *Principles of the Liturgy.* Translated by Matthew J. O'Connell. Vol. 1 of *The Church at Prayer.* Edited by Aime Georges Martimort. 4 vols. Collegeville, MN: The Liturgical Press, 1983.

Judicius [Judisch, Douglas]. "Theological Observer: The Deepening Liturgical Crisis." *Concordia Theological Quarterly* 41 (1977): 50–52.

Kavanagh, Aidan. *The Shape of Baptism: The Rite of Christian Initiation.* New York: Pueblo Publishing Company, 1978.

Klauser, Theodor. *A Short History of the Western Liturgy: An Account and Some Reflections.* Translated by John Halliburton. 2d ed. Oxford: Oxford University Press, 1979.

Koenker, Ernest B. *The Liturgical Renaissance in the Roman Catholic Church.* Chicago: The University of Chicago Press, 1954.

_______. *Worship in Word and Sacrament.* St. Louis: Concordia Publishing House, 1959.

Lindemann, Herbert F. "*CW-2* Passes in Review." *The Lutheran Quarterly* 26 (1974): 221–224.

_______. *The New Mood in Lutheran Worship*. Minneapolis: Augsburg Publishing House, 1981.

Luther, Martin. "An Order of Mass and Communion for the Church at Wittenberg (1523)." *Luther's Works.* American Edition. Vol. 53. *Liturgy and Hymns.* Edited by Ulrich S. Leupold and Helmut T. Lehmann. Translated by Paul Zeller Strodach. Revised by Ulrich S. Leupold. Philadelphia: Fortress Press, 1965.

Lutheran Church—Missouri Synod. *Proceedings of the 46th Regular Convention of the Lutheran Church—Missouri Synod.* Detroit, Michigan, 1965.

_______. *Proceedings of the 53rd Regular Convention of the Lutheran Church—Missouri Synod.* St. Louis, Missouri, 1979.

Mandus, Egge E., ed. *Worship: Good News in Action.* Minneapolis: Augsburg Publishing House, 1973.

Martimort, A. G. "Structure and Laws of the Liturgical Celebration." In *Principles of the Liturgy.* Translated by Matthew J. O'Connell. Vol. 1 of *The Church at Prayer.* Edited by Aime Georges Martimort. 4 vols. Collegeville. MN: The Liturgical Press, 1983.

Megivern, James J., ed. *Worship and Liturgy: Official Catholic Teachings.* Wilmington, DE: McGrath Publishing House, 1978.

"Minutes of the Commission on Worship, Liturgics and Hymnody of the Lutheran Church—Missouri Synod. Concordia Historical Institute, St. Louis, Missouri, May 14–16, 1964. See file: 111.1K.13, Box 1.

_______. Concordia Historical Institute, St. Louis, Missouri, October 11–18, 1962. See file: 111.1K.13, Box 1.

"Minutes of the Sub-Committee on Liturgics of the Commission on Worship, Liturgics and Hymnody." George Hoyer, Secretary. Concordia Historical Institute, St. Louis, Missouri, September 26–27, 1963. See file: 111.1K.13, Box 1.

Mueller, Theodore. "Justification: Basic Linguistic Aspects and the Art of Communicating It." *Concordia Theological Quarterly* 46 (1982): 21–38.

Olson, Oliver K. "Contemporary Trends in Liturgy Viewed From the Perspective of Classical Lutheran Theology." *Lutheran Quarterly* 26 (May 1974): 110–157.

_______. "Liturgy as 'Action.'" *Dialog* 14 (1975): 108–113.

Pfatteicher, Phillip H. *Commentary on the Lutheran Book of Worship: Lutheran Liturgy in Its Ecumenical Context.* Minneapolis: Augsburg Fortress, 1990.

_______. "The New Holy Communion Rite—II: Seven Clear Achievements." *Lutheran Forum* 5 (1971): 14–15.

_______. "Still To Be Tried." *Lutheran Forum* 27 (November, 1993) 22–24.

Pfatteicher, Phillip H. and Carlos R. Messerli. *Manual on the Liturgy: Lutheran Book of Worship.* Minneapolis: Augsburg Publishing House, 1979.

Pittelko, Roger D. and Fred L. Precht. *Guide to Introducing Lutheran Worship.* St. Louis: Concordia Publishing House, 1981.

Pius X. "*Tra le Sollecitudini: Motu Proprio* of Pope Pius X on the Restoration of Church Music." In *Worship and Liturgy.* Edited by James J. Megivern. Wilmington, DE: McGrath Publishing Company, 1978.

Precht, Fred L., ed. *Lutheran Worship: History and Practice.* St. Louis: Concordia Publishing House, 1993.

Reed, Luther D. *The Lutheran Liturgy: A Study of the Common Service of the Lutheran Church in America.* Revised Edition. Philadelphia: Fortress Press, 1959.

"Report and Recommendation of the Special Hymnal Review Committee." St. Louis: Concordia Publishing House, 1977–1978.

"Report of the Commission on Worship, Liturgics, and Hymnology." *Convention Workbook (Reports and Overtures) 46th Regular Convention of the Lutheran Church—Missouri Synod*, Detroit, 1965.

"Report of the Committee on Hymnology and Liturgics." *Reports and Memorials of the 44th Regular Convention of the Lutheran Church—Missouri Synod*, San Francisco, 1959.

"Report on the Consultative Meeting between the Commission on the Liturgy and Hymnal (National Lutheran Council) and the Commission on Worship, Liturgics and Hymnody (LCMS) on April 25, 1963." Concordia Historical Institute, St. Louis. See file 111.1K.13, Box 1.

Resolution 2-08, "To Publish Supplement to *The Lutheran Hymnal* Field Testing." *Convention Proceedings: 47th Regular Convention of the Lutheran Church—Missouri Synod*, New York, 1967.

Resolution 3-04, "To Deal with the Proposed *Lutheran Book of Worship*." *Convention Proceedings: 52nd Regular Convention of the Lutheran Church—Missouri Synod*, Dallas, 1977.

Rusch, William G. "A Background Paper for a Theological Review of Materials Produced by the Inter-Lutheran Commission on Worship." Unpublished paper. Copy available in Concordia Seminary Library, St. Louis, 1977.

Sasse, Hermann. *This Is My Body: Luther's Contention for the Real Presence in the Sacrament of the Altar*. Revised edition. Adelaide: Lutheran Publishing House, 1977.

Schalk, Carl. *The Roots of Hymnody in the Lutheran Church—Missouri Synod*. St. Louis: Concordia Publishing House, 1965.

Schmemann, Alexander. *Introduction to Liturgical Theology*. New York: St. Vladimir's Seminary Press, 1986.

Searle, Mark, ed. *Alternative Futures for Worship*. Vol.2. *Baptism and Confirmation*. Collegeville, MN: The Liturgical Press, 1987.

Senn, Frank C. "An End for Confirmation?" *Currents in Theology and Mission* 3 (1976): 45–52.

_______. *Christian Worship and Its Cultural Setting*. Philadelphia: Fortress Press, 1983.

_______. "Confirmation and First Communion: A Reappraisal." *Lutheran Quarterly* 23 (1971): 178–191.

_______, ed. *New Eucharistic Prayers: An Ecumenical Study of Their Development and Structure.* New York: Paulist Press, 1987.

_______. "The Shape and Context of Christian Initiation: An Exposition of the New Lutheran Liturgy of Holy Baptism, *Dialog* 14 (1975): 97–107.

_______. "Teaching Worship in Seminaries: A Response." *Worship* 55 (June, 1981): 325–332.

Shepherd, Massey Hamilton Jr., ed. *The Liturgical Renewal of the Church.* New York: Oxford University Press, 1960.

Spinks, Bryan. *Luther's Liturgical Criteria and His Reform of the Cannon of the Mass.* Grove Liturgical Study 30. Bramcote, Nottinghamshire, England: Grove Books, 1982.

Stauffer, S. Anita. *Lutherans at Worship.* Minneapolis: Augsburg Publishing House, 1978.

Taft, Robert. "The Dialogue Before the Anaphora in the Byzantine Eucharistic Liturgy. I: The Opening Greeting." *Orientalia Christiana Periodica* 52 (1986): 299–324.

Tappert, Theodore G., ed. *The Book of Concord: The Confessional Writings of the Evangelical Lutheran Church.* Philadelphia: Fortress Press, 1959.

Van Loon, Ralph R. *Assisting Ministers Handbook.* Edited by S. Anita Stauffer. Philadelphia: Parish Life Press, 1986.

Van Unnik, W. C. "Dominus Vobiscum: The Background of a Liturgical Formula." *Sparsa Collecta: The Collected Essays of W. C. van Unnik,* Part II. Supplements to *Novum Testamentum* 31. Leiden: E. J. Brill, 1983, 362-391.

White, James F. *A Brief History of Christian Worship.* Nashville: Abingdon Press, 1993.

_______. *Introduction to Christian Worship.* Nashville: Abingdon Press, 1990.

Index of Subjects

Index of Names

About the Author

TIMOTHY C. J. QUILL studied at Concordia Seminary in St. Louis, Missouri where he received the Masters of Divinity (1980) and Masters of Sacred Theology (1993). He was ordained in the Lutheran Church—Missouri Synod in 1980 and served parishes in New Hartford, Connecticut (1980–85) and St. Louis, Missouri (1985–94). In 1994 he entered Drew University's Liturgical Studies Program. He received his Masters of Philosophy from Drew University in 1996 and is currently working on his Ph.D. dissertation on the liturgical writings of Theodosius Andreas Harnack (1817–89). In 1996 he also received a call to Concordia Theological Seminary, Fort Wayne, Indiana. He has written articles for *Concordia Pulpit, Concordia Pulpit Resources, Concordia Journal* and *Logia: A Journal of Lutheran Theology.*